Published by

Publisher's Cataloging-in-Publication Data

Carr, Dr. Douglas E.

Deliverance ministry / Dr. Douglas E. Carr.

p. cm.

1. Exorcism. 2. Pentecostalism. 3. Spiritual healing.

BV873.E8 C37 2008
235`.4—dc22   2006925410

Unless otherwise noted:
Scripture taken from the HOLY BIBLE, NEW INTERNATIONAL VERSION. (niv) Copyright © 1973, 1978, 1981 International bible Society. Used by permission of Zondervan Bible Publishers.

Other scripture quotations:
KING JAMES VERSION. (kjv) Authorized King James Version.

The Journey Guide Inventory used by permission of Touch Publications: "Your Journey Guide," Touch Outreach Ministries, 1998. For more details about Your Journey Guide, visit www.touchusa.org or call 800-735-5865 for a catalog.

The Questionnaire is based on a text by Doris Wagner, and is used by her permission: "How to Cast out Demons, A Beginner's Guide, "Wagner Institute for Practical Ministry, 1999. For more details about this book, or more information about Doris Wagner's audio cassette seminar by the same name, please visit Arsenal@cpwagner.net or call toll free 1-888-563-5150.

ACKNOWLEDGMENTS

I acknowledge my lovely wife and helpmate, Pamela J. Carr, and thank God for her. Her encouragement, intercession, support, in addition to the biography she compiled for this book have helped me more than she will ever realize this side of eternity.

TABLE OF CONTENTS

ACKNOWLEDGMENTS.................................iii

FOREWORD..ix

INTRODUCTION xiii

CHAPTER ONE 1
**POWER AND AUTHORITY
FOR DELIVERANCE MINISTRY**

CHAPTER TWO 3
JESUS, A MODEL TO FOLLOW

CHAPTER THREE................................... 11
**UNDERSTANDING THE NEED
OF DELIVERANCE MINISTRY**

CHAPTER FOUR.................................... 15
THE HEAT OF THE BATTLE

CHAPTER FIVE.................................... 19
THE THREE MAJOR BATTLEGROUNDS

v

CHAPTER SIX 31
CASE STUDY FROM MARK 4:35 - 5:22

CHAPTER SEVEN 39
STANDING STRONG IN BATTLE

CHAPTER EIGHT 49
THE OPPONENTS OF OUR BATTLE

CHAPTER NINE 53
EXAMPLES OF THE BATTLE

CHAPTER TEN 57
STRONGHOLDS

CHAPTER ELEVEN 61
THE STORY OF KING SAUL

CHAPTER TWELVE 69
DEALING WITH STRONGHOLDS

CHAPTER THIRTEEN 73
MAJOR TYPES OF STRONGHOLDS

CHAPTER FOURTEEN 75
PERSONAL SPIRITUAL INVENTORY

CHAPTER FIFTEEN 79
GAINING VICTORY OVER STRONGHOLDS

CHAPTER SIXTEEN 85
**FIND OUT WHO IS IN CHARGE —
THEOLOGY OF THE HUMAN MAKEUP**

CHAPTER SEVENTEEN 91
THE WORK OF REPROBATION

CHAPTER EIGHTEEN 95
GOD'S CURE FOR REPROBATION

CHAPTER NINETEEN 99
RESTORATION

CHAPTER TWENTY 101
EVERY CHRISTIAN'S BATTLE

CHAPTER TWENTY-ONE 103
SECURING ADEQUATE PROTECTION

CHAPTER TWENTY-TWO 107
THREE TYPES OF PEOPLE

CHAPTER TWENTY-THREE 111
LEARNING TO WALK IN RIGHT ALIGNMENT

CHAPTER TWENTY-FOUR 113
THE BENEFITS OF RIGHT SPIRITUAL ALIGNMENT

CHAPTER TWENTY-FIVE 117
PREPARING TO BE FREE INDEED

CHAPTER TWENTY-SIX 123
**GAINING FREEDOM
IS AN ACTIVITY OF CHRIST'S BODY**

CHAPTER TWENTY-SEVEN 125
**REVERSING THE CURSE BY REPLACING
AHAB & JEZEBEL WITH CHRIST-LIKENESS**

CHAPTER TWENTY-EIGHT 149
DEALING WITH REJECTION ISSUES

CHAPTER TWENTY-NINE. 159
FORGIVING ALL WHO HAVE REJECTED YOU

CHAPTER THIRTY. 163
MINISTERING TO MENTAL AND EMOTIONAL ISSUES

CHAPTER THIRTY-ONE. 171
MINISTERING TO CULT AND OCCULT ISSUES

CHAPTER THIRTY-TWO 177
BREAKING CURSES

CHAPTER THIRTY-THREE. 179
DEALING WITH ADDICTION

CHAPTER THIRTY-FOUR. 187
LUST AND SEXUAL BONDAGE ISSUES

CHAPTER THIRTY-FIVE. 195
FORGIVING THOSE WHO HAVE HURT YOU SEXUALLY

CHAPTER THIRTY-SIX 199
BAPTISM IN LOVE

APPENDIX 207
**The Free Indeed Deep Healing
Questionnaire Worksheet**

INDEX 245

FOREWORD
by Dr. Doris M. Wagner

I am frequently asked to read, critique, and/or write forewords to books written by students of Wagner Leadership Institute. Often these students have attended our seminars and classes and spent considerable time and money to complete their training. I am particularly pleased when one of our students has learned the teaching well, has improved on it considerably, has begun to minister successfully and has produced what I would consider might well be a future textbook in the field of deliverance. To date there have been just a few, but such is the case with Douglas Carr and the book you hold in your hands.

I am even more pleased when a man undertakes ministering in the field. It seems as though there are over twice as many women laboring in the field of deliverance. I'm not sure why — I have conjectured possible reasons might be that God has gifted more women with mercy and compassion, perhaps their nurturing instincts kick in somehow, perhaps it's because deliverance and intercession seem to go hand in hand and we know that there are many more female intercessors than male — all guesses, to be sure. Most of the illustrations we have in Scripture are of men taking on the tough job of deliverance. It just felt very good to read Douglas's book.

First of all, I was thoroughly impressed with the superb intertwining of Biblical truth and teaching with prolific personal examples and experiences. Deliverance and the setting of captives free is so frequently mentioned in Scripture that I am convinced it is often overlooked today just because people don't know where to begin. It was simply understood in Jesus' time that people were afflicted with demons but they didn't know what to do about it. Jesus taught and trained his disciples how to do it, and then told them to go and minister to the afflicted. And they did.

Douglas is doing much the same through his Free Indeed seminars and the production of this book. His passion is to see a deliverance ministry established in the local church. He provides a wonderful head start with this teaching and especially the questionnaire in the back of the book. He has gleaned the best of the best and put it together. This has made for a marvelous how-to handbook for churches to begin a deliverance ministry.

I especially appreciated the theological underpinnings for deliverance ministry in chapters five and six. What gems! Many folks need an adjustment in their worldview to make room for modern day deliverance and this is solid teaching.

I also appreciate a good theological explanation of how Satan, **our** enemy, operates. Frankly, I get a little annoyed when I hear the "toothless lion" and "defeated foe" carried on ad nauseam. We are still at war with Satan and deliverance is the hand-to-hand combat that beats him back from the lives of individuals today. One need only take part in setting one person free from demonic bondage, and usually that person has an insatiable thirst to keep on doing it!

To illustrate how Satan operates was clearly presented in the case study chapter on the demoniac from Gerasenes, as well as chapters on the hierarchy of demonic beings and the definition and dealing with spiritual strongholds. The clear and thorough teaching concerning the Ahab and Jezebel spirits is another topic I have not found in other deliverance books.

Douglas's treatments of the topics of rejection, the cult and occult, breaking of curses, addictions, and generational issues were very well handled in a new, fresh way.

I especially liked his section on probably the most pervasive problem in the church today – that of lust. Christian counselors who do not have deliverance as part of their tool bag are frequently laboring with one hand tied behind their backs. The acknowledging of the problem and confession of sin is but one part of a solution and freedom from the bondage of lust. The task is complete after the breaking of soul ties and the casting out of all associated demons. Demons are not counseled out — they are cast out. As a matter of fact, some demons enjoy **receiving** attention **through counseling** and dig in deeper. Having said that, however, let me state that once the deliverance and inner healing task is complete, Christian counseling is frequently a valuable tool to assist the newly freed person in gaining skills to avoid future contamination.

I hope "Free Indeed" goes on to become a major textbook in the field. It is worthy to do so, and has gained a spot on my reading list for future students.

    Doris M. Wagner, Doctor of Practical Ministry
    Wagner Leadership Institute and Executive Vice President,
    Global Harvest Ministries
    Colorado Springs, Colorado
    October, 2008

INTRODUCTION

People often say that they wish they would have known the contents of the Free Indeed Seminar 25 years ago. I understand what they mean. Had I understood the ministry of deliverance when I first started my family and entered the ministry countless lives would have been spared heartache, despair and defeat.

But God, in His infinite wisdom, doesn't release new revelation to his children until they are ready to receive it. Therefore I pray that this book will fall into the hands of those who are ready to receive the revelation of how important deliverance ministry is for every person who wants break away from Satan's schemes and fully enjoy the abundant life that Jesus came to give.

The contents of this book closely parallel the Free Indeed Seminar that I developed to introduce deliverance ministry in local churches. Many churches have discovered a whole new walk in power and authority through the Seminar and it is my prayer that many Christians will discover the same thing as they read this book.

CHAPTER ONE

POWER AND AUTHORITY FOR DELIVERANCE MINISTRY

Jesus released power and authority to his church that is far greater than most Christians understand or practice. We can quote verses from the Bible but we often fail to grasp the liberating truths they contain. For example; Jesus gave His church the authority to release forgiveness and deliverance to those who truly seek God. *"Again Jesus said, 'Peace be with you! As the Father has sent me, I am sending you.' And with that he breathed on them and said, 'Receive the Holy Spirit. If you forgive anyone his sins, they are forgiven; if you do not forgive them, they are not forgiven'"* (John 20:21-23). Christians have known these verses but many have never known how to apply them.

The most liberating thing Jesus said to the woman caught in adultery (John 8:1- 12) was "neither do I condemn you, go and sin no more". We can release the same freedom to people when we simply follow the Spirit's lead and tell people that their confessed sins are forgiven.

Jesus also released great power for his disciples to heal the sick. God transformed my own ministry of healing when I learned to walk in His delegated authority. I used to beg God to heal people and occasionally would see healing come. But when I began to walk with the Spirit I learned that we can know when God is ready to release healing through us. Consequently I now see people healed on a regular basis.

I memorized John chapters 14 and 15 several years ago and put myself to sleep each night meditating on the things Jesus said. One section particularly stood out to me.

Jesus said *"I tell you the truth, anyone who has faith in me will do what I have been doing. He will do even greater things than these, because I am going to the Father. And I will do whatever you ask in my name, so that the Son may bring glory to the Father. You may ask me for anything in my name, and I will do it".* (John 14:12-14.)

This passage troubled me because it spoke of power and authority that simply wasn't manifesting among the churches and Christians I knew. I asked my own pastor about this passage and he cautioned me to not take it too seriously. But God impressed me that I was to take it seriously.

Then the day came when I asked God to heal a person and I sensed the Spirit of God speaking to my spirit "No — you heal him". That didn't fit my theology but the impression was so strong that I finally laid hands on the person and said "in Jesus' name you are healed". I'm not sure who was more amazed — the man who was healed or me. But since that day I've ministered healing to scores of people under the prompting of the Spirit.

Jesus meant it when He said *"As you go, preach this message: 'The kingdom of heaven is near.' Heal the sick, raise the dead, cleanse those who have leprosy, drive out demons. Freely you have received, freely give"* (Matthew 10:7-8).

Benny Hinn, who is being greatly used by God in healing evangelism, simply says "we need to do things the way Jesus did them". Jesus wants to set us free from powerless religious thinking and bring us into the fullness of His love and power. He wants to do a great work in our personal lives so He can greatly work through us as we minister to others. The central message of the entire Free Indeed Ministry is to live out the words of Jesus *"So if the Son sets you free, you will be free indeed."* John 8:38.

CHAPTER TWO
JESUS, A MODEL TO FOLLOW

The generation that experienced Woodstock in the 1960's may be the most demonized generation to ever walk on American soil. Sin is on the increase and consequently there are more demons at work. One can compare the way viruses contaminate computers to how demons contaminate people. To be effective in today's world, we must move in the power of the Holy Spirit to cast out demons and set captives free.

The Holy Spirit Descended Upon Jesus.
Jesus clearly taught the connection between deliverance ministry and the kingdom of God saying, *"But if I drive out demons by the finger of God, then the kingdom of God has come to you"* (Luke 11:20). Luke uses the word finger as a euphemism for the Spirit of God. Matthew makes it even more clear. *"But if I drive out demons by the Spirit of God, then the kingdom of God has come upon you"* (Matthew 12:28).

The ministry of deliverance is a ministry done through the Holy Spirit. We can not do it without him and He usually won't do it without our participation.

Jesus left us an example to follow. Remember; Jesus did not consider equality with God something to be grasped. He made himself nothing, taking on the very nature of a servant, being made in human likeness. Jesus never quit being divine, but while He walked this earth; He did not use his divine nature. He became just like you and me, except that He never sinned.

There are fables about Jesus performing miracles when He was a boy. One said He would whittle birds out of wood and then touch them and they would fly away. But those were fables. Jesus, in human flesh, needed the Holy Spirit to do miracles.

To be successful in deliverance ministry we need to follow the six major steps Jesus took as the Father prepared him for ministry.

1) The first thing that happened while Jesus was being prepared for great ministry was that the Holy Spirit descended upon him. Before his baptism people didn't think Jesus was anyone other than the illegitimate son of Joseph and Mary. Even though He was the Son of God He didn't have any distinguishing features that made his friends and neighbors think He was anyone special. Luke says it this way. *"When all the people were being baptized, Jesus was baptized too. And as he was praying, heaven was opened and the Holy Spirit descended on him in bodily form like a dove. And a voice came from heaven: "You are my Son, whom I love; with you I am well pleased." Now Jesus himself was about thirty years old when he began his ministry. He was the son, so it was thought, of Joseph, the son of Heli"* (Luke 3:21-23).

Jesus had not yet begun his earthly ministry because He had emptied himself and became a man. As a man even Jesus could not do the kind of ministry He was destined to do without the Holy Spirit. Jesus never did a miracle before the Spirit descended upon him because He was limited like any other person apart from the power of the Holy Spirit.

2) Jesus was filled with the Spirit, but still did no miracles.

The Bible says that *"Jesus, full of the Holy Spirit, returned from the Jordan and was led by the Spirit in the desert, where for forty days he was tempted by the devil. He ate nothing during those days, and at the end of them he was hungry"* (Luke 4:1-2).

Even after Jesus was baptized and filled with the Holy Spirit He didn't start casting out demons. Instead He was led into the desert by the Spirit and fasted for forty days. At the end of the forty days Jesus was tempted by the devil but overcame.

I don't think a forty day fast is a prerequisite to walk in the power of God but I do know that my life was transformed after I came off a forty day fast. It was after that fast that I really began walking in Divine Authority and Power. It was also shortly after my forty day fast that the doors were opened for me to attend Wagner Leadership Institute where I earned my Masters and Doctorate with proficiencies in deliverance and intercession.

3) Jesus returned in the power of the Spirit.

Something happened during Jesus' fast and he returned and began the greatest ministry ever. *"Jesus returned to Galilee in the power of the Spirit, and news about him spread through the whole countryside. He taught in their synagogues, and everyone praised him."* Luke 4:14-15. Everyone praised Jesus because He had new power. He used that power to cast out demons, heal the sick and teach with authority.

4) Jesus recognized his mission.

Luke records how Jesus stepped into his ministry after reading from Isaiah at the synagogue. *"He went to Nazareth, where he had been brought up, and on the Sabbath day he went into the synagogue, as was his custom. And he stood up to read. The scroll of the prophet Isaiah was handed to him. Unrolling it, he found the place where it is written: "The Spirit of the Lord is on me, because he has anointed me to preach good news to the poor. He has sent me to proclaim freedom for the prisoners and recovery of sight for the blind, to release the oppressed, to proclaim the year of the Lord's favor"* (Luke 4:16-19).

From that day on, Jesus walked in the authority and power of God to preach the good news, heal the sick and set captives free. I truly believe that God wants to bring us to a pivotal point in our lives where we will begin walking in the authority and power of God to continue Jesus' ministry of healing and deliverance on earth.

5) Jesus Released His Mission to Us.

Jesus said that we would do everything He did and even greater things. *"I tell you the truth, anyone who has faith in me will do what I have been doing.* **He will do even greater things than these**, *because I am going to the Father. And I will do whatever you ask in my name, so that the Son may bring glory to the Father. You may ask me for anything in my name, and I will do it. "If you love me, you will obey what I command"* (John 14:12-15.) (Emphasis mine).

When Jesus was on earth he could only be at one place at a time. He could be by the pool healing a blind man, or at the well calling a woman to repentance, or with the man whose son needed deliverance. But he couldn't be everywhere at once. But now Jesus works in and through every Christian everywhere who will accept his mission and walk in the power of God.

6) Jesus released his authority to us.

a) Jesus gave Christians the authority to forgive sins. The Roman Catholic Church seems to understand this better than many Protestant Churches and that may be why there is less mental illness among Catholics than there is among Protestants. People need to know that they are forgiven.

The King James Version uses the better word "remit" in John 20:21-23. There is a very real way that we can deliver people from the power of sins by speaking the forgiveness of Jesus over them to such an extent that they will realize that they are set free from their sin. *"Whosoever sins ye remit, they are remitted unto them; [and] whosesoever [sins] ye retain, they are retained"* (John 20:23) (KJV).

b) Jesus also released the authority to heal the sick to his followers. He said *"Heal the sick, raise the dead, cleanse those who have leprosy."* Matthew 10:8a.

I realize that Paul left Trophimus sick in Mellitus and that he told Timothy to drink a little wine for his stomach sake because of his frequent illness. Paul himself struggled with a thorn in the flesh for a season. There are times when I sense the Lord doesn't want me to pray for the sick but when he does the sick are usually healed because He has given true believers the authority to heal.

c) The authority to drive out demons has also been released to those who choose to follow in the footsteps of Jesus. He said *"... drive out demons. Freely you have received, freely give"* (Matthew 10:8b).

I didn't believe in deliverance when I cast out my first demon. My eyes were just beginning to be opened to the things of God when a woman came to me and said she was addicted to gambling. I was so naïve that I didn't even think there was any place to gamble around my city.

My wife and I were leaving for vacation right after church that day and it was after service that the woman came to me for help. She had already come a long way since I had led her to the Lord a couple of years previous. She was an alcoholic when she came to Jesus and was living with a man out of wedlock. But Jesus cleaned her up! She had been dry since shortly after she was saved and had moved her boyfriend out and was living a pure life. She was faithful in church and had gone through discipleship. Therefore I was totally shocked when she told me she was addicted to gambling. She said she "ate, slept and drank gambling". It was all she could think about.

I confess that all I could think about is getting out of there to go on vacation. Besides that, I felt powerless to do anything about her gambling. But a little voice kept whispering to my spirit "cast out the spirit of gambling". I had an inner argument with that voice, telling it that I didn't believe in deliverance. The voice continued, however, and grew louder until I finally offered to pray for the woman and in my prayer bound and cast out the spirit of gambling.

We went our separate ways and I figured that when I returned home from vacation I would spend months counseling her about her gambling. Imagine my surprise when I found out that she had not even been tempted to gamble after I cast out the spirit of gambling. That caught my attention and started my lifelong study of deliverance.

d) Jesus also gave us the authority to minister in his place. He actually meant it when *"He said to them, "Go into all the world and preach the good news to all creation. Whoever believes and is baptized will be* *saved, but whoever does not believe will be condemned. And **these signs will accompany those who believe: In my name they will drive out demons**; they will speak in new tongues; they will pick up snakes with their hands; and when they drink deadly poison, it will not hurt them at all; **they will place their hands on sick people, and they will get well.**" After the Lord Jesus had spoken to them, he was taken up into heaven and he sat at the right hand of God. Then the disciples went out and preached everywhere, **and the Lord worked with them and confirmed his word by the signs that accompanied it**"* (Mark 16:15-20 — Emphasis mine).

I've probably "caught more than I've been taught" concerning deliverance and so will you. I've learned a lot from the books, tapes and ministries of men and women who were engaged in healing and deliverance ministry before I even believed in it. At the same time, the Holy Spirit is the world's best teacher and he is ready to teach those who desire to advance in the power ministries.

Some people think that deliverance and healing ministries are only for those who are specifically gifted for such ministry. It is true that the Holy Spirit gifts certain members of the Body with gifts of healing and/or deliverance. But the Bible teaches that all Christians can have power and authority for healing and deliverance.

God's gifts and authority, however, need our participation. We can't do it without him and he won't do it without us. Serving people through delegated authority and through gifts of the Spirit is a two-fold proposition. The Holy Spirit gives the power, authority and gifts but we need to exercise them.

Peter said something about speaking in tongues in Acts 2 that applies to all ministries that are dependent upon the Spirit of God. "*All of them were filled with the Holy Spirit and* **(they) *began to speak** in other tongues **as the Spirit enabled them**"* (Acts 2:4 — Emphasis mine).

They began to speak as the Spirit enabled them. It was their co-operation with what the Holy Spirit was doing that enabled them to do what God wanted them to do. Likewise, in deliverance and healing ministry we do the ministry as the Holy Spirit enables us. We can do greater things as the Spirit of God enables us to carry on the ministry of Jesus on earth.

It is important to be circumspect when doing deliverance ministry because the demons that work in a person will also work to make you treat the person the way a demon is treating them. For example, you may be tempted to reject someone who has a spirit of rejection or you may have impure thoughts toward someone with a spirit of lust or victimization. God will use such things both to help us understand the other person's need of deliverance and areas in our own lives that need special attention.

CHAPTER THREE
UNDERSTANDING THE NEED OF DELIVERANCE MINISTRY

Many people know Jesus as Savior but too few know him as Deliverer. But Jesus came to deliver people from sin and Satan. Even his name comes from the same root as "Joshua", the mighty deliver who led Israel in the conquest against the warring tribes that resisted her progress into the Promised Land. There are several passages that explain that Jesus came to destroy the works of Satan as we journey toward the Promised Land of Heaven.

Hebrews 2:14-15 states that Jesus' ministry focus was to destroy the devil and deliver people from the bondage that Satan causes: *"Since the children have flesh and blood, he too shared in their humanity so that by his death he might destroy him who holds the power of death — that is, the devil — and free those who all their lives were held in slavery by their fear of death."*

John was even clearer about the purpose of the Lord's appearance. *"The reason the Son of God appeared was to destroy the devil's work"* (I John 3:8b). As ambassadors for Christ, every Christian is to carry on the work of destroying the devil's work — in people, homes, neighborhoods, communities and in the world.

Jesus clearly stated that the Spirit of the Lord anointed him, to set people free from their bondage. *"The Spirit of the Lord is on me, because he has anointed me to preach good news to the poor. He has sent me to proclaim freedom for the prisoners and recovery of sight for the blind, to release the oppressed, to proclaim the year of the Lord's favor"* (Luke 4:18-19).

People need to be set free from the bondages of past hurts, addictions, hurtful self-images, etc. as well as from literal demons. Jesus calls every Christian to carry on deliverance ministry just like Jesus modeled for us.

One of the primary purposes of deliverance and spiritual warfare is to set people free so they can respond first to the Gospel of the Kingdom and then to the work of the Kingdom. Many lost souls are held in such bondage that they do not even have a hope of salvation unless someone does spiritual warfare on their behalf.

The Apostle Paul was one of the greatest soul winners ever. Consider his observation. *"And even if our gospel is veiled, it is veiled to those who are perishing. The god of this age has blinded the minds of unbelievers, so that they cannot see the light of the gospel of the glory of Christ, who is the image of God"* (II Corinthians 4:3-4).

The Greek word for veiled is "kaloopto". It refers to a literal covering that hides what is under it even as skin covers our bodies. Paul says that the gospel is hidden to those who are perishing. Note that he says that the God of this age has blinded the minds of unbelievers so that they *can* not see. It isn't that they *will* not see but that they *cannot* see. The word blinded refers to something almost like a smoke screen. The Greek word for revelation is "ap-ok-al'-oop-sis" which adds the negative to "kaloopto" and therefore literally means the unveiling.

It takes believing prayer to tear down the veils so people can see the light of the gospel. The Greek word for light here is "photismos" which is the root of photography. As Christians pray and do warfare for the lost, the apertures of their souls are snapped open so they can receive a photographic imprint of the gospel.

I think of two cases where I could not win a person to the Lord without engaging in spiritual warfare. The first was a lady who attended our church every Sunday but wasn't saved. I could talk with her about anything except the Lord and she would understand but when I tried to talk with her about her need to be born again it was like talking to a brick wall.

One day when I had an appointment with her the Spirit reminded me of the veil. That day I asked her if I could pray for her before we talked. When she agreed I asked the Lord to remove the veil from her heart so she could see the hope of the Gospel. After we prayed and broke the veil off from her it was easy for her to be born again.

The second case involves a sweet relative of mine who was brought up as a Jehovah's Witness. I repeatedly tried to share the Gospel with her to no avail until one day I called on some intercessors to pray that the veil would be broken off her when I witnessed to her. It was amazing to see how the Lord opened her eyes that day. She even decided to renounce her Jehovah's Witness baptism and readily accepted the Lord immediately after she did so. She has been walking faithfully with the Lord every since.

Deliverance ministry can actually be a prerequisite for some people to be saved. Some people can't seem to get a hold of Jesus until we make the devil let go of them. Paul compares this to warfare. *"For though we live in the world, we do not wage war as the world does. The weapons we fight with are not the weapons of the world. On the contrary, they have divine power to demolish strongholds. We demolish arguments and every pretension that sets itself up against the knowledge of God, and we take captive every thought to make it obedient to Christ"* (II Corinthians 10:3-5).

Let's look at some of the interesting words and concepts from this passage to better understand the spiritual warfare that Jesus calls the Church to do. First we need to realize that we can't fight the way the world does. We won't persuade people to follow Christ through nipulation or nagging control. But we do have divine weapons that will demolish strongholds.

The Greek word for demolish means to bring down with great violence. The same word is used to describe someone who is being impeached or forcibly removed from office. The word for stronghold does not describe a demon but a literal place from which demons may rule. A stronghold is a real place like a prison in people that gives Satan a place to hold on to. If we don't deal with the stronghold we won't have victory over the strongman. We will study strongholds in chapter twelve.

The Greek word for arguments (imaginations in the King James) is "logismos" which is the root word for the English word "logic". The devil actually builds false logic systems in people that keep them from responding to the Gospel. There are arguments like "I do more good than I do evil, so I guess I will go to heaven" or "it doesn't matter what I believe as long as I'm sincere". Such logic holds people in darkness until we pray it off from them.

The Greek word translated "pretension" or "high thing" in the King James refers to an elevated high place or root of pride that keeps the lost from responding to the Gospel. Before I was saved my "high place" was that I thought I was every bit as good as the man who witnessed to me so I didn't think I needed to be saved.

Our duty as Believers is to learn how to war with the weapons which have the divine power to demolish the wrong belief systems, etc. that keep people from walking in the fullness of the Gospel of the Kingdom.

We will study weapons for battle in chapter seven.

CHAPTER FOUR
THE HEAT OF THE BATTLE

Thinking Christians need to answer the question: "why do many Christians struggle so much"? Why do some struggle in certain areas and others in other areas? Is the struggle simply against the sinful nature? If so, why does one person's sinful nature tempt him to addictions while another person's sinful nature tempts him to lust?

Is the battle against a sinful world? Are people simply the victims of an ungodly society? Is it truly society's fault when a teenage gunman lashes back at society and kills some of his classmates and teachers? If so, why do some people come from terrible circumstances to become outstanding citizens while others with similar situations become psychopaths?

Are there demons behind every bush tempting people to sin and ruin? Was Flip Wilson right when he said "the devil made me do it"? If so, why can the devil make some people do bad things but not others?

Our answer to those questions depends on our world view. There are two world views that go to unbalanced extremes and must be rejected. There is one world view that is Scriptural and right and we need to line up with that one. Unfortunately many Christians don't have a truly Scriptural world view.

In my seminars I ask people to think of some things that God has created. Most people name things like: stars, lakes, trees, people, animals and things like that. Few people ever mention unseen things like gravity, power, authority, time, angels or demons. That shows that most people have a materialistic world view.

1. <u>The Materialistic World View</u> believes that only what is seen is real. America and most developed countries hold this view. The natural world view says "only that which can be observed is real". If you cannot see it, taste it, hear it, buy it or sell it, it is not real. This view leaves no room for angels or spirits and little room for God. Dr. Gott's medical advice column in the Sturgis Journal 1/15/98 reflected this view:

> Dear Dr. Gott: Have you every talked to someone who was cursed by a witch? I have been. What can I do to clear myself of it?
>
> Dear Reader: Witches' curses are nothing more than superstitions. If you don't believe in them, they won't affect you at all. On the other hand, the mind is a powerful instrument and strong beliefs can certainly alter one's attitude, life — even health. In certain African cultures, a person cursed by a witch doctor will often become ill and die. Western scientists have yet to discover the basis for this phenomenon, but it happens nonetheless, probably because the victims are utterly convinced that they will die. What you need is a counter spell, the most effective which is for you to recognize that such curses are simply inane ramblings. Once you stop believing in this foolishness, you can devote your energies to more productive pursuits, such as getting on with your life and realizing that more positive attitudes will serve you better.

The error of the materialistic world view is that it ignores the spiritual. Have you ever seen God? Have you ever tasted God? Have you ever smelled God? If not, the natural world view will tell you that there is no God. But have you felt God? Of course you have. Now let me ask you this: Have you ever seen pain? Have you ever tasted pain? Have you ever smelled pain? No, but you have felt it. Have you ever seen a demon? Have you ever tasted a demon? Have you ever smelled a demon? Perhaps not, but without a doubt you have felt the work of demons, whether or not you have identified its source.

2. <u>The Spiritualistic World View</u> believes that true reality is unseen. This world view sees a demon behind every bush. It believes that everything that happens is caused by unseen spiritual forces. People become pawns in the hands of the spirit world. There are several forms of the spiritualistic world view. Christian Science teaches that all matter is illusion and that only the spiritual which is unseen is truly real. Pantheism thinks God is the transcendent reality of which the material universe and man are only manifestations. It denies God's personality and expresses a tendency to identify God and nature as one.

The greatest error of the spiritualistic view is that it ignores personal human responsibility. I think of a funeral I did for one of two boys who died in a drunken automobile wreck. At the visitation people were trying to comfort one another from the spiritualistic world view. They said things like "it was their time to go" and "God knows best" as if it was God's fault that these boys broke the commandments of God; ignored the laws of the land and drove their car into a tree at a high rate of speed.

3. <u>The Scriptural World View</u> states that both the seen and the unseen are real. Paul indicated this in several passages. Referring to Jesus he said *"For by him all things were created: things in heaven and on earth,* **visible and invisible,** *whether thrones or power or rulers or authorities; all things were created by him and for him. (Colossians 1:16* — Emphasis mine).

We need a basic understanding of the Scriptural world view if we are going to understand deliverance ministry and spiritual warfare.

It is important that we pay more attention to what is unseen. Paul said it this way, *"So we fix our eyes not on what is seen, but on what is* *unseen. For what is seen is temporary, but what is **unseen** is eternal"* (II Corinthians 4:18 — Emphasis mine).

To be effective in healing and deliverance ministry we need to focus on the unseen things that are eternal.

There is a whole realm and hierarchy of unseen demonic forces that God calls us to war against. Only those who recognize them and war against them will walk in victory over the kingdom of darkness. The Bible gives us a concise overview of what we are up against. *"Finally, be strong in the Lord and his mighty power. Put on the full armor of God so that you can take your stand against the devil's schemes. **For our struggle is not against flesh and blood, but against the rulers**, against the **authorities**, against the **powers** of this dark world and against the **spiritual forces of evil** in the heavenly realms"* (Ephesians 6:10-12 — Emphasis mine).

We will discuss this hierarchy of demonic beings further in chapter eight.

CHAPTER FIVE
THE THREE MAJOR BATTLEGROUNDS

Success in battle requires an understanding of our opponents. There are three major battlegrounds that Christians face. First is the battle ground of the sinful nature, second is the battleground of our sinful world, and lastly is the battleground in the heavenly realms. Let's take a look at them.

1. *The battleground of our sinful nature.* There are three major parts of the sinful nature that we need to understand: the Adamic sin nature, the acquired sin nature, and evil desires which come from the sinful nature.

a. *The war with the Adamic sin nature.* The Adamic refers to the sinful condition of every heart that has been passed down through Adam's sin. Romans describes it as follows, *"Therefore, just as sin entered the world through one man, and death through sin, and in this way death came to all men, because all sinned"* (Romans 5:12).

Everyone, thanks to Adam, is born with a general tendency to sin. Even "innocent" little babies have a sinful nature. Put two young children in a crib with a couple of toys and you will soon have a fight. Why? Because of the Adamic sin nature.

b. ***The war with our acquired sin nature.*** We've all learned that specific tendencies to sin can be passed down from birth parents. The children of alcoholics tend to become alcoholics. The children of child abusers tend to become child abusers. It is fascinating to note how this acquired sinful nature is passed down by the birth parents even if the child doesn't know his or her birth parents.

One of my dearest friends illustrates this. I won him and his wife to the Lord a few years ago and they have grown into wonderful Christians. The man had a son through a woman he never married. They broke up before the boy ever knew his father and the mother kept the boy and his father apart until the boy became a young adult. Then, through the hand of God, the boy and his father were reunited. It is amazing to see how alike they are — right down to the acquired sin nature. The son, even though he just recently met his father, has inherited the specific sin nature that the father was held captive to before he was born again. God's Word explains this. *"Those of you who are left will waste away in the lands of their enemies because of their sins; also because of their fathers' sins they will waste away. "'But if they will confess their sins and the sins of their fathers — their treachery against me and their hostility toward me, which made me hostile toward them so that I sent them into the land of their enemies — then when their uncircumcised hearts are humbled and they pay for their sin, I will remember my covenant with Jacob and my covenant with Isaac and my covenant with Abraham, and I will remember the land"* (Leviticus 26:39-42).

To be effective in ministry to whole persons we need to minister to the acquired sin nature. We will take a deeper look at this in chapter twenty-five. For now we just need to consider how the sins of the parents are visited to their children. *"See, it stands written before me: I will not keep silent but will pay back in full: I will pay it back into their laps — both your sins and the sins of your fathers, says the Lord."* Isaiah 65:6-7a.

c. ***Our war with evil desires.*** Evil desires may be triggered by outward stimulation but the outward stimulation actually appeals to the evil desire within. James addressed this. *When tempted, no one should say, "God is tempting me." For God cannot be tempted by evil, nor does he tempt anyone; but each one is tempted when, by his own evil desire, he is dragged away and enticed. Then, after desire has conceived, it gives birth to sin; and sin, when it is full-grown, gives birth to death* (James 1:13-15.)

Thorough ministry will address the Adamic sin nature, the acquired sin nature, and the war with evil desires.

2. ***The battleground of our sinful world.*** The Apostle John sums up the battleground of the sinful world in I John. *"Do not love the world or anything in the world. If anyone loves the world, the love of the Father is not in him. For everything in the world — the cravings of sinful man, the lust of his eyes and the boasting of what he has and does — comes not from the Father but from the world. The world and its desires pass away, but the man who does the will of God lives forever"* (I John 2:15-17.)

The battleground of the sinful world includes the war with sinful cravings, the war with the lust of the eyes and the war with the pride of life.

a. ***The war with our sinful cravings deals with things that we want that are not good for us.*** They may even be good things that get in the way of better things. For example, just before I was called into the full time ministry in 1973 the devil launched an all out attack on me to make me crave things that would have put me in such debt I would not have been able to go to college or take the drastic cut in pay that was necessary when I entered the ministry. There were a lot of things that I craved: a nice house in the country, a new car, a fast motorcycle and expensive vacations and fishing trips. But the thing that summarized my deepest cravings was that I wanted a brand new canoe.

On New Year's Eve of 1972, I was working with a youth group and we showed a movie on the life of Christ. One scene still really stood out to me where the rich young man approached Jesus and asked "Good teacher, what must I do to inherit eternal life?" Jesus spoke to him about the lesser commandments and the man claimed to have kept all of them. Jesus looked at him and loved him. "One thing you lack," he said. "Go, sell everything you have and give to the poor and you will have treasure in heaven. Then Come, follow me" (Mark 10:17-22). In the movie the rich young man looked over his shoulder at his vast treasure, looked sadly back at Jesus, turned and then walked away. Then Jesus turned toward the camera and a tear was running down his cheek. I vowed in that moment that I would never again allow sinful cravings to draw me away from the Lord's call on my life. Less than six months later I was called into the ministry and registered for college. I took a 27% cut in pay, paid my way through college and never missed a meal or a payment and a few years later even ended up with a boat that was better than any canoe ever could be. But I would have missed it all had I fallen into the credit debt and fulfilled my cravings outside of God's timing.

A lot of people from affluent generations have never really resisted the battleground of sinful cravings and that has caused many to fall into the trap of debt — buying things that they crave but which usually aren't best for them.

b. *The war with the lust of our eyes.* Like kids in a candy store, we sometimes want everything we see. I think that is part of the lure of pornography and lust — wanting things that you can see with the eyes. It is interesting that the Greek word for idolatry comes from two Greek Words. "Idon" which means to see and "latria" which means to worship. Idolatry means "to worship that which you can see".

The advertising business appeals to the lust of the eyes so that millions of dollars are invested in advertisements for the Super Bowl each year. Idolatry truly lurks within the hearts of many people — including many Christians.

c. *The war with the pride of life.* Worldly people find their significance by what they do or in what they own. Ask a worldly person who they are and they will probably describe themselves by what they do, what they have built or what they have acquired. For years I found my identity in the ministry and in my family. I was proud of the church I was building and I was proud of my wife and children. There's certainly nothing wrong with being pleased with your church or family but I failed miserably because I did not find my personal identity in Christ alone.

Most churches and denominations will agree concerning the first two battlefields: the battlefield of the sinful nature and the battlefield of our sinful world. They fit in pretty well with the materialistic world view. But people with a materialistic world view have trouble understanding the battlefield of spiritual warfare even if they are Christians and go to church.

Here is where I need to ask, "Are you going to believe what a sinful world has taught you, or are you going to believe the revelation given in the Word of God?" I have a wonderful pastor friend who used to pray with a group of pastors that I met with weekly. He finally decided to leave the group because I was doing too much spiritual warfare. He said he didn't believe in a literal devil and demons. He thought they were just a personification of evil. But that isn't what the Bible teaches.

3. ***The battleground in the heavenly realms.*** People with a materialistic world view do not think much about the heavenly realms — even if they claim to be Christian. The Bible, however, teaches that our greatest blessings are found in the heavenly realms. Paul wrote *"Praise be to the God and Father of our Lord Jesus Christ, who has blessed us in the **heavenly realms** with every spiritual blessing in Christ"* (Ephesians 1:4 — Emphasis mine).

Christians will never be as effective as they can be until they realize that they are seated in the heavenly realms with Christ. *"And God raised us up with Christ and seated us with him in the **heavenly realms** in Christ Jesus"* (Ephesians 2:6 — Emphasis mine).

True deliverance ministry and spiritual warfare are actually done from the position of being seated in the heavenly realms.

Paul taught that God's intent was for Christians to declare the manifest truth of God into the heavenly realms by how we do our business for the Kingdom on earth. As we walk in right spiritual authority and declare "thy kingdom come, thy will be done on earth as it is heaven" we make known the manifold wisdom of God in the areas where we manifest such authority. *"His intent was that now, through the church, the manifold wisdom of God should be made known to the rulers and authorities in the **heavenly realms**,"* (Ephesians 3:10 — Emphasis mine).

The battleground in the heavenly realms is many fold and we will spend some time looking at it. The first thing to consider is spiritual bondage.

a. **Our war with spiritual bondage.** Satan can hold people in bondage in their minds, will, emotions and bodies. He takes them captive to his thoughts and schemes. This captivity can even be physical. One third of the healings in Mark are done through deliverance and we will look at just one from Luke that happened to a woman that Jesus called a "daughter of Abraham". *"On a Sabbath Jesus was teaching in one of the synagogues, and a woman was there who had been crippled by a spirit for eighteen years. She was bent over and could not straighten up at all. When Jesus saw her, he called her forward and said to her, 'Woman, you are set free from your infirmity.' Then he put his hands on her, and immediately she straightened up and praised God. Indignant because Jesus had healed on the Sabbath the synagogue ruler said to the people, 'There are six days for work. So come and be healed on those days, not on the Sabbath.' The Lord answered him, 'You hypocrites! Don't each of you on the Sabbath untie his ox or donkey from the stall and lead it out to give it water? Then should not this woman, a daughter of Abraham,* **whom Satan has kept bound** *for eighteen long years, be set free on the Sabbath day from what bound her?'"* (Luke 13:10-16 — Emphasis mine).

This woman's physical healing came when Jesus ministered to her spiritual bondage.

b. **Our war with spiritual captivity.** Are you a saint or a sinner? Your answer to that question reveals whether you are trusting in your good works for salvation or if you are trusting in the Lord's perfect work. The devil loves to tempt people to believe that holiness is a list of man made do's and don'ts. But the minute they do that they are taken captive to works religion apart from grace.

Both God and Satan know that if they can control how people think, they will control what they do. "As a man thinketh in his heart, so is he". Many people are held captive in their minds. If they think that they are sinners destined to fall, they will fall. But if they realize that Jesus made them saints when they were born again, they will realize their destiny to walk in victory as children of the light. The biggest battleground for most people is in their minds. That is probably why Paul wrote *"see to it that no one takes you captive through hollow and deceptive philosophy, which depends on human tradition and the basic principles of this world rather than on Christ"* (Colossians 2:8).

The devil and his demons love to hold people captive to make them do works of darkness. Paul warned Timothy about this. *"Those who oppose him he must gently instruct, in the hope that God will grant them repentance leading them to a knowledge of the truth, and that they will come to their senses and escape from the trap of the devil, who has taken them captive to do his will"* (II Timothy 2:25-26). Referring back to a verse used earlier, we need to destroy the logic systems that hold people captive. *"We demolish arguments and every pretension that sets itself up against the knowledge of God, and we take captive every thought to make it obedient to Christ"* (II Corinthians 10:5).

c. **Our war with demons.** Just as there are heavenly angels, so are there fallen angels. Demons are made up of angels that were thrown from heaven — and possibly their offspring. We will not cover that fully, other than to give you a few verses to challenge your thinking. *"The great dragon was hurled down — that ancient serpent called the devil, or Satan, who leads the whole world astray. He was hurled to the earth and his angels with him"* (Revelation 12:9).

We need to be careful when we study the Bible. The materialistic world view causes well meaning Christians to paste or cut things from their Bibles by making them see things that are not really there. For example, Job 40:15-24 gives a clear description of a dinosaur whose tail sways like a cedar tree. But most Bible notes suggest that it an elephant or a hippopotamus because scholars do not have room for dinosaurs in their thinking because they have believed the lie that dinosaurs became extinct millions of years before man evolved. Anyone who has seen an elephant or hippopotamus knows that they do not have tails that swing like a cedar — they have little curly tails.

The same thing is true of Genesis Six where the Bible says that the sons of God had children through the daughters of men and produced a powerful race of giants. Most commentators explain away the implications of that because their world view won't allow them to take it literally. Some suggest that Jesus said that the angels cannot marry humans, but Jesus qualified that statement by saying that the angels *of heaven* cannot intermarry with people. He didn't say anything about the fallen angels of hell. To me, this is one of those things that is not worth arguing about, so I will just give you the verses and let you come to your own conclusion. *"The **sons of God** saw that the **daughters of men** were beautiful, and they married any of them they chose... The Nephilim were on the earth in those days — and also afterward — when the **sons of God** went to the **daughters of men** and had children by them. They were the heroes of old, men of renown"* (Genesis 6:2, 4 — Emphasis mine).

*"At the resurrection people will neither marry nor be given in marriage; they will be like the angels in **heaven**"* (Matthew 22:30 — Emphasis mine).

Whether or not one believes that demons can have children with humans, honest Christians have to admit that the New Testament often mentions demons. Some people wonder whether or not Christians can have demons. Charles Kraft answers, "Why would they want one?"

There are entire denominations that teach Christians cannot be demonized because they have the Spirit of God. Part of their misunderstanding is terminology. The terms "demon possessed or demon possession" are not the best terms to use when describing how demons influence Believers. A better term would be "demonized". I have delivered over two hundred Christians from demons that were causing them problems.

But rather than argue with those who don't believe Christians can have demons, I ask them if Christians can be tempted, tormented or tested by demons. I ask them how they think God wants us to resist the devil like it says in James 4:7.

I Once had a long talk with a woman who was being emotionally, verbally and sometimes physically abused by her husband. He was insanely jealous and prone to outbursts of anger, criticism and accusation. She felt like she had to walk on eggshells to avoid his outbursts. She told me that she thought things would get better after he became a Christian. In some ways they had, but in other ways she never realized how big an enemy the devil was until he started following Christ.

Ephesians 2:1-2 indicates that all people are under the control of the ruler of the kingdom of the air before they are born again. The devil doesn't have to fight those he already controls. But he does oppose everything that Believers do for God.

In my seminars I illustrate the battle that begins when we decide to follow Jesus. I call on one of the biggest men present and ask him to follow me across the front of the room. I tell him that I am playing the devil and he is playing an unsaved person. The man follows me and I don't resist him at all until he 'gets saved' and begins to walk in the opposite direction to indicate that he is now following Jesus instead of the devil. I then start pushing him back in every way I can. I always end the illustration by mentioning that the big man could have knocked my socks off but chose to endure my wrong treatment instead. That is the way Christians behave when they don't resist the devil. Jesus resisted the devil and expects us to as well.

Think of how Jesus ministered to people who had demons: *"News about him (Jesus) spread all over Syria, and people brought to him all* who were ill with various diseases, those suffering severe pain, the **demon-possessed**, those having seizures, and the paralyzed, and he healed them" (Matthew 4:24 — Emphasis mine).

One particularly interesting story is of the two demon-possessed men that Jesus ministered to. Let's look at Matthew's account of them, beginning with where Jesus approached them: *"When he arrived at the other side in the region of the Gadarenes, two **demon-possessed** men coming from the tomb met him"* (Matthew 8:28 — Emphasis mine).

Consider the nature of these demonized men. They were so violent that no one could pass them by. Could it be that some of the heinous acts that people commit might be done under the power of demons? People say "I totally lost control of myself". If they weren't in control, who was?

You may remember how those demons asked to be sent into a herd of pigs. Demons always look for another living host when they are cast out. That is why it is so important to pray protection for other people and even pets before you do deliverance. (We will explore a case study of a demonized man in the next chapter)

When my wife and I first began practicing deliverance ministry there was a night that I was led to pray protection for our cat "Aristotle". But I thought that I was getting too weird so I didn't do it. We ministered deliverance individually to a young unmarried couple that had been involved in promiscuity. After we brought the man and woman back together I was again led to pray for our cat. Again I thought that would be too radical so I didn't do it. The next morning my wife called me at the office and told me that she was afraid of our cat. I asked her why and she explained how our normally docile cat had been pacing the floor all morning and how it had been staring her down with a weird look in its eyes. It literally kept Pam captive in the bathroom by staring her down whenever she tried to approach the door.

I immediately knew in my spirit what was going on so I told Pam to command the evil presence to leave the cat and our house. Pam rebuked the spirit, it left and the cat lay down and slept for the rest of the morning and most of the afternoon.

A few weeks later we ministered deliverance to a young lady at a cell group held in another person's home. We didn't know that the home owner had a cat. The next morning she called and told how she had bent over to pick up her normally loving cat. This time it became wild and began to scream and scratch at her until her husband came and rebuked the spirit that had left the young lady and entered the cat. Now we always pray protection over all the people and pets in a home before we minister deliverance.

Demons are more active and prevalent than we think even when it comes to physical aliments. Many illnesses and physical handicaps are not caused by demons, but some are. Physical ailments that are caused by demons will be healed when the person finds freedom in Christ and when we learn to exercise our authority over the devil.

I had one preacher bring another minister to me for deliverance. I had already conducted a deliverance appointment with the first preacher and he wanted his friend to find the freedom he now had. Shortly into the appointment the second preacher told us he had such a terrible headache that he could hardly hear us, so I asked the first preacher to pray for him. He started out with a long, unbelieving prayer — that kind that leaves you off the hook if God doesn't answer. So I interrupted and said "heal him, in Jesus' name!" So he said, "In Jesus' Name I command this headache to stop". And it did instantly. Now we minister physical healing along with deliverance — after all, isn't that what Jesus did?

There are three different battlegrounds and we need to minister to all three - including the battleground in the heavenly realms if we want to be successful in life and ministry.

CHAPTER SIX
CASE STUDY FROM MARK 4:35 - 5:22

Let's take a look at a longer Scripture and please allow me to make amplification right as we go through the text. I will use italics for the Scripture and regular print for my comments.

35 That day when evening came, he said to his disciples, "Let us go over to the other side." (Jesus was very intentional about moving into an area where deliverance was needed. God sent Jesus from heaven into a sinful world and Jesus never stayed in the "safe sanctuaries" but moved into the areas of greatest darkness.)

36 Leaving the crowd behind, (Even though we practice some corporate deliverance, deliverance is a ministry of the individual more than it is a ministry of the multitude. Jesus was ready to go a great distance, even when it meant leaving his opportunities for mass evangelism to reach out to one demonized man) *they took him along, just as he was,* (we have to be authentic and not put on pretenses when we are doing deliverance) *in the boat. There were also other boats with him.* (There are usually other people hanging around deliverance ministry who really don't have a clue as to what is happening.)

37 A furious squall came up and the waves broke over the boat, so that it was nearly swamped. (Consider the opposition the enemy brought to this team that was destined to minister deliverance. You can expect storms to brew if you move into deliverance. The devil doesn't like it when we learn how to set people free but Jesus modeled that he was willing to face this type of storm to help even one demonized individual)

38 Jesus was in the stern, sleeping on a cushion. The disciples woke him and said to him, "Teacher, don't you care if we drown?" (Notice how the disciples started thinking ill of their leader when the storms came. Deliverance ministry is not a ministry for the fainthearted and if the devil can't get directly to the minister of deliverance he will try to work through those who are closest to him.)

39 He got up, rebuked the wind (Notice that Jesus didn't pray about the storm. Instead he rebuked it like a demon!) *and said to the waves, "Quiet! Be still!"* (Again, he didn't pray — he told them to be still) *Then the wind died down and it was completely calm.* (People working deliverance never cease to be awed at the power of God but they do come to a point where they are seldom surprised at anything people have experienced.)

40 He said to his disciples, "Why are you so afraid? Do you still have no faith?" (Fear is the opposite of faith and is one of the quickest things to hit people moving in deliverance. Jesus addressed this lack of faith head on with his disciples.)

41 They were terrified and asked each other, "Who is this? Even the wind and the waves obey him!" (Fear is working if we are frightened when God does the miracle of deliverance. Deliverance ministry, like healing, is a work of faith.)

5:1 They went across the lake to the region of the Gerasenes. (Later we will examine how demons work regionally)

2 When Jesus got out of the boat, a man with an evil spirit came from the tombs to meet him. (People with evil spirits are often drawn to those who might help them. One of the challenges I have as a teacher of deliverance is that so many people want personal appointments when my true calling is to teach local churches how to minister deliverance — because the need is so great.)

3 This man lived in the tombs, and no one could bind him any more, not even with a chain. (Demonized people can manifest super-human strength. Jails have chairs and cots with extra strong straps to restrain people who get out of hand when they are being booked. I remember one man that was causing a terrible disturbance while I was visiting another man in jail. We were several cells away from the man causing the disturbance and there was no way that he could hear me. But I finally I spoke to the demon that was working in the man and simply said "in Jesus' Name, stop it, now!" The disturbance stopped immediately!)

4 For he had often been chained hand and foot, but he tore the chains apart and broke the irons on his feet. No one was strong enough to subdue him. (Demons can give people supernatural strength.)

5 Night and day among the tombs and in the hills he would cry out and cut himself with stones. (This man was obsessed with death, was supernaturally strong and uncontrollable. He cried out and cut himself with stones. Demons often cause people to dig at themselves or cut themselves. We have cast demons from several people, especially women, who have scars everywhere on their bodies that they could reach with their fingernails.)

6 When he saw Jesus from a distance, he ran and fell on his knees in front of him. (Some people think he was being religious or that he fell in worship, I think he may have fallen under the power of the Holy Spirit. I did a seminar where a key leader of the church came to me for ministry and confessed that he had a voice that had been telling him to run up and murder me but the power of God held him back. When I started rebuking the spirits of anger, hatred and rage, the demons of the man glared at me with a look that I don't think I will ever forget — but the spirits in the man were unable to come against the power of Jesus who lives in me.)

7 He shouted at the top of his voice, "What do you want with me, Jesus, Son of the Most High God? Swear to God that you won't torture me!" (Demons are used to the tortures and torment of hell. They feared Jesus might use his greater power to hurt them.)

8 For Jesus had said to him, "Come out of this man, you evil spirit! (The word "said" is in the present tense and would better translated "Jesus had been saying to him". Sometimes you have to continue speaking to a demon until it comes out.)

9 Then Jesus asked him, "What is your name?" (Jesus operated in human flesh and evidently the Holy Spirit hadn't revealed the name so Jesus asked. I seldom ask a demon for its name because demons are liars and you can't trust them) *"My name is Legion,"* (A legion was the largest unit of a Roman army with between 3,000 and 6,000 soldiers. It is common to cast 50 or more demons out of an individual) *he replied, "for we are many."* (Note that the demon didn't use a common name like Dick or Henry. Instead their name reflected what they did and how they worked. Jesus often cast out demons by calling them according to how they worked. For instance, he commanded the spirit of infirmity to leave a suffering woman as in Luke 13:11.)

10 And he begged Jesus again and again not to send them out of the area. (The word area here comes from the Greek word "topos" that we get our word "topography" from. Ephesians 6:11-12 shows that there is a hierarchy of demons. These demons did not want to be sent into unfamiliar territory where another gang of demons was ruling.)

11 A large herd of pigs was feeding on the nearby hillside. (Demons are opportunist and they seek an unclean living host to attach to.)

12 The demons begged Jesus, "Send us among the pigs; allow us to go into them." (Demons are disembodied spirits and they always seek living hosts to "go into".)

13 He gave them permission, and the evil spirits came out and went into the pigs. (I believe it can be dangerous to send demons into other living hosts. This was not a standard practice for Jesus either. I personally like to send them to the feet of Jesus and actually think doing so helps quicken the return of Jesus. (See Psalm 110:1, and Hebrews 1:13 and 10:13.)

14 Those tending the pigs ran off and reported this in the town and countryside, and the people went out to see what had happened. (You would expect people to be excited about such a remarkable deliverance, but some people, especially religious people, seem to get upset rather than rejoicing.)

15 When they came to Jesus, they saw the man who had been possessed by the legion of demons, sitting there, dressed and in his right mind; and they were afraid. (This man had been anti-social, had superhuman strength, and had been uncontrollable and indecent. Now he is dressed and normal and the people were afraid. Why were they afraid when they should have been rejoicing? Demons always seek a living host, so perhaps the legion of demons left the pigs when they drowned and attached to the town's people, making them afraid of the wonders of God.)

16 Those who had seen it told the people what had happened to the demon-possessed man — and told about the pigs as well. 17 Then the people began to plead with Jesus to leave their region. (There are times when people, especially religious people, fail to see the wonderful changes that take place when people are delivered from demons. These people — or perhaps the demons working through the people — actually pleaded with Jesus to leave after He did this deliverance)

18 As Jesus was getting into the boat, the man who had been demon-possessed begged to go with him. (There is always the temptation for people who have been delivered to become dependent on the person who works deliverance for them rather than becoming secure in Christ.)

19 Jesus did not let him, but said, "Go home to your family and tell them how much the Lord has done for you, and how he has had mercy on you." (The best witness of deliverance is the testimony of one who was bound but is now free. I will never forget the powerful testimony of a woman who was delivered on the very day she was going to commit suicide. She spoke at a camp meeting where two or three hundred people, including children and teens, clung to her every word as she spoke. Another lady who had undergone deliverance drove two hours to testify to our church how Jesus had set her free through our deliverance ministry. She held up a paper plate with 29 psychotropic drugs she used to take before she could get out of bed each morning. Her deliverance was so effective that her psychiatrist had her down to three pills in less than three months. Such testimonies are powerful.)

20 So the man went away and began to tell in the Decapolis how much Jesus had done for him. And all the people were amazed. (People responded to the actual testimony of the person delivered better than they did to Jesus who did the deliverance.)

21 When Jesus had again crossed over by boat to the other side of the lake, a large crowd gathered around him while he was by the lake. (Jesus left a crowd to help the demonized man, but there was another crowd waiting when he was done. He didn't lose opportunities for large group ministry by taking time to work deliverance with an individual.)

22-24 Then one of the synagogue rulers, named Jairus, came there. Seeing Jesus, he fell at his feet and pleaded earnestly with him, "My little daughter is dying. Please come and put your hands on her so that she will be healed and live." So Jesus went with him. A large crowd followed and pressed around him. (When word gets out that people are being delivered and really helped under your ministry, people seem to come out of the woodwork seeking help.)

We know that not everyone who is anti-social, extra strong, uncontrollable, indecent, self-abusive or religious is demonized. But we just studied the story of one man who was. How many times do secular treatment plans fail because the etymology of a disorder is demonic? I think more often than our western minds are willing to admit.

The proof is in the pudding. We have seen people delivered from all sorts of addictions, self-defeating behaviors, hurtful actions and physical afflictions when we have dealt with the spiritual issues behind their problems. Doesn't it make sense that we find out what the Bible says about demons and deliverance?

d. ***Our war with the strongman.*** In the context of deliverance ministry Jesus spoke about the strong man. *"Or again, how can anyone enter a strong man's house and carry off his possessions unless he first ties up the strong man? Then he can rob his house."* Mt 12:29. I've learned that the strongman spirit is usually a weak spirit that has gained strength by grouping other demons around itself. When we do deliverance we like to bind the strongman from giving directions and help to lesser demons. Then we cast out all the demons that support the strongman. After they are gone, the strongman's grip is weakened and they are easily cast out. This works really well when dealing with spirits of fear. First we bind the strongman of fear and then deal with all the supporting spirits of fear like: fear of snakes, fear of men, fear of spiders, fear of the dark, etc. Once we have cast out the lesser spirits of fear the strongman of fear (or phobia) comes out easily.

e. ***Our War with Footholds.*** There are some things that give the devil footholds — places in our lives where he can stand and gateways through which demons can come. Unresolved anger is mentioned in Ephesians. *"In your anger do not sin": Do not let the sun go down while you are still angry, and do not give the devil a **foothold***. (Emphasis mine). (The Greek word is "topon" from which we get the English root of topography. Ongoing anger gives the devil a literal place to stand in our lives) Eph 4:26-27.

CHAPTER SEVEN
STANDING STRONG IN BATTLE

*Therefore put on the full armor of God, so that when the day of evil comes, you may be able to stand your ground, and after you have done everything, to stand (*Ephesians 6:13).

Deliverance ministry, whether it is for yourself or for others, is not for the timid or the unprepared. It is foolish to enter deliverance ministry with sin or strongholds in the heart. It is crucial to be under proper authority and covering when doing deliverance ministry.

1. WEAPONS FOR THE BATTLE:

A hunter would never go into the woods without the proper weapons — especially if hunting dangerous game. Demons are dangerous game and we must be careful to put on the full armor of God and walk with divine weapons when we move in deliverance. In this chapter we will discuss some of the Christian's weapons for the battle.

a. *The cross of Jesus Christ.* We can with the battle with our sinful nature by crucifying our sinful selves on the Cross of Calvary. Jesus did go to the Cross on our behalf — but he did not go there so we would not have to. He went there so we could also make it to the Cross. He bore our sins on the tree so that we might die to sin and self and be crucified with Christ so we can live new lives. *He himself bore our sins in his body on the tree, so that we might die to sins and live for righteousness; by his wounds you have been healed (*1 Peter 2:24).

Our belief in Jesus' crucifixion and resurrection should lead to our personal crucifixion and resurrection by faith to the victorious Christian life. Paul said *"I have been crucified with Christ and I no longer live, but Christ lives in me. The life I live in the body, I live by faith in the Son of God, who loved me and gave himself for me"* (Galatians 2:20).

The Christian's death and resurrection is not automatic. We need to apply and appropriate our identification with Jesus' death and resurrection to our personal lives. The Book of Romans says *"What shall we say, then? Shall we go on sinning so that grace may increase? By no means! We died to sin; how can we live in it any longer? Or don't you know that all of us who were baptized into Christ Jesus were baptized into his death? We were therefore buried with him through baptism into death in order that, just as Christ was raised from the dead through the glory of the Father, we too may live a new life".* Romans 6:1-4.

During one Good Friday Service I had the people write any sin they were struggling with onto a piece of paper and then nail it to a wooden cross that was made by an ex-drug dealer in the congregation. I thought it was a really neat idea. Later on, however, I realized that just nailing our sins to the cross does not bring victory. To walk in victory we must nail ourselves to the cross of Christ. That means dying to self. It means taking self off the throne of our lives and putting Jesus Christ at the command center of our hearts.

b. ***Confess and renounce acquired sin.*** The early church knew the importance of not only confessing sin but also renouncing the works of the devil. Early baptism services included the phrase "I renounce the devil and all his works". But now we want everything the fast and easy way. We wrongly think that simply confessing our sins takes care of everything, but confession is only part of the path to freedom. Confession takes care of things between us and God, but complete confession will address the sins that have been inherited from our ancestors. And it will also renounce and break down the strongholds of the devil.

The Bible has several verses that deal with confessing the sins of the fathers. Both Daniel and Nehemiah demonstrate confessing the sins of their forefathers. They saw the need to confess the sins of their fathers even if they were not practicing them personally. Daniel, for example, was not stiff-necked and he did not worship idols like many of his forefathers did.

- *Our sins and the iniquities of our fathers have made Jerusalem and your people an object of scorn to all those around us* (Daniel 9:16b).
- *They stood in their places and confessed their sins and the wickedness of their fathers* (Nehemiah 9:2b).

The wisest man who ever lived taught the importance of renouncing sin. *"He who conceals his sins does not prosper, but whoever confesses and renounces them finds mercy* (Proverbs 28:13).

While confession is made to God the Father for forgiveness of sins, renouncing is a way of resisting the devil and canceling his hold because of past sins. In confession we submit to God and in renouncing we resist the devil as James taught us to. *"Submit yourselves, then, to God. **Resist** the devil, and he will flee from you"* (James 4:7 — Emphasis mine).

c. **Set your mind on the Spirit.** Nature abhors a vacuum. It isn't enough to take your mind off evil desires. You must also fill it with right desires from the Holy Spirit. Whenever we pray with people and come against strongholds or demons, we always try to pray the opposite of their previous condition. If they are anxious, we pray for peace. If they struggle with doubt, we pray for faith, etc.

We can choose either to set our mind on the Spirit or on the sinful nature and that choice determines the outcome of our lives. We have a choice and we need to choose daily to focus on the Spirit. As Paul wrote, *"Those who live according to the sinful nature have their minds set on what that nature desires; but those who live in accordance with the Spirit have their minds set on what the Spirit desires. The mind of sinful man is death, but the mind controlled by the Spirit is life and peace..."* (Romans 8:5-6).

The only way we can enjoy daily victory is to so set our minds on the Spirit that we actually live by the Spirit. *"So I say, live by the Spirit, and you will not gratify the desires of the sinful nature. For the sinful nature desires what is contrary to the Spirit, and the Spirit what is contrary to the sinful nature. They are in conflict with each other, so that you do not do what you want"* (Galatians 5:16-17).

d. **Seek Sanctification.** It's not enough to confess the "big three": the pride of life, the lust of the eyes and sinful cravings. When we confess our sins, God forgives us and purifies us from them. But in seeking sanctification, we are set apart from sin. We can all pray Paul's prayer for ourselves and for others. *"May God himself, the God of peace, sanctify you through and through, may your whole spirit, soul and body be kept blameless at the coming of our Lord Jesus Christ"* (I Thessalonians 5:23).

When a person is born again it is their spirit that is made new. Jesus said that the Spirit gives birth to spirit. After people are born again, their souls still need to be saved which means that their souls need to come into alignment with their converted spirits. In other words, they need to work with God to let the work He has done in their converted spirits work its way into their souls which are "being saved".

But we are not of them who draw back unto perdition; but of them that **believe to the saving of the soul** (Hebrews 10:39 KJV — Emphasis mine).

Our spirits are born again by faith the instant we believe but our souls are *being* born again as we believe God for the transformation of the way we think, the way we feel, and the way we choose.

First Thessalonians 5:23 shows the order of sanctification. First spirit, then soul and finally the body is cleansed and restored. God's renewing work begins from the inside out. The spirit is the eternal part of us that communicates with God. The soul, (which is our mind, will emotions and memories) is gradually changed as we die to sinful desires, submit to God and grow. And finally, these changes in our spirits and souls bring hope of renewal even to our bodies until their redemption.

God redeems us in reverse order in which he gives us up. Notice the order of "giving up" from Romans chapter one.

First God gives people over in their bodies. *"Therefore God **gave them over** in the sinful desires of their hearts to sexual impurity for the degrading of their **bodies** with one another.* (Romans 1:24 — Emphasis mine).

Next God gives people over to shameful lusts which are a work of the soul — the mind, will emotions and memories. *"Because of this, God **gave them over** to shameful lusts..."* (Romans 1:26a — Emphasis mine).

God finally gives people over to a depraved mind which does not retain the knowledge of God — which is a work of the spirit. Therefore God gives man over in spirit. *"... He **gave them over** to a depraved mind..." (*Romans 1:28b — Emphasis mine).

Sanctification reverses this process of giving up as it restores spirit, soul and body in that order.

   e. **Put on the armor to stand against the forces of evil.** Ephesians 6:14-20 speaks about the Christian's armor. Some people tell you to put on the armor every morning. I suggest that you never take it off, for the armor is probably more important at night when you are in a semi-conscious state than it is when you are alert. Let's take a brief look at the armor.

> ➤ The Belt of Truth. The word for truth here means "reality" — knowing who you really are in Christ. It includes the truth that you are a saint, that nothing can separate you from the Love of God, that you can do all things through Christ who strengthens you and the like. The belt of truth guards your loins and keeps you from tripping over yourself.

- The Breastplate of Righteousness. This means right standing in God with Christ which guards your heart. A secret here is that it is not enough to just stand with imputed righteousness — we have to wear it and live it in our daily lives. True righteousness begins with right standing with God through faith but it moves into being in the right places at the right times doing the right things with the right people.
- The Sandals of the Gospel of Peace. Like the knobby soles of a soldier's boot, the Gospel of peace keeps you from slipping in your Christian walk. We have learned how important it is to speak God's peace into our home, our church and into our daily lives.
- The Shield of Faith. The shield protects you from the enemy's arrows and covers all your vitals. Chuck Pierce wrote about the shield of faith in the excellent book *Restoring Your Shield of Faith* that I highly recommend.
- The Helmet of Salvation. The Greek word for salvation means so much more than our English understanding of salvation. "Sozo" refers to God rescuing and saving us in every way. The helmet protects your head and the way you view life. When people tell me they are saved I like to ask them "what are you saved from — and to?".
- The Sword of the Spirit which is the word of God. The Greek word translated "word" is "rhema" which means the spoken or illumined word of God which guides your offense. This is the first of the offensive weapons that helps you gain your ground. Rhema includes words that the Spirit brings to mind from Scripture or prophetic words.
- Prayer in the Spirit. People may disagree about what praying in the Spirit means — but almost everybody knows what it is like to listen to prayer that is not done in the Spirit. Praying in the Spirit means praying however the Spirit guides you and with His help. Such prayer helps you capture new territory.

f. **Repentance.** Sin gives the devil footholds. Continued sin allows him to set up strongholds. The only way to stay free from the devil is to go and sin no more. Christians need to stay connected to one another. Young Christians should always be assigned a mature Christian mentor to help them in their walk.

We need to understand what true repentance is. It is not just a 180 degree change of direction. People can do that without having a change of heart. People often come into the church because they are under conviction. They stop doing the wrong things and start doing the right things and everybody presumes that they are born again. But many times that is not really the case. They have had a life change but not a heart change. Without a heart change they soon fall away.

True repentance is a change of heart that leads to a change of behavior. It breaks the power of sin in our lives and leads us into times of refreshing from the Lord. *"Repent, then, and turn to God, so that your sins may be wiped out, that times of refreshing may come from the Lord"* (Acts 3:19).

g. Deliverance. People in spiritual bondage often need help to find spiritual freedom. God wants every Believer to have victory in Christ. But He never meant for us to operate independently. God gifts different members of the body differently so we can help each other and because He wants the members of the body to depend on each other.

Anything less than total freedom from demonic bondage leads to a substandard Christian life. Paul chastised the Galatians saying, *"It is for freedom that Christ has set us free. Stand firm, then, and do not let yourselves be burdened again by a yoke of slavery"* (Galatians 5:1).

Jesus wants us to experience the truth that sets us free. *"Then you will know the truth, and the truth will set you free"* (John 8:32).

We need to reject the proud Protestant error that we can deal with our sins secretly. The Bible says we need to confess our sins to each other and pray for each other. *"Therefore **confess your sins to each other and pray for each other so that you may be healed.** The prayer of a righteous man is powerful and effective"* (James 5:16 — Emphasis mine).

h. ***Resisting the Devil and His Demons.*** Demons won't let go of any area of your life unless you tell them to. Simply uttering the words "spirit of _____, I resist you" will make them leave. I wanted to use the words "rebuking and rebuke" where I used "resisting and resist: here. The reason I chose not to was because of the temptation of pride. We do have the authority of Christ over demons and they must obey. When we resist the devil, he has to flee. But pride comes before a fall and if we begin rebuking demons from a stance of pride rather than a stance of Spirit-led authority, we set ourselves up for spiritual battles that cannot be won apart from true humility.

James understood the link between humility and spiritual authority when he wrote *"But he gives us more grace. That is why Scripture says: "God opposes the proud but gives grace to the humble." Submit yourselves, then, to God. Resist the devil, and he will flee from you"* (James 4:6-7).

i. ***Binding the Strong Man.*** We are the body of Jesus on earth today. He does his work through us. We can't rebuke a demon or bind a strongman in our own power but, thank God, we don't have to. We have his power and can do it in Jesus' name. Jesus meant it when He said *"I will give you the keys of the kingdom of heaven; whatever you bind on earth will be bound in heaven, and whatever you loose on earth will be loosed in heaven"* (Matthew 16:19).

We usually take binding and loosing in a negative sense but we can also apply it positively. Proverbs 3:3 speaks about binding good things about your neck. We've learned to bind certain Scriptures and spiritual fruits to people that we pray for. We may pray something like, "today I bind peace to my wife as she cares for her mother who has Alzheimer's disease".

j. ***Making Your Salvation Sure.*** Far too many Believers walk in insecurity. They think they are saved. They hope they are saved. But they are plagued with doubts. Anyone who doubts his or her salvation will not have much power against the devil and demons. It's when you come to realize who you are in Christ that you can face the enemy and take authority over him in Jesus' Name.

Assurance of salvation is a matter of taking God at his word. I knew a dear Christian woman who was afraid of having surgery for fear that she might die and not be ready. She had grown up in a Pastor's family but had been taught that brand of work's salvation that teaches you are saved by faith but that you keep your salvation by not doing certain things.

As an adult the woman did her best to follow Jesus and prayed through out the days and nights. But she was still plagued with doubt. I asked her if she had Jesus and she told me yes, that she couldn't make it without him. So I quoted First John to her. *"And this is the testimony: God has given us eternal life, and this life is in his Son. He who has the Son has life; he who does not have the Son of God does not have life"* (I John 5:11-12). I asked her, "Do you have Jesus?" She said yes, so I assured her "then you have eternal life". And eternal life is… eternal! We don't need to argue about eternal security or apostasy. We just need to believe in real security. If we really have Jesus we are really secure!

God tells us that we need to do two things to become his children. We simply need to receive Jesus and believe in him. When we do that we become children of God. *"Yet to all who received him, to those who believed in his name, he gave the right to become children of God"* (John 1:12).

When I lead people to Jesus I often illustrate the truth of John 1:12 by giving them a pencil and asking "when did that pencil become yours?" They usually say "when you gave it to me". So I take it back and try it again and again until they realize that it became theirs the moment they took it. God already gave his Son to be our savior — but Jesus doesn't really become our personal savior until we receive him.

Some people struggle with doubt because they have confessed Jesus as their Savior but have not recognized him as Lord. Larry Kreider says that the word "Savior" is mentioned 37 times in the Bible. The word

"Lord" is found 7,736 times. Savior is mentioned 22 times in the New Testament and Lord is found 433 times. Paul said that we need to confess Jesus as "Lord", not "Savior". *"That if you confess with your mouth, 'Jesus is Lord,' and believe in your heart that God raised him from the dead, you will be saved. For it is with your heart that you believe and are justified, and it is with your mouth that you confess and are saved... For, 'Everyone who calls on the name of the Lord will be saved'"* (Romans 10:9-10, 13).

Jesus is Savior, but we don't truly walk in victory until we know him as Lord. You can remove all doubt now by confessing Jesus as Lord. "Lord Jesus, I receive you as my Savior and will follow you as Lord. I place my faith in you to help me live and grow as a Christian. Amen."

CHAPTER EIGHT
THE OPPONENTS OF OUR BATTLE

Every good coach makes it his business to study the opposing team. Can you imagine lining up on the football fields with both teams wearing the same uniforms? You might line up right, but you would get sidetracked in the battle. Many of us are averted from the real enemy. Take a look at a familiar verse.

- *For our struggle is not against flesh and blood...* (Ephesians 6:11a).
- *For we wrestle not against flesh and blood, but against...* (Ephesians 6:11 KJV).

Our biggest drawback as we follow Christ is not that we have evil spirits to fight, but that we "wrestle not". We may fight, but we often end up fighting each other rather than the spiritual forces of evil.

a. ***Our Struggle is NOT Against People.*** Why is it that two people, who love each other so much that they are married, fight as if they are enemies? This happens even in the church — why? Because we don't always recognize who the real enemy is. When we do, we join forces and fight our common enemy together rather than fighting each other.

Why is it that Christians from the same Church struggle to get along? They believe in the same Lord, they love the same church. They get mad at the same Pastor and read the same Bible. So why do so many Christians act like bullies or babies in so many board and committee meetings? Why do they nurse their hurt feelings rather than looking on Christ and living? It is because they think that they are fighting with each other, when they are really contending with the devil and demons.

God began teaching me this lesson one time when it was my day off and I was in a really bad mood and didn't know why. I spent most of the day outside because I didn't want my wife to witness what I was feeling. I truly love her, but that day I didn't like her — and couldn't figure out why. It didn't seem like she could do anything right, even though she wasn't doing anything wrong. When I came in for lunch I was determined to not let her in on the black cloud I felt was suffocating me.

After eating a quiet lunch she asked "is something wrong". I shouted "no" and slammed my way out and went back in the woods to cut wood. But the Lord started ministering to me and I soon realized something was wrong and Pam could see it even when I didn't understand it. I finally confessed to her how I was feeling. At first she thought that she must be doing something wrong but I assured her that the black cloud was not coming from her but from the enemy. When we finally grasped the truth of the battle we were in we joined forces and fought the enemy off together. It worked that day and has ever since. It sounds too good to be true, but negative feelings and reactions have almost entirely become a thing of the past since we've learned to really pray for each other.

b. ***Our Struggle IS against a Hierarchy of Demonic Beings.*** Paul said it this way, *"Our struggle is not against flesh and blood, but against the rulers, against the authorities, against the powers of this dark world and against the spiritual forces of evil in the heavenly realms.* (Ephesians 6:11b-12).

Paul mentions four categories of spiritual enemies here. First are *the rulers or principalities* (Greek "archai") which rule over Entire Nations and/or Territories. These rulers are spiritual forces of evil which stand behind the natural forces of territorial government. Daniel recognized this force when he spoke about the "king of Persia" in Daniel 10. The context shows that he was speaking about the spiritual forces behind the human ruler. *"But the prince of the Persian kingdom resisted me twenty-one days. Then Michael, one of the chief princes, came to help me, because I was detained there with the king of Persia"* (Daniel 10:13). A check of the context in Daniel 10:1-11:1 shows that even God's angels struggle against demonic rulers when God's people pray.

The second category of spiritual enemy is *authorities* (Greek exousia) which are over supernatural & human governments on a smaller scale. They seem to target smaller areas like The United States rather than all of America. These are the forces that work behind the scenes to fulfill Satan's purposes through human governments and organizations. Think about it: why was the Bible and prayer taken out of schools in the United States? It wasn't just Madelyn O' Hare; it was the spiritual forces working through her.

Why is witchcraft entering our schools in the U.S.A. and tempting our children? It's not just Ms. Rawlings and Harry Potter; it is the spiritual authorities that are using books on sorcery in an attempt to lead a very important generation astray.

There are a lot of reasons given for the rise of drug use. But the word sorcery comes from the Greek word "pharmakaia" which means there are literally demonic authorities working behind illicit drug trade.

If Christians are going to be as shrewd as serpents and as innocent as doves they must learn to see the demonic forces working behind gang activity. They need to understand what stirs up the pro-choice crowd so much. They need to pray about the powers working behind the scenes to legalize sodomy in the form of gay marriages.

The third category of demons is called powers (Greek — dunamis) which are over people groups within their specific cultures. These are the spiritual forces working behind the scenes in countries and cultures. Each place and people seems to have their own corner on behaviors that dishonor God. Think about it. Most people in the USA are materialistic. Most Amish practice healing magic. France is sensuous and Africa is superstitious. The Irish are known to be hot-headed and the Germans are called stubborn. It is never fair to over generalize and with God there are exceptions to every rule. But there are powers working over people groups and they are determined to keep people in bondage. Somehow these "powers' continue working in people of certain cultures even when they move to different regions of the world.

The last category of demons listed in Ephesians Six is the one that is the greatest focus of personal deliverance ministry. It is called the *spiritual forces of evil* (Greek kismokratoras) which work in, through and against individuals.

These are the common every day "household" demons. They are the lower level spirits that pick on people. They are portrayed by little red suited devils that sit on a person's shoulder in the cartoons. They are more real than we imagine. Why do some really good people do such awful things? Where do thoughts of murder and suicide come from? Where do shocking thoughts of sin come from? Have you ever had the urge to jump off a high place or to swing into the oncoming line of traffic? Why? When you aren't in control — who is?

CHAPTER NINE
EXAMPLES OF THE BATTLE

The Apostle Paul, inspired by the Holy Spirit, did his very best to help us understand how demonic forces work against God's people. Let's take a deeper look at the familiar text from First Corinthians 10:1-13 to understand how demons work to bring havoc to our lives.

"For I do not want you to be ignorant of the fact, brothers, that our forefathers were all under the cloud and that they all passed through the sea. They were all baptized into Moses in the cloud and in the sea. They all ate the same spiritual food and drank the same spiritual drink; for they drank from the spiritual rock that accompanied them, and that rock was Christ."

Our daily victory has to center on the person of Jesus Christ. He does not need to go back to the cross. We just need to appropriate the victory he already purchased for us through the cross.

I used to think God was a little unfair with Moses for banning him from the Promised Land because Moses struck the rock the second time just like he did the first time — even though God had told him to speak to the rock so the water would come out for the people. (Exodus 17:1-6 and 20:8-12). But Paul explained "that rock was Christ". Jesus did not need to be smitten and crucified twice. After he went to the Cross all we have to do is declare its power to receive its benefits.

Paul continues, *Nevertheless, God was not pleased with most of them; their bodies were scattered over the desert. Now these things occurred as examples to keep us from setting our hearts on evil things as they did. Do not be idolaters, as some of them were; as it is written; "The people sat down to eat and drink and got up to indulge in pagan revelry." We should not commit sexual immorality, as some of them did — and in one day twenty-three thousand of them died. We should not test the Lord, as some of them did — and were killed by snakes. And do not grumble, as some of them did — and were killed by the destroying angel.*

God wants us to see the consequences of setting our hearts on evil things like idolatry, partying, sexual immorality, testing the Lord and grumbling. The same things that happened to the Israelites when they lost their way to the Promised Land illustrates what will happen to us if we are not steadfast in the spiritual battle we are in. Paul says *"These things happened to them as examples and were written down as warnings for us, on whom the fulfillment of the ages has come. So, if you think you are standing firm, be careful that you don't fall! No temptation has seized you except what is common to man, and God is faithful; he will not let you be tempted beyond what you can bear. But when you are tempted, he will also provide a way out so that you can stand up under it.* 1 Corinthians 10:11-13.

Someone said that the New Testament is in the Old Testament concealed and the Old Testament is in the New Testament Revealed. I think that proves true as we study Exodus chapter six and First Corinthians chapter 13 to see how the Old Testament passage relates to the New Testament one.

Then the LORD said to Moses, "Now you will see what I will do to Pharaoh: Because of my mighty hand he will let them go; because of my mighty hand he will drive them out of his country." God also said to Moses. "I am the LORD. I appeared to Abraham, to Isaac and to Jacob as God Almighty, but my name the LORD I did not make myself known to them. I also established my covenant with them to give them the land of Canaan, where they lived as aliens. Moreover, I have heard the groaning of the Israelites, whom the Egyptians are enslaving, and I have remembered my covenant. Therefore, say to the Israelites: 'I am the LORD, and I will bring you out from under the yoke of the Egyptians. I will free you from being slaves to them, and I will redeem you with an outstretched arm and with mighty acts of judgment. I will take you as my own people, and I will be your God. Then you will know that I am the LORD your God, who brought you out from under the yoke of the Egyptians, and I will bring you to the land I swore with uplifted hand to give to Abraham, to Isaac and to Jacob. I will give it to you as a possession. I am the LORD.'" Moses reported this to the Israelites, but they did not listen to him because of their discouragement and cruel bondage" (Exodus 6:1-9).

This is the beginning of the story of how the Israelites could have escaped from bondage. They got a good start, but unfortunately they allowed discouragement to take their minds off the promises of God and most of them did not make it all the way into the Promised Land.

Their story leaves an example that encourages us to not give up until we are totally free from bondage and every stronghold of the enemy is torn down.

To fully understand Exodus Six and First Corinthians 10 we need to understand the pattern of the Examples.

Pharaoh is a pattern of the devil. He thought of himself as God and sought to pervert the things of Jehovah for his own liking.

Egypt is a pattern of the world. The Israelites had been held in bondage in Egypt for four hundred years. After that many years that were not only in Egypt but they were also of Egypt. Even when they came out of Egypt, Egypt did not fully come out of them and that led to numerous downfalls.

The Israelites are a pattern of the called out ones. The very name "church" means "called out ones" Christians are called out of this world's system and into the Kingdom of God's system. As "called out ones" Christians are to advance the Kingdom of God on earth so His will is done on earth as in heaven.

The exodus and the wandering in the desert is a pattern of our daily battle. I once did a study of all the Canaanite Tribes that resisted, opposed and oppressed the Israelites as they tried to set up residence in the Promised Land. Each one of those tribes is a pattern of particular spiritual schemes we face as we advance the Kingdom of Heaven.

The Promised Land is a pattern of heaven. As citizens of heaven and ambassadors for Christ we are to represent the heavenly pattern on earth.

The rock is a pattern of Christ. Jesus provided the living water by being crucified on the Cross. We appropriate the living water by declaring the victory of the Cross over our lives.

Going through the sea is a pattern of our water baptism. When Christians are baptized they should renounce the devil and all his works.

Their lives are a pattern of the spiritual warfare we face. As you study the victories and defeats of the Nation of Israel you will see that whichever side they chose to identify with and walk with became the side that won. When we truly choose to set our minds on the Spirit and take up our crosses to follow Jesus we will enjoy victory over the devil and his demons.

CHAPTER TEN
STRONGHOLDS

A stronghold is an area of continued defeat in a Believer's life. A stronghold is not a demon but may be an area that a demon works through. Common strongholds include lust, unforgiveness, anger, and feelings of rejection, inferiority, addictions and the like.

God has the power and the desire to destroy every stronghold in our lives. Micah spoke about tearing down strongholds. *"In that day," declares the LORD, "I will destroy your horses from among you and demolish your chariots. I will destroy the cities of your land and tear down all your strongholds. I will destroy your witchcraft and you will no longer cast spells. I will destroy your carved images and your sacred stones from among you; you will no longer bow down to the work of your hands* (Micah 5:10-13).

John stated that the very reason for Jesus' time on earthy was to destroy the devil's work. *He who does what is sinful is of the devil, because the devil has been sinning from the beginning. The reason the Son of God appeared was to destroy the devil's work* (I John 3:8).

Still, many Christians have pockets of resistance in their lives that hinder them from enjoying the total victory God wants them to have. Whether these strongholds are attitudes, addictions or actions; they seem to hold people in continual or at least periodic defeat.

The writer to the Hebrews tells us to throw off these strongholds that hinder us from enjoying God's best and entangle us in Satan's schemes. *Therefore, since we are surrounded by such a great cloud of witnesses, let us throw off everything that hinders and the sin that so easily entangles, and let us run with perseverance the race marked out for us* (Hebrews 12:1).

I was thoroughly saved on March 17, 1972. I was brought into the Kingdom of Light and was made a new creation. Most of the old was gone, most of the new had come. I answered the call to full time youth-ministry less than 12 months later and worked full time for Youth For Christ while going to college full time. I took my first pastorate between my junior and senior years at college. I worked hard, studied hard and every church I pastored grew. I learned a lot but I never learned the things of the Spirit and certainly was not taught about demons and deliverance.

Nobody was more surprised than I when my first marriage of eighteen years broke up in 1987. I left the ministry and never thought God could use me again. I struggled with thoughts of suicide and immorality. I discovered I was addicted to the need to be in a relationship — no matter how bad.

My life was a ruins and I felt like a spiritual sham. But right when I got down to my lowest point, the Lord Jesus Christ reached out and picked me up. He began teaching me about my own need of deliverance. He showed me areas where I had allowed the enemy to build strongholds.

In the back of this book my wife wrote an "about the author" biography of me. She basically says that God taught me about demons because I had them all. Maybe I did, but I've found out that I'm not the only person who thought they had God by the hand even though Satan was intent on destroying their life.

There are so many Christians who are caught in a sin-confess; sin-confess pattern. They try their hardest to overcome prevailing sin through confession and they promise to repent. But when the prevailing sin comes from strongholds that demons are working through, deliverance is a prerequisite to victory.

You can tell when you are dealing with demons when you hear them speaking to your spirit in the second person. They will whisper things like "you are no good", "there's no hope for you", etc.

I've ministered to many preachers and Christian leaders who were caught in a pattern that drove them to their own altars every Saturday night where they begged God to forgive them one last time and promised to "never do it again".

Christians can be like an abusive spouse who goes to his or her mate and says "if you will just forgive me one more time, I will never do it again". But the pattern remains the same because most Christians have never been taught how to break the strongholds and cast out the demons that feed the pattern.

Many believers have besetting sins. These are the sins that they may able control in public, but that keep creeping up in private. Hebrews 12 speaks of them and refers to them as "the sin that so easily entangles", or as the King James says, "the sin which doth so easily beset us".

When there is an area of defeat that a Believer can't seem to maintain victory over it is a stronghold. A stronghold is a mindset impregnated with hopelessness about something that denies the Word of God and results in faithlessness and a place of darkness that we have no hope for.

CHAPTER ELEVEN
THE STORY OF KING SAUL

Saul's story is found in First and Second Samuel, in First Chronicles, and is referred to in several Psalms. Saul was tall and handsome, standing a head taller than any of his peers. The Bible says that he was without equal and was God's choice to be the first King of Israel. At first he was humble, winsome and a bit fearful. He tried to hide among the luggage when he was about to be anointed king. At first he relied heavily on God for counsel, guidance and strength. God changed his heart and poured His Spirit on him to the point that he prophesied with the prophets.

But something got into to Saul. He went from good to bad and from bad to worse. He became insanely jealous, abusive, proud and fanatical. Dr. Ed Murphy, who has spent his lifetime teaching and counseling in spiritual warfare and deliverance, believes that Saul was a Believer who became increasingly demonized. (I recommend Ed Murphy's book: *The Handbook for Spiritual Warfare*.)

But Saul did not follow God whole-heartedly. He became lukewarm and carnal. He sought God's blessings, but also looked for answers from the psychics. How did such a godly man, anointed of the Lord, filled with the Spirit and gifted to prophesy become the spiritual wreck that eventually committed suicide? I believe it is because he became progressively controlled by demons.

Things started off well before Saul was demonized. The first thing young King Saul did was get serious with God. Does that surprise you? Satan didn't bother Saul much until after God began working in him. The devil doesn't waste much time on people who aren't committed to God — he already has them. But Saul became a servant of the Almighty. At first he was a man of God, humble and zealous for God's honor and the salvation of the people. He was transformed by the power of God.

Saul was given a new heart which is an Old Testament pattern of conversion. *As Saul turned to leave Samuel, God changed Saul's heart, and all these signs were fulfilled that day* (I Samuel 10:9).

The Scripture clearly says that Saul was given the Spirit of God and was changed into a new person. *The Spirit of the LORD will come upon you in power, and you will prophesy with them; and you will be changed into a different person... When they arrived at Gibeah, a procession of prophets met him; the Spirit of God came upon him in power, and he joined in their prophesying* (I Samuel 10:6, 10).

Saul received the spiritual gift of prophecy and was empowered to prophesy among the prophets. *When all those who had formerly known him saw him prophesying with the prophets, they asked each other "What is this that has happened to the son of Kish? Is Saul also among the prophets?* (I Samuel 10:11).

People were amazed at Saul's transformation. He followed God, was transformed by God and led the entire nation back to God. No one could doubt that the Lord had done a real work in Saul's life. But this man became a real basket case as he opened himself up to demonization.

Saul's real problems with demons began when he assumed authority that wasn't his. Rebellion is the sin of witchcraft. When a person assumes authority that has not been granted him, it opens him up to the work of Satan. That happened to Saul when he assumed Samuel's role as a priest and prophet. Judgment was pronounced on Saul and the whole nation because of his rebellion. *So he said. "Bring me the burnt offering and the fellowship offerings." And Saul offered the burnt offering. Just as he finished making the offering, Samuel arrived, and Saul went out to greet him. "What have you done?" asked Samuel. Saul replied, "When I saw that the men were scattering, and that you did not come at the set time, and that the Philistines were assembling at Micmash, I thought, 'Now the Philistines will come down against me at Gilgal, and I have not sought the LORD'S favor.' So I felt compelled to offer the burnt offering." "You acted foolishly," Samuel said. "You have not kept the command the LORD your God gave you; if you had, he would have established your kingdom over Israel for all time* (I Samuel 13:9-13).

Saul became a religious fanatic after being judged by Samuel (I Samuel 14:24-46). The devil loves religion. He stirs people to fanaticism that is not based on Christ and the truths of the Bible. He deceives people through new age movements and heresies that are so close to the truth that they trap even sincere believers. He is behind cults like the "Heaven's Gate" cult that committed mass suicide to be released to follow the Hale Bopp comet. Satan continues to use things like the Heaven's Gate cult and the Jonestown mass suicide to bring accusation and suspicion toward authentic works and workers of God that go beyond the accepted religious norms in a church or community. When true apostles or prophets step up to do the works of God, Satan moves religious people to bring accusations and comparisons to cult leaders like Jim Jones, etc.

Saul, seeking God's blessing after losing it through judgment, was ready to kill his own son Jonathan because of a rash oath he had made to try to appease God. This is common among fanatics — an unholy mixture of self-assertion and zeal for God.

God gave Saul plenty of chances to repent but Saul stepped over the line. The sad story of Saul's self-centeredness and pride is told in 1 Samuel 15. You may remember how Samuel gave Saul the Lord's order to attack the Amalekites and totally destroy everything that belonged to them. He did attack them, but was unwilling to destroy the material goods. So they kept King Agag and the best of the sheep, cattle, lambs and everything good.

The word of the Lord came to Samuel that Saul had disobeyed and that Jehovah was grieved that he had made Saul King. Samuel spent a sleepless night and rose early the next morning to go and admonish Saul.

Saul greeted him with "the Lord bless you, I have carried out the Lord's instructions". So Samuel asked about the bleating of the sheep and pronounced judgment on Saul. *But Samuel replied: "Does the LORD delight in burnt offerings and sacrifices as much as in obeying the voice of the LORD? To obey is better than sacrifice, and to heed is better than the fat of rams. For rebellion is like the sin of divination, and arrogance like the evil of idolatry. Because you have rejected the word of the LORD, he has rejected you as king"* (I Samuel 15:22-23).

Saul's pride and rebellion manifested through his growing jealousy of David. Chapters 18 and 19 of First Samuel tell the sad tale of how Saul became an egomaniac and repeatedly tried to kill David. Saul became very unstable. At times he called David "son" and promised not to harm him. Then he turned around and tried to track him down with his armies.

You might think that all these bad traits are the result of a sinful human nature. But if you look closely you will see that evil spirits were taunting Saul. At first you will notice that David's spiritual music could drive the demons away.

This happened to me when I was being restored to the Lord. One Sunday morning I woke up with such a heavy weight on my chest that it felt like Satan himself was sitting there. I couldn't breathe, I had trouble praying and my mind was clouded with doubt and despair. With some effort I finally got up, showered and dressed for church. On my way to church I stopped at a friend's house and shared what I was going through.

My friend turned on the tape player and started playing Petra's song "I exalt thee". I listened to that song over and over until the demonic presence was totally gone. The same thing happened at first for Saul when David played spiritual music for him. But as Saul's demonization progresses, spiritual music only serves to agitate Saul and the demons that were in him. All through his life, Saul had to choose whether to repent and deal with the demons in his life or to continue in his sinful ways. Unfortunately, he made the wrong choices.

Now the Spirit of the LORD had departed from Saul, and an evil spirit from the LORD tormented him. Saul's attendants said to him, "See, an evil spirit from God is tormenting you. Let our lord command his servants here to search for someone who can play the harp. He will play when the evil spirit from God comes upon you, and you will feel better." So Saul said to his attendants, "Find someone who plays well and bring him to me." One of the servants answered, "I have seen a son of Jesse of Bethlehem who knows how to play the harp. He is a brave man and a warrior. He speaks well and is a fine-looking man. And the LORD is with him." Then Saul sent messengers to Jesse and said, "Send me your son David, who is with the sheep." So Jesse took a donkey loaded with bread, a skin of wine and a young goat and sent them with his son David to Saul. David came to Saul and entered his service. Saul liked him very much, and David became one of his armor-bearers. Then Saul sent word to Jesse, saying, "Allow David to remain in my service, for I am pleased with him." Whenever the spirit from God came upon Saul, David would take his harp and play. Then relief would come to Saul; he would feel better, and the evil spirit would leave him. 1 Samuel 16:14-23.

It is interesting that this evil spirit was from God. Jehovah is sovereign over all, including evil spirits. God can make evil spirits do his will. God used the demons to bring David, the shepherd boy who was destined to be King, into Saul's service. At first Saul received temporary relief while David played spiritual music. It was during these periods of relief that Saul could have turned his heart back to God. *The next day an evil spirit from God came forcefully upon Saul. He was prophesying in his house, while David was playing the harp, as he usually did.*

Saul had a spear in his hand and he hurled it, saying to himself, "I'll pin David to the wall." But David eluded him twice. Saul was afraid of David, because the LORD was with David but had left Saul (I Samuel 18:10-12).

STAGES OF SAUL'S DEMONIZATION.

Demonization doesn't usually happen all at once. It is usually progressive as people give in to the things of darkness. The first stage of Saul's demonization was mild. At first, Saul had periods of attack mixed with periods of normality. God's purpose here was to give him chances to repent. This state is typified in 1 Samuel 16 for Saul but it is also illustrated in the New Testament with Hymenaeus and Alexander. *Among them are Hymenaeus and Alexander, whom I have handed over to Satan to be taught not to blaspheme* (I Timothy 1:20).

There have been three times that I have handed people over to Satan because they have openly and purposely chosen to reject God's will for their lives. The results have not been pretty but in each case my purpose was redemptive, hoping that the people come to their senses and repent.

The second stage of Saul's demonization was intense. He became more irrational and destructive in his personal relationships. *But an evil spirit from the LORD came upon Saul as he was sitting in his house with his spear in his hand. While David was playing the harp, Saul tried to pin him to the wall with his spear, but David eluded him as Saul drove the spear into the wall. That night David made good his escape. Saul sent men to David's house to watch it and to kill him in the morning. But Michal, David's wife, warned him, "If you don't run for your life tonight, tomorrow you'll be killed." So Michal let David down through a window, and he fled and escaped. Then Michal took an idol and laid it on the bed, covering it with a garment and putting some goat's hair at the head. When Saul sent the men to capture David, Michal said, "He* is ill." *Then Saul sent the men back to see David and told them, "Bring him up to me in his bed so that I may kill him." But when the men entered, there was the idol in the bed, and the head was some goat's hair* (I Samuel 19:9-16).

Saul's slippery slide into demonization got so bad that he even tried to kill his own son. *Saul's anger flared up at Jonathan and he said to him, "You son of a perverse and rebellious woman! Don't I know that you have sided with the son of Jesse... But Saul hurled his spear at him to kill him* (I Samuel 20:30, 33a).

The third stage of Saul's demonization was occultism. In First Samuel 28, without ever denying faith in the Lord, Saul slips into cultic mediumistic practices. He was like many Christians who go to church on Sunday and read their horoscope on Monday. Saul was dabbling in the things of Satan while trying to maintain the appearance of a follower of God.

The final stage of Saul's demonization was that he was a severely demonized believer. Even after Saul was severely demonized, the Spirit of the Lord would come on Saul so he would prophesy continually. The gift and calling of God are without recompense. So Saul becomes a mystery man. At times he acted spiritual and other times he was obviously controlled by demons. *Saul died because he was unfaithful to the LORD; he did not keep the word of the LORD and even consulted a medium for guidance, and did not inquire of the LORD. So the LORD put him to death and turned the kingdom over to David the son of Jesse* (I Chronicles 10:13-14).

Please don't think that Saul's example does not apply to us because it is Old Testament. Remember, those things happened as an example for us who believe. The New Testament gives pictures of Christians, who like Saul, are true believers, but have so many strongholds that they fall into rebellion and pride and lead truly miserable and hurtful lives. This can even lead to premature physical death.

When the Bible speaks of the death of Christians it calls it "sleep". There is something that we read in Communion Services that we need to understand. *That is why many among you are weak and sick, and a number of you have fallen asleep* (I Corinthians 11:30). Strongholds can literally lead to premature physical death. I truly believe that many Believers have strongholds that bring early death so they go to heaven without fully accomplishing God's destiny for their lives.

CHAPTER TWELVE
DEALING WITH STRONGHOLDS

A stronghold is an area of continued defeat that leads to hopelessness. It may be an addiction like drinking, gambling or tobacco, or it may be an area of emotional defeat like bitterness or depression. It can also be in the thought life like lust, insecurity, doubt or self-hatred.

One of the devil's biggest schemes against believers is for them to nurse their hurts and offenses. I once attended a Power Healing Conference in Denver. It was a great conference and we closed it by gathering around the Lord's Table for communion. One speaker got up and said before we shared the Lord's Supper that anyone who had been hurt by a Christian minister should come forward. I was totally shocked when more than half of the attendees flocked to the altar. And these were supposed to be the cream of the crop who were being trained to minister divine healing to others!

I think of Numbers 21 where the people of Israel started whining about the way things were going in their "church". They complained about the potlucks, they complained about the leadership and they complained about the journey God had them on. This made Jehovah so angry that he sent poisonous snakes to bite them and many of the people started dying. I think this gives a picture for today to the people who are jumping from church to church or flocking to altars nursing their wounds because somebody has offended them. It is time to quit picking at our scabs and start looking to Jesus who carried our grief and sorrows!

Then the LORD sent venomous snakes among them; they bit the people and many Israelites died. The people came to Moses and said, "We sinned when we spoke against the LORD and against you. Pray that the LORD will take the snakes away from us." So Moses prayed for the people. The LORD said to Moses, "Make a snake and put it up on a pole; anyone who is bitten can look at it and live." So Moses made a bronze snake and put it up on a pole. Then when anyone was bitten by a snake and looked at the bronze snake, he lived (Numbers 21:6-9).

A lot of people have a stronghold of offense because they keep looking at their hurts and picking at their scabs rather than looking on Jesus so they can move beyond their offenses and become useful for the Kingdom.

When people receive Christ there are always areas not completely surrendered to the Lord. Although they seek to sincerely follow Christ, there may be hurts, habits or long standing attitudes that need Christ's healing and deliverance. These strongholds may be tiny pockets of resistance, or they may be lasting fortified areas that hinder a person from becoming what they want to be in the Lord. The picture of Israel entering the Promised Land and warring against ungodly nations is an example of strongholds. They were in the Promised Land, but there still remained some nations which either did not honor God or openly resisted Him. Another example comes from the close of World War II. There were still pockets of Japanese troops that continued to fight vigorously. They didn't know they had lost the war. The same thing happens in the lives of many Christians. The way has been won by Jesus Christ himself. But there are still pockets of resistance that will remain until they learn that the victory is already theirs to be claimed in Christ.

Strongholds are sinful thought patterns, actions or addictions that don't seem to improve through prayer alone. I've worked with Christian leaders who've had strongholds of pornography, lust or masturbation.

A typical pattern began when the pastor was young and played with pornography or immorality. They got saved, answered the call to ministry but never really dealt with areas of defeat where Satan has a place to stand in their lives. They may ask for forgiveness time and again but they won't break the pattern unless they destroy the stronghold and cast out the demons.

Strongholds come through a variety of gateways. There are countless gateways for demons. Some are the believer's fault but many are not. Demons are not fair in the way they take advantage of their victims. For example, children who were abused often turn into adults with strongholds that need to be broken. Those who were repeatedly sexually abused may have dissociative identity disorder. Demons have not played fairly with them.

The sins of the fathers are passed down to the fourth generation along with the strongholds inherent in them. Sexual sin and unforgiveness create strongholds that open gateways to demons as does cult or occult involvement.

There are ways that we can identify strongholds. A rule of thumb that I've used is that you cannot cast out the flesh and you cannot discipline a demon. If a destruction pattern of attitude or action doesn't break through prayer and self-discipline it is probably a stronghold where deliverance is needed.

CHAPTER THIRTEEN
MAJOR TYPES OF STRONGHOLDS

The devil is crafty and will try to sneak in wherever he can. But there are a few areas that always lead to demonic strongholds.

One of the most powerful types of strongholds is soul ties. A soul tie is an unhealthy uniting of two persons. Soul ties are usually caused either by unhealthy dependence on others or through illicit sexual relations. They are created when a person has a devotion to another person that replaces their love, worship and dependence on Christ.

Co-dependence leads to such soul ties. A person may be a weak victim or a strong rescuer that "needs" another person to make them complete. This causes a soul tie. Some married children retain unhealthy soul ties with their parents, looking to a parent for support that they should be receiving from their spouse. *"If anyone comes to me and does not hate his father and mother, his wife and children, his brothers and sisters — yes, even his own life — he cannot be my disciple. And anyone who does not carry his cross and follow me cannot be my disciple* (Luke 14:26-27).

I used to struggle with the verse that told me to love God more than my spouse and children. Then the Lord explained to me, "If you love me most, you will love your spouse and children more."

Sexual intimacy outside of marriage always creates a soul tie — even when sex is forced upon an unwilling victim. When a person has sex they become one flesh with their partner. This creates a soul tie. Within marriage that is glue that helps hold a couple together. Outside of marriage it creates spiritual bonding which opens gateways to demons. And it can also affect the children of the person who fornicates: *For the unbelieving husband has been sanctified through his wife, and the unbelieving wife has been sanctified through her believing husband. Otherwise your children would be unclean, but as it is, they are holy* (I Corinthians 7:14).

We will take a deeper look at this in chapter thirty-four. For now it is important to understand that God warns us against sexual sin because of the soul tie it creates. *Why be captivated, my son, by an adulteress? Why embrace the bosom of another man's wife? For a man's ways are in full view of the LORD, and he examines all his paths. The evil deeds of a wicked man ensnare him; the cords of his sin hold him fast* (Proverbs 5:20-22).

A second type of stronghold is created through idolatry. Idolatry is excessive attachment, admiration or infatuation for material things. This includes idol worship. But it extends to any material thing that comes between a person and God. Any "thing" that is worshiped or loved more than God is an object of idolatry. Many Christian open their homes to hard core idolatry through paintings, face masks, artifacts and things that have been dedicated to false gods or used in the occult.

Occultism also creates strongholds. This includes some forms of magic, fortune telling, contact with spirits, spells, healing magic, Ouija Boards, tarot cards, séances, Satanism and the like. The devil never seems to run out of tricks. Now he is using Pokemon, Angel Boards, Harry Potter books and the like.

Many people have strongholds of rejection that make them think of themselves in a perverted way. Others have strongholds of addiction or lust that continue to lure them away from purity even after they are saved.

CHAPTER FOURTEEN
PERSONAL SPIRITUAL INVENTORY

Some people hesitate to use any guide when doing deliverance, thinking that it hinders the Holy Spirit. They believe it is best to just meet with little or no preparation and to minister however the Spirit leads. I have no doubt that people who minister that way have some success in casting out demons.

But I have found that the Holy Spirit can work as well through process as he can apart from it. I too have times when there isn't opportunity to prepare to do deliverance — just like there are times when I don't have a warning that someone may need personal counseling. But the most effective deliverance ministry I think people can do is when they can prepare in advance.

Since I completed my doctoral work at Wagner Leadership Institute I've developed and repeatedly revised my Deep Healing Questionnaire, which I began with a questionnaire that Doris Wagner used (with her permission). That questionnaire has been revised several times as I've ministered deliverance over the past decade. I use the questionnaire to help people complete a personal spiritual inventory to help the deliverance worker discern where prayer is needed. The Questionnaire has proven to be a great tool and I've also developed a Questionnaire Worksheet that proves helpful for the deliverance minister in determining which areas, strongholds and demons need the most prayer attention. The Questionnaire Worksheet is included in the appendix to this book and the Questionnaire is simply the Worksheet without the bulleted "things to look for" that the deliverance minister might use.

Ralph Neighbour Jr. developed *The Journey Guide Inventory* that provides a less intrusive model that helps people realize that Satan may have developed strongholds in the lives of those he works with. I have used it often to help make people aware of the need to take a serious look at the need for deliverance and deep healing. I use his inventory with permission from Touch Ministries.

The Journey Guide Inventory:
- ☐ I had a poor relationship with my father/mother. Perhaps that's why I find it hard to believe that God truly loves me.
- ☐ I have a hard time forgiving myself for things I've done in the past. I constantly dislike myself.
- ☐ I have been wrongly treated and hurt in the past. I find it hard to be set free of the inner anger I feel when remembering it.
- ☐ I have a sin or bad habit in my life that controls me. I try hard, but I really feel like a captive in this situation.
- ☐ I have a hard time with a sexual problem. I have never been able to break its control and the bad habits that go with it.
- ☐ I have some addictive behavior: e.g. overeating, gambling, exaggerating, smoking, drugs, alcohol, etc.
- ☐ I sometimes feel that my desire for money and possessions has a powerful control over me.
- ☐ Sometimes I find that I cannot control my anger. It seems to well up from within and explodes before I can stop it.
- ☐ I have many fears in my life. Like: fear of the dark, being alone, fear of sickness and death, etc.
- ☐ I have contemplated suicide on several occasions.
- ☐ I have a problem with anxiety. Sometimes I don't even know why I am so anxious. I get anxious even about little things.
- ☐ I have been involved in homosexuality.

- ☐ I find it hard to concentrate when I'm reading the Bible and praying. If feels like drowsiness comes on me.
- ☐ In the past, I have been involved in occult practices (e.g. séances, witchcraft, Ouija boards, etc.) or have been member of a cult.
- ☐ I have been abused physically, mentally, or emotionally.
- ☐ I still have pornography or sensual books or materials in my home.
- ☐ I have had disappointing experiences with former churches.
- ☐ I hold up work as my most important activity. My life is consumed by my performance and achievement level.
- ☐ I find myself sleeping more than normal and have no desire or motivation to do anything productive.
- ☐ I have a great fear of speaking up or stating my opinion.
- ☐ I have felt like I constantly have to be in a romantic relationship with a person of the opposite sex.

I believe that *The Journey Guide Inventory* is extremely helpful in helping people realize they have some personal issues that they need to address. The Deep Healing Questionnaire is a tool that helps both the minister and the one receiving ministry to look deeper within so they might be more thorough in addressing issues that might have led to spiritual bondage.

CHAPTER FIFTEEN
GAINING VICTORY OVER STRONGHOLDS

There are five distinct steps necessary for gaining victory over strongholds.

1. ***Taking spiritual inventory.*** Before one can deal with personal strongholds he needs to recognize what those strongholds are. The first step in gaining victory is to identify all strongholds and areas of bondage. Discerning personal strongholds comes through self-examination. A person needs to take personal inventory to see what long lasting struggles or sin patterns are in his or her life. Just noting how one feels and reacts to different situations can be a great help here.

The next step of self-examination is through spiritual discernment. The Holy Spirit never condemns a person who is following the Lord but He will convict the person of needed changes. It is wise to pray like David did and say "search me O God and see if there be any wicked way in me" (Psalm 139:23-24).

The final step of uncovering personal strongholds is through personal discernment and spiritual discernment of others. Other people can see what we cannot see. They can observe the reality of our blind spots and can often receive words from the Spirit of God that we aren't personally ready or willing to receive.

2. ***Recognizing your authority and position in Christ.*** Neil Anderson has done a wonderful job of introducing the Church to bondage breaking truth encounters. I don't know of anyone who has done a better job of helping people see the biblical promises and the truth about their position in Christ that will set them free.

In my seminars I usually have people make the following truth declarations about themselves according to the Word of God.

- *I was a sinner, but now I am a saint, saved by grace through faith.* Ephesians 2:8-9.
- *I have been put right with God by faith and have peace with him.* Romans 5:1.
- *I have been saved by Christ's life.* Romans 5:10.
- *I have died to sin.* Romans 6:2.
- *I now have no condemnation.* Romans 8:1.
- *I will put on immortality.* 1 Corinthians 15:53.
- *I have received God's Spirit as a guarantee.* 2 Corinthians 5:1.
- *I have received mercy.* 2 Corinthians 4:1.
- *I am a new creation.* 2 Corinthians 5:17.
- *I am Christ's Ambassador.* 2 Corinthians 5:20.
- *I am holy and blameless in God's sight.* Ephesians 1:4.
- *I am God's child.* John 1:12-13.
- *I am a fellow citizen with God's people and a member of his household.* Ephesians 2:19.
- *God will never leave or forsake me.* Hebrews 13:5.
- *I have been born again into a living hope.* 1 Peter 1:3.
- *I have been bought with a price and belong to God.* 1 Corinthians 6:19-20.
- *I am complete in Christ.* Colossians 2:10.
- *I cannot be separated from the love of God.* Romans 8:35-39.
- *I am established, anointed, and sealed by God.* 2 Corinthians 1:21-22.
- *I am hidden with Christ in God.* Colossians 3:3.

- *He is still working on me.* Philippians 1:6.
- *I am born of God, and the evil one cannot touch me.* 1 John 5:18.
- *I am the salt of the earth and the light of the world.* Matthew 5:13-16.
- *Jesus chose me and appointed me to go and bear fruit that will last.* John 15:16.
- *I am God's Temple.* 1 Corinthians 3:16.
- *I am seated with Christ in the heavenly realm.* Ephesians 2:6.
- *I am God's workmanship.* Ephesians 2:10.
- *I can do all things through Christ who strengthens me.* Philippians 4:13.

3. **Repenting of all known sin.** People cannot get free or stay free from demonic bondage if they continue in sin. Receiving forgiveness or deliverance apart from true repentance brings temporary relief at best. John the Baptist told people to *"produce fruit in keeping with repentance. And do not begin to say to yourselves, 'We have Abraham as our father.' For I tell you that out of these stones God can raise up children for Abraham. The ax is already at the root of the trees, and every tree that does not produce good fruit will be cut down and thrown into the fire"* (Luke 3:8-9).

It does little good to pray against the spirit of lust if the person receiving prayer is unwilling to break off a promiscuous relationship. Prayer does not set a person free unless he or she is willing to forsake an addictive habit after deliverance. Ministry apart from repentance will bring nothing more than short lived victory.

4. **Confess and renounce every sin and stronghold.** The Bible is clear that we are to confess and forsake sin. The same applies to breaking the power of personal strongholds. Confessing is simply admitting to God that what we have done is sinful. Renouncing includes telling the devil that sin has been confessed and that he no longer has a right to attack you in that area. *"He who conceals his sins does not prosper,*

but whoever confesses and **renounces** *them finds mercy"* (Proverbs 28:13 — Emphasis mine).

5. ***Forgiving all those who have hurt you.*** Unforgiveness is something that actually gives the devil a foothold. The most common hindrances to healing and deliverance that I have discovered are unforgiveness, unbelief and unwillingness to repent.

I will never forget the senior citizen who came to me for prayer at a Free Indeed Seminar. She was a beautiful woman, a faithful Christian who had been married to the same man for sixty years. She was also tormented by arthritic pain. When she came for prayer she told me that she had arthritis in the shoulder. I asked her to try lifting her arm and she winced as she struggled to lift her hand shoulder high.

I prayed a prayer of faith over her and asked her to try it again. She tried lifting her arm again but there was no improvement. I wondered why prayer wasn't making a difference so I asked God and the Holy Spirit spoke one word "unforgiveness". I asked the woman who she needed to forgive and she said "I will never forgive her". I asked the woman who she was unwilling to forgive. She explained that she wouldn't forgive her deceased mother for not protecting her when her stepfather molested her as a child. She said "Mother had to have known what he was doing to me".

I explained how God turns people over to the tormentors if they refuse to forgive others from the heart even as God has forgiven them. After a short time of counsel she decided to willfully forgive her mother.

Then I asked her to try lifting her hand again so I could measure the difference before and after I prayed a second time. She lifted her hand straight up above her head without any pain, looked up at her outstretched hand with amazement and declared "I am healed!"

Every since that day when prayer for healing or deliverance is hindered I question people to see if there is someone they need to forgiven.

I usually bind demons from talking when I am doing deliverance but there have been times that I have asked them what right they have to stay in a person when they refuse to come out. Time and again the demons have indicated that the person has unforgiveness in their heart.

a. People need to forgive others for personal hurts they have received. Jesus gave the parable about the tormentors. *"In anger his master turned him over to the jailers to be tortured* (KJV "tormentors"), *until he should pay back all he owed. "This is how my heavenly Father will treat each of you unless you forgive your brother from your heart"* (Matthew 18:34-35).

b. People also need to let God execute revenge. God will not let the guilty go unpunished but when people hold grudges their unforgiveness seems to delay God's vengeance. Paul wrote *"Do not take revenge, my friends,* **but leave room for God's wrath***, for it is written: "It is mine to avenge; I will repay," says the Lord. On the contrary: "If your enemy is hungry, feed him; if he is thirsty, give him something to drink. In doing this, you will heap burning coals on his head." Do not be overcome by evil, but overcome evil with good"* (Romans 12:19-21 — Emphasis mine).

c. The final thing people need to do is receive personal grace to extend God's forgiveness when possible: *"If you forgive anyone his sins, they are forgiven; if you do not forgive them, they are not forgiven"* (John 20:23.

We know a lot about forgiveness but we haven't really learned enough about our part in helping others know they are forgiven. Ministering forgiveness is a huge and necessary part of the ministry of deliverance. People need to leave prayer sessions knowing that they are forgiven. After someone confesses sin to God before a counselor, it helps for the counselor to declare "Your sin is forgiven in Jesus' Name".

CHAPTER SIXTEEN

FIND OUT WHO IS IN CHARGE — THEOLOGY OF THE HUMAN MAKEUP

We were created to walk with God. He wants to guide us through life that is abundant, free and eternal. But He didn't make us to be robots or pawns in the hand of destiny. Instead He made us to be Sovereign, under him, over all things. He even made our submission to Him voluntary. We can choose Him and His ways or ourselves and our ways.

God's ways are so much higher than our ways. Man's first or natural instinct is almost always the opposite of God's will. People think they will get ahead by holding on to what they have. God says "Give and it will be given unto you." Human instinct says "Don't get mad, get even." God says "Turn the other cheek, pray for those who misuse you, bless those who persecute you.

An intricate part of freedom comes from voluntary submission to God and His ways. A funny truth is that Freedom equals being captive to obedience in Christ while captivity equals being free from obedience to Christ.

If we are honest, most of us will admit to an ongoing struggle. The Holy Spirit in us prompts us to obey God while the sinful nature and

Satan prompt us to disobey God. In Free Indeed Seminars I explain to people how they can tell who is holding the reins in their lives:

When self or Satan is master we say: "not thy will but mine be done. But when Jesus is our master we say: "not my will, but thine be done." *"So I say, live by the Spirit, and you will not gratify the desires of the sinful nature. For the sinful nature desires what is contrary to the Spirit, and the Spirit what is contrary to the sinful nature. They are in conflict with each other, so that you do not do what you want"* (Galatians 5:16-17).

We've heard and read verses like these for years, but who has taught us HOW to walk in the Spirit? Freedom comes from bringing all things under the control of Christ. God made man in His own image but every since the fall, people have been trying to remake God in their own image. That will never work.

Then God Said, "Let us make man in our image, in our own likeness, and let them rule over the fish of the sea and the birds of the air, over the livestock, over all the earth, and over all the creatures that move along the ground." Genesis 1:26.

Man was created in the image of God. We need to take a deeper look at this familiar truth.

1. **God is Creator; in His image He made us co-creators.** God created the world and everything that is in it. Then He made man in His own image. Only humans have the creative image of God. There is no end to the creativity of man. From planes to trains to cities and computers, man demonstrates the likeness of his creator. The theory of evolution tries to undermine God's creative power. It forgets that God made Adam as a full grown man. He could have created rock formations that were thousands of years old when they were created! Many are convinced that they are products of chance and evolution. That simply cannot be true. We were created in the image of God, not some Neanderthal Man.

It seems like a lifetime ago that I attended Spring Arbor College and Professor Darrell Moore quoted the following in class.

Evolution

Three monkeys dining once in a coconut tree
Were discussing some things that they heard true to be.
"What do you think? Now, listen you two:
Here, monkeys is something that cannot be true.

"That humans descend from our noble race!
Why, it's shocking — a terrible disgrace.
Whoever heard of a monkey deserting his wife
And leaving a baby to starve and ruin its life?"

"And have you ever known of a mother monk
To leave her darling with strangers to bunk?
Their babies are handed from one to another,
And some scarcely know the love of a mother."

"And I've never known a monkey so selfish to be,
As to build a fence around a coconut tree.
So other monkeys can't get a wee taste,
But would let all the coconuts there go to waste.

"Why, if I'd put a fence around this coconut tree,
Starvation would force you to steal from me.
And here is another thing a monkey won't do,
Seek a cocktail parlor and get on a stew."

"Carouse and go on a whoopee disgracing his life,
Then reel madly home and beat up his wife.
They call this all pleasure and make a big fuss —
They've descended from something, but not from us!"

— Author Unknown

Man is created in the creative image of God but sin, self and Satan have done a remarkable job at marring God's image in humans.

2. ***God is sovereign and in His image we are sovereign.*** When God created humans, He gave them dominion over the animals, the birds of the air, and the fish of the sea. He told mankind to tend the earth and take care of it. God wanted people to be stewards of the earth. But Satan usurped his authority to become ruler of the earth. In Christ we take it back!

Jesus said "All authority in heaven and on earth has been given to me — therefore go…" That is why we need to pray before God works — He has delegated His authority to us over the earth realm. Think of how God sought for a man to stand in the gap so He wouldn't have to destroy the land. He needed a human being to exercise the imputed authority God has released to mankind.

3. ***God is triune and in His image we are triune.*** The godhead consists of three persons: God the Father, God the Son and God the Holy Spirit. In God's image, we have three parts: spirit, soul and body.

Part one: our human spirits. Our spirits communicate with God. *"The Spirit himself testifies with our spirit that we are God's children."* (Romans 8:16).

Our spirits are saved for the day of the Lord. As Paul wrote, *"… Hand this man over to Satan, so that the sinful nature may be destroyed and his spirit saved on the day of the Lord"* (I Corinthians 5:5).

Our spirits make us one with Christ. *"But he who unites himself with the Lord is one with him in the Spirit"* (I Corinthians 6:17).

Part two: our souls. Our soul is our mind, our will, our emotions and our memories. The Greek word that we get psychology from is "psyche". It is usually translated soul or life. The Bible has a lot to say concerning the soul. Here are just a few of the verses with the Greek word for soul added for emphasis.

Do not be afraid of those who can kill the body but cannot kill the soul (psyche). *Rather, be afraid of the One who can destroy both soul and body in hell* (Matthew 10:28).

What good will it be for a man if he gains the whole world, yet forfeits his soul? (Psyche) *Or what can a man give in exchange for his soul* (psyche)? (Matthew 16:26).

He answered; "'Love the Lord your God with all your heart and with all your soul (psyche) *and with all your strength and with all your mind': and, 'Love your neighbor as yourself'"* (Luke 10:27).

For the word of God is living and active. Sharper than any double-edged sword, it penetrates even to dividing soul (psyche) *and spirit, joints and marrow; it judges the thoughts and attitudes of the heart* (Hebrews 4:12).

CHAPTER SEVENTEEN
THE WORK OF REPROBATION

Once we understand the theology of the human makeup we can begin to see how God desires for His image to manifest through the human spirit, soul and body. But Satan constantly works to destroy God's image. The word "reprobation" isn't used as often as it used to be when the King James Bible was the most common Bible used in most homes and churches.

In the King James Bible the Greek word "adokimos" is translated "reprobate" six times and "castaway" and "rejected" one time each. It means "not standing the test, not approved", "that which does not prove itself such as it ought" or "unfit for, unproved, spurious, or reprobate".

A deeper study of the word "adokimos" comes from ancient days when all money was made from soft metals. Many people would shave small portions of the metal off from their coins for personal gain. This became so prevalent that in one century over 80 laws were passed in Athens, Greece to stop the shaving down of coins.

There were honorable money changers who refused to accept money that had been shaven down — they would only put money into circulation that was of full weight and value. Such men were called "dokimos" or "approved". The word "adokimos" puts a negative "a" in front of "dokimos" and means "not approved". Therefore, when we speak of a person being reprobate or, as the New International Versions says of a "depraved mind" we are speaking of someone who has become void of proper judgment.

The work of reprobation is that work of the sinful nature and of the devil where people lose God's likeness to the extent that they can no longer make proper righteous judgments in their daily lives.

1. ***How people lose God's likeness.*** (Romans 1:24-32)

a. People can lose God's likeness in their bodies: *"Therefore God gave them over in the sinful desires of their hearts to sexual impurity for the degrading of their bodies with one another"* (Romans 1:24). When people lose God's likeness in their bodies they mistreat their bodies or use them in ways that are dishonoring to their Maker.

b. People can lose God's likeness in their souls: *"Because of this, God gave them over to shameful lusts..."* (Romans 1:25-27). The soul includes the mind, will, emotions and memories. When people lose God's likeness in these areas they begin to give into all kinds of shameful desires.

3. The last area where people lose God's likeness is in their human spirits. Paul says: *"furthermore, since they did not think it worthwhile to retain the knowledge of God, he gave them over to a **depraved mind**, to do what ought not to be done"* (Romans 1:28 — Emphasis mine).

The word translated mind comes from the Greek word "nous" that goes far deeper than just the gray matter of the human brain. It means "mind or disposition" in the sense of inner orientation or moral attitude. It controls the subconscious mind that controls about 80% of our actions and reactions.

When people begin to lose God's likeness that reprobation begins in the body, moves into the soul and finally on to the human spirit.

2. Spiritual, soulish or reprobate people. People may move to and from being spiritual, soulish or reprobate several times before becoming truly spiritual, soulish or reprobate. It is easy to backslide from God's likeness but it takes grace and commitment to maintain true spirituality.

a. A truly spiritual person is one whose human spirit is strongest, whose soul is kept in check by the human spirit and whose body is held in submission to the soul.

The Greek word "pneumatikos" is translated "spiritual" several times in Scripture, of which we mention two here. *"The spiritual (pneumatikos) man makes judgments about all things, but he himself is not subject to any man's judgment: "For who has known the mind of the Lord that he may instruct him?" But we have the mind of Christ. Brothers, I could not address you as spiritual (pneumatikos) but as worldly (sarkinos) — mere infants in Christ* (I Corinthians 2:15-3:1). This verse assures the spiritual person that they make right judgments and that they have the mind of Christ. Paul addresses the Corinthians as "sarkinos" which means fleshly or worldly. He says they are controlled by the flesh rather than by the spirit.

A second verse makes a distinction between people living in sin and those who are truly spiritual. *"Brothers, if someone is caught in a sin, you who are spiritual (pneumatikoi) should restore him gently. But watch yourself, or you also may be tempted"* (Galatians 6:1).

3. Soulish (psuchikos) Luke warm, carnal, or sin controlled) Believers. The word translated "soulish" is "psuchikos" which is related to the words psychology, psyche, and the like. The Greek root "psuche" is usually translated "soul" or "life".

A soulish person may be a Believer but they are living according to their soulish nature rather than according to the Spirit of God. Paul says that *"The man without the Spirit (psuchikos) does not accept the things that come from the Spirit of God, for they are foolishness to him, and he cannot understand them, because they are spiritually discerned"* (I Corinthians 2:14).

In a soulish person the human spirit is weaker, the sensual mind, will, emotions and memories grow stronger and the physical or sensual fights for control. At this point the two opposing forces of spirituality and sensuality results in double-mindedness and instability. James says we become double-souled. *He is a double-minded* (dipsukos), *unstable in all he does* (James 1:8).

4. **Reprobates.** When God gives people over to reprobation, their spirits are quenched, their souls become philosophical or religious apart from the spirit, and their physical bodies become sensual and perverted. They come to the point where they do not even want to retain the knowledge of God.

When I was a boy there was a cartoon character named Tommy who wore a funnel upside down on his head. The funnel was portrayed as a sort of "thinking cap". In reality we filter all incoming data either through our spirit, through our soul or through our body. In a sense we either have our "funnels" funneling information either into our human spirits, our souls or through our physical senses alone and that controls how easily we receive revelation. If we receive through our spirits, we can easily receive the things of God. But if we receive through our soul or body it becomes easier to receive sensual data.

Spiritual people can evaluate or "judge" themselves easily. Since they receive things from God through their spirits they are easily convicted when they move contrary to God's image or nature. Soulish people have more difficulty in discerning God's will and likeness, and reprobates simply don't realize how sinful sin really is.

CHAPTER EIGHTEEN
GOD'S CURE FOR REPROBATION

God's desire is that all people turn from their sensual, soulish or reprobate ways and He provides grace that offers hope for the spirit, soul and body.

1. ***The human spirit can be born again.*** Jesus said *"Flesh gives birth to flesh, but the Spirit gives birth to spirit. You should not be surprised at my saying, 'You must be born again'"* (John 3:6-7). It has to start here! God cleanses a person from the inside out. At the center of each person is the very life of the person — the human spirit. Until a person is born again his or her spirit is lost and under the control of the ruler of this world (Ephesians 2:1-3). But when they are born again, God's Spirit brings life to them by taking up residence in their human spirits (Romans 8:9). That is instantaneous and happens the moment they are born again. The apostle Peter said it this way *"For you have been born again, not of perishable **seed** but of imperishable, through the living and enduring word of God* (I Peter 1:23 — Emphasis mine).

Peter uses the graphic Greek word "sperma" to describe God's seed. When a person is born again they are born anew of God's "sperm" — they literally take on God's DNA!

2. ***The Soul Can Be Saved.*** After a human spirit is born again, the Holy Spirit who is newly resident in the person begins working on

the human soul. Remember, the soul is our mind, will, emotions and memories.

After we are born again in spirit our souls are <u>being</u> converted. This "saving of our souls" is a process that begins when we are born again and accelerates when we are sanctified and filled with the Spirit and continues until we are glorified.

It is important to realize that being born again and having your soul saved are not synonymous. When a person is born again in spirit the process of "saving the soul" has just begun. It was to born again people that Peter wrote *"For you are receiving the goal of your faith, the salvation of your souls"* (I Peter 1:9). Jesus talked about "losing our souls" for the gospel. *"For whoever wants to save his life* (a translation of psuche which is often translated "soul") *will lose it, but whoever loses his life for me and for the gospel with save it* (Mark 8:35).

James clearly urges us to partner with God by receiving the engrafted word which is able to save our souls. *"Wherefore lay apart all filthiness and superfluity of naughtiness, and receive with meekness the engrafted word, which is able to save your souls"* (James 1:21, KJV).

We engraft the word of God when we learn it, meditate on it and allow it to mold our lives back into the image of God. My wife and I have a large garden which includes several fruit trees. Most of them come from grafted stock. Skilled gardeners take a strong root stock and graft sweet fruit branches to it so they will have the strength of the stock and the sweetness of the fruit. In a similar way we can engraft the word of God into our lives so it will release the power of God and the fruit of the Spirit in our souls.

3. *The body can be crucified and will be redeemed.*

While we remain on earth we are to "reckon ourselves dead to sin" by "crucifying our bodies with Christ". This is an act of faith whereby we identify with the death of Jesus on the cross. The glorification of our bodies will take place at the rapture of the church. The Bible encourages us to crucify ourselves with Christ:

I have been crucified with Christ and I no longer live, but Christ lives in me. The life I live in the body, I live by faith in the Son of God, who loved me and gave himself for me (Galatians 2:20).

Do you not know that your body is a temple of the Holy Spirit, who is in you, who you have received of God? You are not your own; you were bought at a price. Therefore honor God with your body (I Corinthians 6:19-20).

In the same way, count yourselves dead to sin but alive to God in Christ Jesus. Therefore do not let sin reign in your mortal body so that you obey its evil desires. Do not offer the parts of your body to sin, as instruments of wickedness, but rather offer yourselves to God, as those who have been brought from death to life; and offer the parts of your body to him as instruments of righteousness (Romans 6:11-13).

Baptism is the one way that we identify with the death, burial and resurrection of Jesus Christ. I believe it is very important that every believer relate with Christ in baptism through immersion.

Let's quickly review. We were created in God's image. God is triune as Father, Son and Holy Spirit. We are triune with spirit, soul and body. Sin causes us to lose God's image in our spirit, soul and body. God gives people up to the degree to which they have ignored Him and His holy will for their lives. Still, it is God's desire to restore us to His image. He calls us to be born again in spirit, converted in soul and crucified with Christ. God wants us to be like Jesus! John said it this way. *"We know that we live in him and he in us, because he has given us of his Spirit. In this way, love is made complete among us so that we will have confidence on the day of judgment, because in this world we are like him"* (I John 4:13, 17).

CHAPTER NINETEEN
RESTORATION

1. **Jesus wants to restore God's likeness in us.** The heresy so prevalent in the Christian Church that "everybody sins everyday" must be debunked. Jesus did not save us so we could continue in sin but so we could leave the life of sin and live unto righteousness by whose stripes we were healed. (I Peter 1:24) Jesus wants us to live as children of God!

"*But when the time had fully come, God sent his Son, born of a woman, born under law, to redeem those under law, that we might receive the full rights of sons. Because you are sons, God sent the Spirit of his Son into our hearts, the Spirit who calls out, "Abba, Father"* (Galatians 4:4-6).

In English speaking countries the first words that babies often say is "daddy". I'm not sure that is fair because in many homes the mother changes most of the diapers and does much of the bathing, feeding and middle of the night chores with the baby. In Hebrew speaking countries the first word babies usually say is "Abba — Abba" which means "father — father". Truly spiritual people are ones who call on their "Abba Father" and desire to be more like him. Jesus instructed us to "B*e perfect, therefore, as your heavenly Father is perfect*" (Matthew 5:48).

Taking on God's perfect nature is the goal of truly spiritual people. Paul said "*We proclaim him, admonishing and teaching everyone with all wisdom, so that we may present everyone perfect in Christ"* (Colossians 1:28). The writer of Hebrews adds *"Because by one sacrifice he has made perfect forever those who are being made holy"* (Hebrews 10:24).

So, we have these beautiful promises from God's Word that challenge us to live above reproach. God calls us to holiness. He says we are to be like Jesus. He wants us to present everyone perfect in Christ. So why do so many people live defeated, unholy lives? What holds Christians back from the full and abundant life that God wants for them? Could it be that they do not realize the battle that they are in? Or do you think they haven't been taught how to fight the battle? God has given the Free Indeed Seminar and this book to teach us how to fight and win!

CHAPTER TWENTY
EVERY CHRISTIAN'S BATTLE

When people are born again they have God's Spirit living in their human spirits prompting them to holiness. But they also have sin and Satan prompting them to ungodliness. Every Believer has this battle to fight and the winning side is whichever side he or she joins. Someone has rightly said that when we are fighting *for* victory rather than *from* victory that we have entered the battle on the wrong ground — we already have victory in Christ and need to "flesh it out" by faith.

Satan's scheme is to lure us to join his side. The Bible says that rebellion is as the sin of witchcraft (I Samuel 15:23). Peter warns us to *"Be self-controlled and alert. Your enemy the devil prowls around like a roaring lion looking for someone to devour* (I Peter 5:8).

Believers often go to one of two extremes when dealing with the devil. The first extreme wants to go into personal hand to hand conflict with the enemy. Christians are sometimes lured into territories they have not been assigned to where they fight with demons they have not been given orders to deal with. This is an error of presumption — moving in areas and against enemies before receiving specific instructions from the Lord or adequate protection and covering by those in authority over them.

The second extreme where Believers are deceived is in thinking that they do not have the authority to go into personal conflict against the devil and his demons. This group cites verses like the one in Jude where even the archangel Michael didn't personally rebuke the devil in the fight over Moses' body but said "the Lord rebuke you" (Jude 1:9).

Some people do become needless casualties of war against the kingdom of darkness because they walk in presumption and do not seek the right protection and covering. But there are others who refuse to enter the fray because of their fear of the devil and his demons. They lose by forfeit and cannot advance against the enemy. Pacifism does not work in the war against the kingdom of darkness. Those who refuse to fight the devil really help advance his cause.

So, should a person personally confront the devil and his demons or should they pray to God for Him to rebuke the devil and his demons? I asked God that question and He clearly spoke to my spirit saying, "ask me to fight the battle for you unless I ask you to fight it". Since then I think my deliverance ministry and spiritual warfare has been about 50% intercession and 50% direct confrontation through the authority I've been given through Christ.

CHAPTER TWENTY-ONE
SECURING ADEQUATE PROTECTION

A football player who went on to the field with his shoulder pads but not his helmet would be headed for trouble. Christians should not enter the battle against darkness without adequate protection. It isn't enough to cover one part of the body, Christian need to be fully armed for battle.

My prayer partner says "it's about time that we quit worrying about the devil and make him start worrying about us". We can do that if we are fully protected.

1. **We find protection through obedience to God.** God will never bless disobedience. He always blesses obedience. God wants to develop the character in every person. He will give a person a test and if they pass it, He blesses them. But if they flunk the test, he gives them another one. God does this for our good so we might be conformed to the image of Christ.

Christians enter the path of blessing through obedience and come under the curse through disobedience. God warns *"See, I am setting before you today a blessing and a curse — the blessing if you obey the commands of the LORD your God that I am giving you today, the curse if you disobey the commands of the LORD your God and turn from the way that I command you today by following other gods, which you have not known"* (Deuteronomy 11:26-28).

2. ***We find protection through God's Word.*** When Jesus was tempted in the desert by the devil he resisted and overcame by quoting Scripture to him. We can also overcome Satan by the blood of the Lamb and the word of our testimony (Revelation 12:11).

Paul told us to *"take the helmet of salvation, and the sword of the Spirit, which is the word (*rhema*) of God"* (Ephesians 6:17). Several Greek words are translated "word" but the one used here, "rhema" refers to the quickened and spoken word of God. Paul suggests that we speak the words that God puts on our hearts when resisting the devil.

3. ***We find protection by submitting to those in authority.*** God works through authority to make his will known. When we resist authority we are actually resisting God unless the authority is going contrary to the will of God.

Lately I have run into dear people who are deceived into thinking they have no authority over them beyond God himself. Such people become road kill to the devil's schemes because God's word clearly tells every person to submit to the human authority that God has placed over them. (Romans 13:1-3; Hebrews 13:17, etc.).

The choice is ours: we can rebel and leave God's umbrella of protection or we can repent, obey and come under proper authority.

a. God's desire is to give us hope and a future. One of my favorite verses was given through Jeremiah. *"For I know the plans I have for you, declares the LORD, "Plans to prosper you and not to harm you, plans to give you hope and a future"* (Jeremiah 29:11).

God's prophetic destiny for our lives is not automatic, however. He requires us to pray, to submit and to war into our prophetic destinies. As certainly as Jesus came to give us live more abundantly (as we discover and walk in our prophetic destinies), so does Satan try to kill, steal and destroy out prophetic destinies.

Ephesians 2:10 says that we are created in Christ Jesus to do good works that he prepared in advance for us to do. God does have a beautiful plan for every life but his best doesn't come automatically or apart from our personal commitment. We do struggle against spiritual agents of darkness as well as against our own sinful natures.

b. God's plan is to sanctify us through and through! As Paul wrote *"May God himself, the God of peace, sanctify you through and through. May your whole spirit, soul and body be kept blameless at the coming of our Lord Jesus Christ* (I Thessalonians 5:23).

To sanctify means to make holy. It carries the idea of an ordinary man or woman coming out of a life of sin and being transformed from glory unto glory and prepared to do works of ministry. It is a process whereby we can break down every stronghold of the enemy and walk in freedom with Christ. Sanctification is clearly God's will for every Christian. The bible tells us that we need to diligently apply ourselves unto holiness. *"Make every effort to live at peace with all men and to be holy; without holiness no one will see the Lord"* (Hebrews 12:15).

Some Christians dismiss the concept of sanctification because it has been wrongly used to typify a work's religion that considers holiness a list of do's and don'ts. But God is very clear that He wills for us to be sanctified. *"It is God's will that you should be sanctified: that you should avoid sexual immorality; that each of you should learn to control his own body in a way that is holy and honorable"* (I Thessalonians 4:3).

CHAPTER TWENTY-TWO
THREE TYPES OF PEOPLE

God's desire is for every person to be sanctified and to conform completely for God's prophetic destiny. But many people choose the way of sin or soulishness instead. There are basically three types of people.

1. **First are the unsaved.** The Greek word is "sarkinos" which literally means "fleshly". They are ruled by their carnal flesh and by the devil until they are born again. "*As for you, you were dead in your transgression and sins, in which you used to live when you followed the ways of this world and of the ruler of the kingdom of the air, the spirit who is now at work in those who are disobedient*" (Ephesians 2:1).

God's hope and plan for unsaved people is that they get saved. He gave His Son as a sacrifice for our sins that we might die to sin and live unto righteousness by whose stripes we are healed. Paul includes himself among those who are hopeless apart from Christ. He wrote "*We know that the law is spiritual; but I am unspiritual* (sarkinos), *sold as a slave to sin*" (Romans 7:14).

Other words for unsaved would be fleshly or unspiritual. The "hierarchy" of sovereignty in an unsaved person's life is self and Satan, then the soul and finally the spirit. An unsaved person's human spirit is literally dead to the things of God. Jesus has not yet begun His inside out work in their lives.

Unsaved people usually cannot hear God's voice unless he breaks through to call them to repentance. The Gospel is veiled for unsaved people. 2 Corinthians 4:3-4 states that the spiritual condition of an unsaved person makes it so they can not see the light of the Gospel. Remember that when you are witnessing — unsaved people **cannot** see. It isn't that they will not but that they cannot see. They are blinded to the Gospel. Paul said "And even if our gospel is veiled, it is veiled to those who are perishing. The god of this age has blinded the minds of unbelievers, so that they cannot see the light of the gospel of the glory of Christ, who is the image of God".

The veil that keeps lost people from seeing the light of the gospel is a literal covering — much like the skin covers the flesh and blood of our bodies. We can't see what is inside because our skin veils it. The Greek word for veil is "Kalupto". You may understand that word better when you add the negative "a" to it and have "apokalupto" which we get the word apocalypse from. The word that is translated "revelation" in the Bible is "apokalupto" and it literally stands for "unveiling".

The only real spiritual protection an unsaved person has comes through the intercession of others. Paul writes that we have divine weapons to pull down the strongholds (veils) that keep people from seeing and responding to Jesus. "For though we live in the world, we do not wage war as the world does. The weapons we fight with are not the weapons of the world. On the contrary, they have divine power to demolish strongholds. We demolish arguments and every pretension that sets itself up against the knowledge of God, and we take captive every thought to make it obedient to Christ." (II Corinthians 10:3-5).

2. **Second are the soulish.** (psuchikos):

Soulish people are born again, but are not Spirit-filled. They are saved but not sanctified. They are on their way to heaven but are not living in daily victory. Jesus calls them "lukewarm" in Revelation three. He says He is about to spit them out of His mouth. Their souls are exalted over their human spirits. They have pockets of sin and resistance that keep them from living sanctified lives.

Soulish people cannot receive the things of God. They may listen but they are unable to perceive or understand. *"But the natural (psuchikos) man receiveth not the things of the Spirit of God: for they are foolishness unto him: neither can he know [them], because they are spiritually discerned."* (I Corinthians 2:14, KJV).

Soulish people gratify the desires of their sinful natures because they do not live by the Spirit or keep in step with the Spirit. *"So I say, live by the Spirit, and you will not gratify the desires of the sinful nature. For the sinful nature desires what is contrary to the Spirit, and the Spirit what is contrary to the sinful nature. They are in conflict with each other, so that you do not do what you want- Since we live by the Spirit, let us keep in step with the Spirit* (Galatians 5:16-17, 25).

God has something different and better for those who will truly follow God in the process of sanctification. We have to partner with the Lord for our own purification. *"Since we have these promises,"* dear friends, *"let us purify ourselves from everything that contaminates body and spirit,* **perfecting holiness** *out of reverence for God"* (II Corinthians 7:1 — Emphasis mine).

A soulish person is driven by his or her human soul. Incoming data is filtered through his/her mind, will, emotions and memories. The hierarchy of a soulish person is soul, Jesus, human spirit and body. Such people are saved but they are not living in spiritual intimacy with God. Therefore they seldom hear Jesus speaking to them and the joy of absolute surrender to the lordship of Christ is veiled. They may know Jesus as savior but have not recognized him as Lord and Master. Therefore they have little spiritual protection.

3. The third type of person is spiritual (pneumatikos). A truly spiritual person is one who is walking in correct spiritual alignment. They are not only born again, but born again with their spirit, soul and body in right alignment with each other and the Lord. Watchman Nee put it this way "A spiritual Christian is one whose human spirit is yielded to the Holy Spirit and whose soul is aligned with their human spirit and body is aligned with their soul." Paul said it this way. *"Those who live*

according to the sinful nature have their minds set on what that nature desires; but those who live in accordance with the Spirit have their minds set on what the Spirit desires. The mind of the sinful man is death, but the mind controlled by the Spirit is life and peace" (Romans 8:5).

A truly spiritual (fully sanctified) person knows Jesus as Lord and is spiritually aligned with their human spirit at the top and their soul and body submitted to the human spirit in that order. A spiritual person knows God's voice (John 10; 3-4). A spiritual person follows Jesus as Lord and Master and has great spiritual protection.

We would be foolish to think that all the promises of the Bible are for everyone. Heaven is promised to the Believer and not to the unbeliever. A person who walks in sin cannot claim the promise of a way out of temptation when they are tempted — not if they are willfully giving in to temptation. Likewise the promise of spiritual protection applies first to those who truly follow Christ. *"But the Lord is faithful, and he will strengthen and protect you from the evil one"* (II Thessalonians 3:3).

CHAPTER TWENTY-THREE
LEARNING TO WALK IN RIGHT ALIGNMENT

F. F. Bosworth compared the way God works with people to a checker game. He said God will make the first move and then wait for the person to take their move before God moves again. Bosworth applied that concept to appropriating all the promises of God, especially the healing promises. Part of walking in right alignment is making our move after God has made His.

1. God's part is doing that for us that we cannot do for ourselves. Only God can write his laws on our hearts. *"'This is the covenant I will make with the house of Israel after that time,' declares the LORD. 'I will put my law in their minds and write it on their hearts. I will be their God, and they will be my people'"* (Jeremiah 31:33). God spoke through Ezekiel saying *"I will give you a new heart and put a new spirit in you; I will remove from you your heart of stone and give you a heart of flesh. And I will put my Spirit in you and move you to follow my decrees and be careful to keep my laws"* (Ezekiel 36:26-27).

2. Our part has several important steps in moving toward God:

   a. First we need to surrender fully to God. The Church is full of partially surrendered Christians. If we really sang truthfully, many would sing "I surrender some, I surrender some", or "take my life and leave me be". We would sing about sitting on the premises rather than standing on the promises. But God expects better than that from us. He inspired

Paul to write *"Therefore, I urge you, brothers, in view of God's mercy, to offer your bodies as living sacrifices, holy and pleasing to God — this is your spiritual act of worship. Do not conform any longer to the pattern of this world, but be transformed by the renewing of your mind. Then you will be able to test and approve what God's will is — his good, pleasing and perfect will"* (Romans 12:1-2.

b. We also need to guard our emotions and attitudes. This is so important that the wisest man who ever lived wrote *"above all else, guard your heart, for it is the wellspring of life"* (Proverbs 4:23). Our hearts and attitudes determine what comes out of our lives far more than talent or giftedness can. A person with mediocre talent may become great with a right attitude but a person with excellent talent won't amount to much with a bad attitude.

c. Thirdly, we need to engage our wills. Some people come to God with the attitude of "fix me" rather than "work with me". I teach altar workers to inquire "how do you want me to pray?" People being ministered to need to engage in battle for themselves so they will be equipped for battle when we aren't there to fight for them. People doing ministry have to be careful to help people become dependent upon Christ and not upon a minister. To this end I often ask people to pray and tell them that I will agree with them in prayer. People need to engage their wills to keep God's commands. Jesus said *"Whoever has my commands and obeys them, he is the one who loves me. He who loves me will be loved by my Father, and I too will love him and show myself to him"* (John 14:21).

d. We also need to yield our bodies to the Lord. *"Therefore do not let sin reign in your mortal body so that you obey its evil desires. Do not offer the parts of your body to sin, as instruments of wickedness, but rather offer yourselves to God, as those who have been brought from death to life; and offer the parts of your body to him as instruments of righteousness"* (Romans 6:12-13).

> *"A spiritual man is not a man born again, but a man born again and walking in alignment."* — Watchman Nee.

CHAPTER TWENTY-FOUR
THE BENEFITS OF RIGHT SPIRITUAL ALIGNMENT

1. Right spiritual alignment gives people the ability to hear God's voice. God enables people to hear his voice in myriads of ways, but people in right spiritual alignment are able to hear what Jesus is speaking to them.

2. Right spiritual alignment also brings the ability to minister with God's power and authority. The Lord wants to release the anointing upon us so we can heal the sick, cast out demons and speak the word of the Lord. But power ministries require that we walk in right alignment.

I heard the true story of an associate pastor and his wife who were leading a deliverance session when suddenly the person receiving ministry jumped up, grabbed some scissors and started chasing them around and trying to kill them. The senior pastor heard the commotion, walked in and spoke with authority to the raving man "sit down and give me those scissors". The man did as he was ordered and the pastor cast the murderous spirit out. Later the pastor explained to his associates that when fear is an operation of the soul and when they let fear take over they lost their spiritual power and authority.

The greatest secret to the Apostle Paul's outstanding success in ministry is that he walked in the power that comes from walking in right alignment. He said *"my message and my preaching were not with wise and persuasive words, but with a demonstration of the Spirit's power, so that your faith might not rest on men's wisdom, but on God's power"* (I Corinthians 2:4-5).

3. Walking in right alignment also gives us access to all the promises of God. Consider this powerful Scripture. *"His divine power has given us everything we need for life and godliness through our knowledge of him who called us by his own glory and goodness. Through these he has given us his very great and precious promises, so that through them you may participate in the divine nature and escape the corruption in the world caused by evil desires"* (II Peter 1:3-4).

PRAYER OF ALIGNMENT

In Jesus' Name, I tell my body to submit to my soul.
I tell my soul to submit to my spirit.
I yield my spirit fully to the Holy Spirit.
I ask the Father to fill me with His Holy Spirit.
I choose to walk in the Spirit and overcome
Satan by the blood of the Lamb
and by the word of my testimony.
And, Holy Spirit, I ask you to show me
every time I slip out of alignment,
that I may realign with you;
spirit, soul, and body.
In Jesus' Name, Amen.

I have full assurance that if you pray that prayer by faith that you will come into right alignment and that you will be convicted by the Holy Spirit every time you fall out of alignment. There may be times when you don't have time to look up the previous prayer of alignment. In those cases the desperate prayer of alignment might help.

DESPERATE PRAYER OF ALIGNMENT:
Body, submit to my soul, Soul, submit to my spirit.
Spirit, submit to the Holy Spirit. Jesus is my Lord!

There are other areas of alignment that are also important for spiritual victory. One of the first is family. Ephesians 5:18-6:9 shows that the proper alignment comes to families when each person walks in the mutual submission mentioned in 5:21. The right alignment for the family is for each person to be submitted to the Lord and then to their Scriptural roles. Husbands are to love their wives and lead their families. Wives are to submit to their husbands and come alongside them for the well being of their homes. Children are to obey their parents and parents are to provide proper nurture and instruction. Any deviation from God's intended alignment for the family throws it out of alignment.

Another area of alignment is within the church. God is restoring proper apostolic order to his church. He wants leaders to lead and followers to follow — and all with the right spirits and attitudes. *"Obey your leaders and submit to their authority. They keep watch over you as men who must give an account. Obey them so that their work will be a joy, not a burden, for that would be of no advantage to you"* (Hebrews 13:17).

Civil authority is a third area where God wants us to walk in right alignment. We need to willfully reject the lawless and rebellious attitudes that escalated in the sixties and return to a proper love and submission to governmental and civil authority. Paul makes this clear saying *"Everyone must submit himself to the governing authorities, for there is no authority except that which God has established. The authorities that exist have been established by God. Consequently, he who rebels against the authority is rebelling against what God has instituted, and those who do so will bring judgment on themselves"* (Romans 13:1-2).

PRAYER FOR TOTAL ALIGNMENT:
Heavenly Father,
I submit to all those you have put in authority over me,
as unto you.
I also commit to take seriously my authority
and responsibility for others.
As I submit fully to you, I will provide godly leadership for them.
In the Name of the Lord Jesus, amen.

CHAPTER TWENTY-FIVE
PREPARING TO BE FREE INDEED

Anyone who doesn't recognize the great spiritual battle that we are in has already lost the battle. Every segment of society seems to be under the influence of evil and evil spirits.

Government: Politicians have never had a worse name than they do in our day. Things have gotten so bad that even a President of the United States can be impeached for perjury and illicit sexual activities and still have high ranking in his job approval polls. There is immorality, lying, scheming, manipulation, fraud, illegal funding of political campaigns and favors being bought by big contributors. We read of scandal everywhere from the White House to the outhouse.

School: Even with the huge increases in funding, schools are getting poor grades. We've all dealt with high school graduates who can't count change or read with any competency. School children take guns to schools and shoot their classmates and teachers. Some schools have installed metal detectors and have guards at the door to prevent vandalism and violence. Could it be that God won't bless the lottery money that is designated to building stronger schools?

Workplace: There seems to be no end to sexual harassment, favoritism or scandal at almost every workplace. Employers use and misuse their employees and employees pilfer thousands of dollars worth of good every years.

Sports: Big name sports heroes are being arrested for rape, drugs, accepting bribes and violence on the field. Then they strike because their million dollar contracts aren't adequate.

Television: Some people call it "hellevision." Advertisers won't sponsor good wholesome programs because they don't sell. Even when good programs can be found we have to be on guard with the advertisements. When good wholesome programs do win the approval of a large audience they are canceled because they aren't reaching the people with the money.

Church: The Church is on the winning team so the Church should be winning. But is it? More churches are being closed than opened in our country. Islam is growing faster than Christianity and there are as many mosques being built in America as there are new church buildings. Many congregations are struggling with declining attendance and bottomed out budgets. Some whole denominations are fighting to protect ungodly behavior and doctrines. Some denominations have knowingly ordained practicing homosexuals. Divorce is rampant even in the church. Many believers are struggling with guilt because their children are involved in drugs, alcohol and promiscuity. Sometimes it looks like the church can't even keep its own, let alone reach the lost.

Family: A government report released in 1999 said that nearly 65% of Americans own their own homes. Good for them! But too few of those homes have one husband and one wife who cleave together until in death they do part. There has been a lot of talk about dysfunctional families. Perhaps it is time for the church to show the world how families are supposed to function.

What will it take to turn things around? How can a godly remnant raise the standard? What can you and I do to make a difference? It is going to take the help of the Lord! I can't fix it and neither can you. But

Jesus can and He works through men, women and young people who are truly spiritual.

1. Our only hope is in the Lord. But without holiness no one will see the Lord! Hebrews tells us to *"make every effort to live in peace with all men and to be holy; without holiness no one will see the Lord. See to it that no one misses the grace of God and that no bitter root grows up to cause trouble and defile many. See that no one is sexually immoral, or is godless like Esau, who for a single meal sold his inheritance rights as the oldest son"* (Hebrews 12:14-16).

2. God has set his standard for those he will use — radical holiness. Peter mentions how God calls us to be holy in all we do. *"But just as he who called you is holy, so be holy in all you do; for it is written: "Be holy, because I am holy"* (I Peter 1:15-16). Jesus told us to *"be perfect, therefore, as your heavenly Father is perfect"* (Matthew 5:48).

3. Holiness includes closing all personal demonic gateways. I tell people who want to do ministry, especially deliverance ministry, that they cannot set people free from things they personally are not free of. A person addicted to pornography will have little success ministering to others who are addicted to porn.

4. People need to take two essential steps to breaking strongholds. First they need to repent of all known sin and then they need to confess and renounce all demonic gateways. The four most major gateways to demons seem to be:

a. **Rebellion.** Rebellion always opens a person up to the assault of the devil. Continued rebellion will certainly lead to spiritual defeat.

b. **Past or present involvement with a cult or the occult.** Any past or present exposure to Ouija Boards, Psychic Readers, séances, Dungeons and Dragons, healing magic, black magic, Satanism, horoscopes, channeling, spirit guides, water witching and the like creates gateways for the devil. People who understand how much God hates sorcery do not rejoice over Harry Potter's literary success — even if it does encourage children to read. God says *"let no one be found among you who sacrifices his son or daughter in the fire, who practices divination or sorcery, interprets omens, engages in witchcraft, or casts spells, or who is a medium or spiritists or who consults the dead"* (Deuteronomy 18:10-11).

 c. **All sexual sin including the sin of others who may have forcibly abused you.** Satan isn't fair and he even uses the sexual sin of perpetrators to put victims in spiritual bondage. Sexual sin not only makes a personal gateway for demons but it also creates soul ties that allow the demons of sexual partners and perpetrators access. That gateway is not destroyed by mere confession. The confession of sin brings God's forgiveness, but it does not destroy the stronghold Satan has because of the sin. Freedom comes from renouncing the hold the enemy has because of the sexual sin and from closing every gateway opened by the sin. God's word says several things about this. Paul told us to *"flee from sexual immorality. All other sins a man commits are outside his body, but he who sins sexually sins against his own body"* (I Corinthians 6:18). Later he writes *"for the unbelieving husband has been sanctified through his wife, and the unbelieving wife has been sanctified through her believing husband. Otherwise* **your children would be unclean**, *but as it is, they are holy* (I Corinthians 7:14 — Emphasis mine). I shudder at the ramification of this verse when it implies that the children of unbelieving parents are unclean. Thankfully God is willing to save anyone who turns to him in repentance.

 d. **Ancestral sin.** The Bible teaches that the punishment of the sins of the parents are visited down to the third and fourth generation of those who hate God. You've read the verses, but have you made the connection? The children of alcoholics tend to struggle with personal addictions. The children of child-molesters tend to have their own sexual strongholds. People with a natural or materialistic world view blame this all on environment. But they cannot explain why these same tendencies are passed on even when the child doesn't know its birth parents. The Bible gives the real answer. *"You shall not bow down to them or worship them; for I, the LORD your God, am a jealous God, **punishing the children for the sin of the fathers to the third and fourth generation** of those who hate me"* (Exodus 20:5). *"... Yet he does not leave the guilty unpunished; he punishes the children and their children for the sin of the fathers to the third and fourth generation"* (Exodus 34:7b). *"'The LORD is slow to anger, abounding in love and forgiving sin and rebellion. Yet he does not leave the guilty unpunished;* **he punishes the children for the sins of the fathers** *to the third and fourth generation"* (Numbers 14:18). *"You shall not bow down to them or worship them, for I, the LORD your God, am a jealous God,* **punishing the children for the sin of the fathers** *to the third and fourth generation of those who hate me"* (Deuteronomy 5:9 — Emphasis mine).

God does not unfairly punish innocent children for the sins of their fathers — but the resulting punishment of the sins of the fathers is inherent in the children. For example, the children of alcoholics have a greater tendency to carry on the pattern of addiction from their parents.

It is easy to see how ancestral sins can open demonic gateways and erect strongholds in the lives of children and grandchildren. Fortunately, the Bible also demonstrates how God led people to tear down these areas of defeat. *"But if they will confess their sins and the sins of their fathers..."* (Leviticus 26:40).

"... They stood in their places and confessed their sins and the wickedness of their fathers" (Nehemiah 9:2). *"Do not hold against us the sins of the fathers"* (Psalm 79:8).

Part of being set free from ancestral sin is confessing and renouncing as Daniel did in Daniel chapter nine. Since God takes such strongholds so seriously, we would be negligent if we didn't address them as well.

5. Each of us has three major bents (tendencies) in life. First is the bent toward good because we are created in God's image. Next comes

the general bent toward evil because we are born in sin. Finally is the specific bent toward evil because the sins and strongholds of the parents are passed down to the third and fourth generation.

All such gateways can be dealt with through deliverance and deep healing. But I remind you that I cannot set you free, and a deliverance appointment can't set you free. It is Jesus Himself, working through His body that sets you free.

CHAPTER TWENTY-SIX
GAINING FREEDOM IS AN ACTIVITY OF CHRIST'S BODY

People often hesitate to go through a deep healing and deliverance appointment because of their shame and disgrace caused by past failure. Unfortunately, it can be true that you dare not share your deepest secrets with some Christians. There may be some who would use your past against you and that's too bad. Any Christian who does not share the unconditional love, acceptance and forgiveness of God is more like the Pharisees than like Jesus.

If you think about the way the adulterous woman was treated in John eight you will remember that the religious Pharisees accused and condemned her. That wanted to make and example out of her. But Jesus, who could have cast the first stone at her because he was perfect, chose instead to say "neither do I condemn you, go and sin no more". That is the attitude that deliverance ministers carry. They will not condemn you or think ill of you. Our job isn't to judge but to help you find freedom in Christ. To that end, look at these passages:

- *You adulterous people, don't you know that friendship with the world is hatred toward God? Anyone who chooses to be a friend of the world becomes an enemy of God. Or do you think Scripture says without reason that the Spirit he caused to live in us envies intensely? But he gives us more grace. That is why Scripture says: "God opposes the proud but gives grace to the humble." Submit yourselves, then, to God. Resist the devil, and he will flee from you. Come near to God and he will come near to you. Wash your hands, you sinners, and purify your hearts, you double-minded. Grieve, mourn and wail. Change your laughter to mourning and your joy to gloom. Humble yourselves before the Lord, and he will lift you up* (James 4:4-19).

- *Is anyone among you in trouble? He should pray. Is anyone happy? Let him sing songs of praise. Is any one of you sick? He should call the elders of the church to pray over him and anoint him with oil in the name of the Lord. And the prayer offered in faith will make the sick person well; the Lord will raise him up. If he has sinned, he will be forgiven. Therefore confess your sins to each other and pray for each other so that you may be healed. The prayer of a righteous man is powerful and effective* (James 5:13-16).

- *Brothers, if someone is caught in a sin, you who are spiritual should restore him gently. But watch yourself, or you also may be tempted. Carry each other's burdens, and in this way you will fulfill the law of Christ. If anyone thinks he is something when he is nothing, he deceives himself. Each one should test his own actions. Then he can take pride in himself, without comparing himself to somebody else, for each one should carry his own load. Anyone who receives instruction in the word must share all good things with his instructor. Do not be deceived: God cannot be mocked. A man reaps what he sows. The one who sows to please his sinful nature, from that nature will reap destruction; the one who sows to please the Spirit, from the Spirit will reap eternal life. Let us not become weary in doing good, for at the proper time we will reap a harvest if we do not give up.* (Galatians 6:1-9).

In our journey towards deliverance, freedom, sanctification and right alignment it takes the whole body of Christ, working together as all the "one another" verses indicate that we should. We dare not wrongly judge others but walk beside them until all are made complete in Christ.

CHAPTER TWENTY-SEVEN
REVERSING THE CURSE BY REPLACING AHAB & JEZEBEL WITH CHRIST-LIKENESS

No church, school, city or government can be strong if marriages and families are weak. The family made of husband, wife and children is the foundational unit of the world. But Satan does his best to make the family a joke. Please forgive me as I share a few of my favorite stories about marriage.

- Henry Youngman's thoughts about marriage: "I married Miss Right". "I just didn't know that her first name was 'always'."
- Someone said marriage is a three-ring circus. Engagement ring, wedding ring, suffering.
- This is my worst. Why do men die before their wives? They want to!
- Milton Berle said "a good wife always forgives her husband when *she's* wrong".
- Phyllis Diller gave some sage marriage advice. "Never go to bed mad, stay up and fight".
- Somebody said, "I never knew what real happiness was until I got married. And then it was too late."
- Just think, if it weren't for marriage, some people would go through life thinking they had no faults at all.

- Two boys, walking home after church were discussing the Pastor's sermon on the devil. The first boy said "what do you think of all this Satan stuff — do you think it is real?" The second boy answered, "Well, you know how the Santa Claus thing turned out — it's probably just Dad".

If you consider how husbands and wives are portrayed on television you will see that the men are usually emotionally insecure wimps that are sex-crazed and that the wives use their superior intelligence to manipulate and control their husbands. If we use families like "Home Improvement" or "Everybody Loves Raymond" and his manipulative wife and mother as patterns for marriage and family we will be in trouble. The fact is, the church needs to set the example of how families should work, but we need to clean our own closets first.

I doubt that I will ever forget the time my wife and I stopped at a garage sale. I got out of the car and walked over and opened Pam's door and helped her out. As we walked up the young lady who was helping with the sale said "I have never seen anything like that before — are you from a different planet?" I had no idea what she was talking about. It turned out that she was shocked that I treated my wife with simple courtesy and respect. We found a couple of things we didn't need and I went up to pay for them. The young lady told her mother how I had opened Pam's door, helped her out and was even paying for her stuff. It was embarrassing and I was shocked too. I couldn't believe that she considered courtesy so unusual. The Bible encourages courtesy and respect.

Anytime a man tells me that he is having trouble praying or that his prayers don't seem to be getting through, I always ask him how he has been treating his wife. Usually there has been a problem and I point him to I Peter 3:7. *"Husbands, in the same way be considerate as you live with your wives, and treat them with respect as the weaker partner and as heirs with you of the gracious gift of life, so that nothing will hinder your prayers.*

If we take the Bible literally and become doers of the Word and not hearers only, we will be able to demonstrate healthy marriages and families to the world.

- *The time is near when all things will end. So keep your minds clear, and control yourselves. Then you will be able to pray. Most importantly, love each other deeply. Love has a way of not looking at others' sins. Open your homes to each other, without complaining. Each of you received a spiritual gift. God has shown you his grace in giving you different gifts. And you are like servants who are responsible for using God's gifts. So be good servants and use your gifts to serve each other. Anyone who speaks should speak words from God. The person who serves should serve with the strength that God gives. You should do these things so that in everything God will be praised through Jesus Christ. Power and glory belong to him forever and ever. Amen.* (I Peter 4:7-11, ICB).

I once took place in a series of meetings led by counselor Brad Bandemer at Shekinah Christian Church in Ann Arbor. Brad's teaching was so good that I asked him for permission to include some of his ideas in the Free Indeed Seminar and book. Hundreds have been helped through the teaching on Ahab and Jezebel and I am grateful to Brad for his insight and for his friendship.

Ahab and Jezebel are two biblical characters that have come to represent some particular demonic strongholds and spirits that we will look at in this section.

1. The Colossians "Let's Get Started" Lists: Colossians 3:5-17.

Each area where people go wrong in life is a deviation from Scripture. If people, especially husbands and wives, would simply live out the Word of God most of their strife would be ended and Ahab and Jezebel would have no place to stand in their lives. Consider this passage in light of your own personal relationships.

- *Put to death, therefore, whatever belongs to your earthly nature: sexual immorality, impurity, lust, evil desires and greed, which is idolatry. Because of these, the wrath of God is coming. You used to walk in these ways, in the life you once lived. But now you must rid yourselves of all such things as these: anger, rage, malice, slander, and filthy language from your lips. Do not lie to each other, since you have taken off your old self with its practices and have put on the new self, which is being renewed in knowledge in the image of its Creator. Here there is no Greek or Jew, circumcised or uncircumcised, barbarian, Scythian, slave or free, but Christ is all, and is in all. Therefore, as God's chosen people, holy and dearly loved, clothe yourselves with compassion, kindness, humility, gentleness and patience. Bear with each other and forgive whatever grievances you may have against one another. Forgive as the Lord forgave you. And over all these virtues put on love, which binds them all together in perfect unity. Let the peace of Christ rule in your hearts, since as members of one body you were called to peace. And be thankful. Let the word of Christ dwell in you richly as you teach and admonish one another with all wisdom, and as you sing psalms, hymns and spiritual songs with gratitude in your hearts to God. And whatever you do, whether in word or deed, do it all in the name of the Lord Jesus, giving thanks to God the Father through him. Wives, submit to your husbands, as is fitting in the Lord. Husbands, love your wives and do not be harsh with them. Children, obey your parents in everything, for this pleases the Lord. Fathers, do not embitter your children, or they will become discouraged. Slaves, obey your earthly masters in everything; and do it, not only when their eye is on you and to win their favor, but with sincerity of heart and reverence for the Lord... Whatever you do, work at it with all your heart, as working for the Lord, not for men, since you know that you will receive an inheritance from the Lord as a reward. It is the Lord Christ you are serving. Anyone who does wrong will be repaid for his wrong, and there is no favoritism* (Colossians 3:5 - 25).

a. Colossians gives a "clean up" or "get rid of — put to death" list of undesirable behaviors. Check the ones that threaten your relationships. (From Colossians 3:5-11)

- ☐ Sexual immorality, impurity, lust (pornography, never satisfied in marriage relations)
- ☐ Evil desires

- ☐ Greed, which is idolatry (always wanting more and more stuff)
- ☐ Anger and rage
- ☐ Malice and slander
- ☐ Filthy language
- ☐ Lying
- ☐ Prejudice toward other races
- ☐ Prejudice toward other religious groups
- ☐ Prejudice toward the opposite gender
- ☐ Prejudice toward other nationalities

b. Colossians also gives a "put on or dress yourself up" list. Putting on these desirable behaviors and clothing ourselves with these things that will bless our relationships and conform us to the likeness of Christ will play a huge part in defeating Ahab and Jezebel (Colossians 3:12-25).

- ☐ Clothe yourselves with compassion (which is the opposite of indifference)
- ☐ Clothe yourselves with kindness (which is the opposite of ignoring needs — like the husband who hears the car door, listens to his wife and children stumbling through the door with bags of groceries and yells "when's supper?")
- ☐ Clothe yourselves with humility (which is the opposite of pride)
- ☐ Clothe yourselves with gentleness (which is the opposite of being pushy and brass)
- ☐ Clothe yourselves with patience (which is the opposite of rushing others)
- ☐ Bear with each other (which is the opposite of flying off the handle)
- ☐ Forgive whatever grievances you may have (which is the opposite of unfulfilled revenge and/or unforgiveness)
- ☐ Put on love, which binds them all together (which is the opposite of self centeredness)

- ☐ Put on perfect unity (which is the opposite of selfish independence)
- ☐ Let the peace of Christ rule in your hearts (which is the opposite of worry and doubt)
- ☐ Thankfulness (which is the opposite of grumbling)
- ☐ Let the word of Christ dwell in you richly (which is the opposite of letting it bounce off)
- ☐ Teach and admonish one another with all wisdom (which is the opposite of "each one for himself/herself")
- ☐ Whole hearted worship (which is the opposite of going through the motions)
- ☐ Whatever you do, whether in word or deed, do it all in the name of the Lord Jesus (which is the opposite of self directed lifestyle)
- ☐ Wives, submit to your husbands (which is the opposite of pleasing self).
- ☐ Husbands, love your wives and do not be harsh with them (which is the opposite of self-fulfillment)
- ☐ Children, obey your parents in everything (which is the opposite of partial or delayed obedience)
- ☐ Fathers, do not embitter your children, or they will become discouraged (which is the opposite of discipline without love)
- ☐ Slaves, obey your earthly masters in everything; and do it, not only when their eye is on you and to win their favor, but with sincerity of heart and reverence for the Lord (God pleasing, which is the opposite of pleasing self)
- ☐ Whatever you do, work at it with all your heart, as working for the Lord, not for men (which is the opposite of apathy, complacency, and indifference)

2. Ahab and Jezebel strongholds and spirits.

If Satan cannot destroy a Christian directly, he always seems to go after the people closest to him. It is nearly impossible to do good ministry for the Lord if you are having problems at home. So Satan assigns Ahab and Jezebel spirits to work against husbands and wives.

The story of Ahab and Jezebel is found mainly in Kings and Chronicles, though they are also mentioned in Jeremiah, Micah and Revelation. The name Ahab means "brother of father". That certainly speaks of confusion and misplaced identity. Jesus' human lineage came through Ahab and Jezebel, so that gives hope in breaking free from Ahab and Jezebel strongholds.

Ahab reigned for 22 years in Samaria. His father-in-law Ethbaal was a pagan steeped in the vile notions and practices of the Baal cults. Ahab's marriage to Jezebel violated the Levitical law, but Ahab didn't build his life on what the Bible said. There were times that he showed signs of spiritual interest. He sought help from the prophets and manifested sincere repentance after one prophetic rebuke. But he remained wishy-washy at best.

Some say Jezebel's name means "chaste", but she was anything but that. Her name literally means "without cohabitation". She never could really bond with anyone. Instead she used and manipulated people, including her husband, for selfish personal gain.

Jezebel pulled her husband into Baal worship and manipulated him to establish a Baal cult center in Samaria that led the whole nation astray. Revelation 2:20-23 paints the picture of the Jezebel spirit as self-promotion, seductive and deceptive manipulation and control and an unrepentant attitude.

- *Nevertheless, I have this against you: You tolerate that woman Jezebel, who calls herself a prophetess. By her teaching <u>she misleads</u> my servants into sexual immorality and the eating of food sacrificed to idols. I have given her time to repent of her immorality, but <u>she is unwilling</u>. So I will cast her on a bed of suffering, and I will make those who commit adultery with her suffer intensely, unless they repent of **<u>her</u>** ways. I will strike her children dead. Then all the churches will know that I am he who searches hearts and minds, and I will repay each of you according to your deeds. (Revelation 2:20-23 — Emphasis is mine).*

Whether Ahab and Jezebel manifests as a stronghold, mindset or demon is less important than the need to cast down every likeness of Ahab and Jezebel in our lives. Ahab and Jezebel often work in partnership to come against godly relationships. If a husband displays Ahab characteristics, his wife will almost always respond with Jezebel actions and attitudes. The opposite is true as well. Let's take a look at how they plotted together to get what they wanted regardless of whom it might hurt. I will add some of my own observations in regular print.

- *Some time later there was an incident involving a vineyard belonging to Naboth the Jezreelite. The vineyard was in Jezreel, close to the palace of Ahab king of Samaria.* (Covetousness) *Ahab said to Naboth, "Let me have your vineyard to use for a vegetable garden, since it is close to my palace. In exchange I will give you a better vineyard or, if you prefer, I will pay you whatever it is worth."* (Me-first) *But Naboth replied, "The LORD forbid that I should give you the inheritance of my fathers." So Ahab went home, sullen and angry because Naboth the Jezreelite had said, "I will not give you the inheritance of my fathers."* (Not allowing others the right to make their own choices if they don't satisfy your own selfish desires) *He lay on his bed sulking and refused to eat.* (Pouting and trying to make others notice you are hurting) *His wife Jezebel came in and asked him, "Why are you so sullen? Why won't you eat?"* (Playing into the games of others) *He answered her, "Because I said to Naboth the Jezreelite, 'Sell me your vineyard; or if you prefer, I will give you another vineyard in its place.' But he said, 'I will not give you my vineyard.'"* (Blaming personal attitudes on everyone else but yourself) *Jezebel his wife said, "Is this how you act as king over Israel?* (Grabbing on to the offenses of others) *Get up and eat! Cheer up.* (Playing cheerleader for reprobate behavior) *I'll get you the vineyard of Naboth the Jezreelite."* (Forsaking personal conscience in order to "fix" another's problems) *So she wrote letters in Ahab's name, placed his seal on them, and sent them to the elders and nobles who lived in Naboth's city with him. In those letters she wrote: "Proclaim a day of fasting and seat Naboth in a prominent place among the people.* (Taking things into your own hands) *But seat two scoundrels opposite him and have them testify that he has cursed both God and the king. Then take him out and stone him to death."* (Willing to lie, steal and cheat to get your own way) *So the elders and nobles who lived in Naboth's city did as Jezebel directed in the letters she had written to them. They proclaimed a fast and seated Naboth in a prominent place among the people. Then two scoundrels came and sat opposite him and brought charges against Naboth before the people, saying, "Naboth has cursed both God and the king." So they took him outside the city and stoned him to death.* (Able to get others to do what you want through whatever means necessary) *Then they sent word to Jezebel: "Naboth has been stoned and is dead." As soon as Jezebel heard that Naboth had been stoned to death, she said to Ahab, "Get up and take possession of the vineyard of Naboth the Jezreelite that he refused to sell you. He is no longer alive, but dead."* (No remorse over wrongdoing) *When Ahab heard that Naboth was dead, he got up and went down to take possession of Naboth's vineyard.* (Happy as long as I get my way) (I Kings 21:1-16).

Both Ahab and Jezebel were out of spiritual alignment. They were soulish and driven by selfishness. They give a strong example of how marriages should NOT work. But they thought they had something to gain by their ungodly ploys. If you ever watched "Touched by an Angel" you know there was always a time of revelation when the angel would start to glow. It always happened when a person was at the end of their rope and found out they were holding onto the wrong rope. Suddenly they have an "eureka" moment. They realize they have been doing wrong, but they are given new hope and understanding of God that will help them change. I pray that will happen as we deal with the Ahabs and Jezebels in our lives today.

   a. Ahab and Jezebel strongholds and spirits have no assigned gender. Both men and women can be controlled by Jezebel and Ahab strongholds, mindsets and/or spirits. I had some of both in me before the Lord set me free.

   b. Ahab and Jezebel strongholds and spirits do have gender preferences. The curse and the fall in the garden left men and women with tendencies that the devil loves to seize and use to wreck havoc in homes and churches. Men are more likely to have Ahab characteristics and women are more likely to behave like Jezebel.

c. Ahab and Jezebel strongholds and spirits usually work in partnership to curse rather than bless marriages, churches and relationships. Ahab and Jezebel work together to stifle honesty and true vulnerability and the kind of communication that a man and wife should share. They work against each other to bring destruction to homes, families and churches. I believe that Ahab and Jezebel spirits are among the strongest working against homes and churches to keep them from entering God's destiny.

There will be a tendency to think of others and apply this teaching to them. Husbands will probably see their wives in what I'm about to say and wives will think I am describing their husbands perfectly. But this isn't about reinforcing what we think is wrong in others. It is about examining ourselves so we can clean up any Ahab or Jezebel that is working in our personal lives.

3. God's Original Design for Man and Woman:

a. The First account of creation shows clear equality between Adam and Eve.

Then God said, "Let us make man (ADAM-HUMAN) *in our image, in our likeness, and let them rule over the fish of the sea and the birds of the air, over the livestock, over all the earth, and over all the creatures that move along the ground." So God created man* (HUMAN) *in his own image, in the image of God he created him;* **male and female he created them.** *God blessed them and said to them,* **"Be fruitful and increase in number; fill the earth and subdue it. Rule** *over the fish of the sea and the birds of the air and over every living creature that moves on the ground."... God saw all that he had made, and it was very good. And there was evening, and there was morning — the sixth day* (Genesis 1:26-28, 31 — Emphasis mine).

- God gave humans, both male and female, the call and responsibility to govern the earth. His mandate to humans was two fold: 1) rule and subdue, 2) fill and multiply. Ahab and Jezebel spirits are assigned to hinder our dominion and increase for the Kingdom.

b. The second account of creation implies differences in purpose (Genesis 2:15-25).

- The LORD God took the man and put him in the Garden of Eden to work it and take care of it. And the LORD God commanded the man, "You are free to eat from any tree in the garden; but you must not eat from the tree of the knowledge of good and evil, for when you eat of it you will surely die." The LORD God said, "It is not good for the man to be alone. I will make a helper suitable for him." Now the LORD God had formed out of the ground all the beasts of the field and all the birds of the air. He brought them to the man to see what he would name them; and whatever the man called each living creature, that was its name. So the man gave names to all the livestock, the birds of the air and all the beasts of the field. But for Adam no suitable helper was found. So the LORD God caused the man to fall into a deep sleep; and while he was sleeping, he took one of the man's ribs and closed up the place with flesh. Then the LORD God made a woman from the rib he had taken out of the man, and he brought her to the man. The man said, "This is now bone of my bones and flesh of my flesh; she shall be called 'woman' for she was taken out of man." For this reason a man will leave his father and mother and be united to his wife, and they will become one flesh. The man and his wife were both naked, and they felt no shame.

   a. Adam was created first and directly responsible to God as the vassal-king or as his steward of all the earth. The buck stopped with Adam when it came to oversight of the earth.

   2. Adam was incomplete relationally. God said "and it was good" at the completion of most of his creation. But he said of man "It is not good for him to be alone" (Genesis 2:18-20).

   3. Eve was created to come alongside so man would not be alone, and to help him fulfill God's mandate. Together they were to advance God's purposes in the earth.

4. Man's sinful perversion. (Genesis 3:1-12).

God desired for mankind — both males and females — to take dominion over the earth and to fill it with the purposes of God. But God doesn't always get His own way. Even though he destines people for greatness they often fall short of God's glory.

   a. The relationship between man and woman was perverted in the fall. Rather than working together they began to blame, manipulate and work against each other. All sin questions God's Word (which is His character) and His goodness (which is His motive).

   b. The gender specific curses for men and women.

     1. The woman's curse included pain and desire (Genesis 3:16). For her it became an issue of control in the context of relational pain. Sin brought her the desire to master or control her husband (Genesis 4:6-7).

     2. The man's curse included toiling and sweating to provide for his family (Genesis 3:17-19). The issue for him became one of competence and he began questioning whether he would be able to provide for his family. Added to that was the issue of futility of wondering if he would be able to continue to provide for his family. God designed man to be an initiating leader of his family and for dominion, but the curse makes him want to shift responsibility.

Summary: The husband was made to be the servant leader; the curse comes against the ease of leading. The woman was meant to be a relational helper; the curse comes against the ease of responding to her husband.

  5. Ahab issues that are typically male.

The central issue for a man is avoiding inadequacy and incompetence. Men wrestle with whether or not they will be able to be good providers. They will do almost anything right up to the point of death to avoid appearing inadequate or incompetent. Men will always tend to avoid or overcompensate when faced with tough situations. Men tend to run from relationships that might expose their inadequacy in providing for their families spiritually, financially or physically. Consider the two extremes men may take.

They may become passive avoiders — thinking that someone else ought to pull thorns & thistles for them. They feel that it is unfair that they may have to suffer. On the other hand they may become aggressive avoiders. They figure that life is tough and out of control. Therefore they believe that any means of gaining control to make it work is legitimate.

Passive avoidance leads to a perversion of involvement. This may appear as the little boy that just stands back and doesn't offer his thoughts or as the good boy who does what he is told but doesn't interject any of his own thoughts or ideas.

Aggressive avoidance is a perversion of strength and may manifest as a distant boy or as a macho jerk.

The little boy requires his wife to handle anything that is too threatening (finances, religion, children, and sex). He is unwilling to work and either unwilling to find a job or unable to keep a job. He putters around with things but never accomplishes much. He avoids conflict at all costs.

The good boy is a stable, dutiful and passionless problem solver. He smoothes conflict over and seems gifted at making the other person think any problems are their fault. He seems to say things like "I don't care, I don't know," or "it's up to you" a lot.

The distant boy is uninvolved and distant. He somehow communicates "I'm not really here" even when he is. He may have a well controlled temper, yet those around him fear he may lose control. He can be more decisive if present and indecisive if it doesn't involve him personally. He may be a powder keg, given to fits of anger. He tends to be moody according to what's going on around him.

Everyone has experienced a macho jerk. These guys are extremely threatened by authentic relationships. They dogmatically apply rules to others but not to themselves. They can be aggressive, using intimidation and fear to control others. They tend to be arrogant and impulsive and given to fits of anger and are not open to challenge, debate, feedback or introspection.

6. Jezebel issues that are typically female.

The central issue for women tends to be avoiding uncertainty. Women wonder if they will be too vulnerable in their relationships. They're guarded in trusting their hearts and souls with others for fear of being hurt. They may use control for coping with uncertainty. Since they fear being vulnerable or out of control in a relationship with someone that might fail them, they may use control to manipulate others to avoid deep pain. Consider the two extremes women may take.

Women may become helpless controllers. They believe that someone should and will come through for them as long as they make it clear that they cannot function (make decisions, deal with conflict, etc.) They place a high price on failure so they won't even try because they don't dare fail. The helpless controller is never able to really give to others. They become takers and not givers and they can really become a drain on their friends.

Women may also become emasculating controllers. When they do they will destroy anyone who tries to get too close emotionally or physically. Such a woman cannot receive from others and if a man wants a relationship with her, he cannot be the head.

The helpless controller is a prevision of vulnerability and may manifest as a little girl or as a nice girl. The emasculating controller is a prevision of strength and may manifest as a busy girl or as a tough girl.

The little girl is naive in a very manipulatively helpless way. She is seductive in her subtle little girlish flirtiness. She may appear to be frail, petite and not a woman of depth but she consciously plans her every move. She may be the "Southern Belle" stereotype.

The nice girl may be the people-pleasing hostess who looks to satisfy you in any of your needs, wants or desires. She is pleasant, easygoing, kind, generous, supportive and warm. But she avoids all conflict with a passion and lives by the motto "I'm not required to give of my soul, because I have served in other ways".

The busy girl is a competent and thoughtful administrator. She handles conflict by always being in a flurry of activity. It's like she knows that she will be a hard target to hit as long as she stays busy. She is expressive in a way that is more controlled and stiff. She tends to have a cool edge about her.

Finally, the tough girl has a tough edge in her sarcasm and cynicism. She will make you pay if you fail her relationally. She dares you to try to conquer her but if you try it you will wish you wouldn't have. Her survival mentality pushes her to validate herself through performance. She may excel in a male-dominated area like being a surgeon or an executive.

7. Strategy of overcoming Ahab and Jezebel strongholds and/or spirits.

a. God's method and goal is Christ-likeness. The Book of Romans tells us that Jesus became like us so we could become like God! *For those God foreknew he also predestined to be conformed to the likeness of his Son, that he might be the firstborn among many brothers* (Romans 8:29).

To be conformed to the likeness of Jesus there are undesirable thought patterns, attitudes and behaviors that we need to die to. As Paul wrote *"In the same way, count yourselves dead to sin but alive to God in Christ Jesus. Therefore do not let sin reign in your mortal body so that you obey its evil desires. Do not offer the parts of your body to sin, as instruments of wickedness, but rather offer yourselves to God, as those who have been brought from death to life; and offer the parts of your body to him as instruments of righteousness. For sin shall not be your master, because you are not under law, but under grace"* (Romans 6:11-14).

b. We need to train ourselves to overcome evil with good. *"Do not be overcome by evil, but overcome evil with good"* (Romans 12:21).

To repair marriages we need to learn to work on ourselves rather than on our mates. I need to deal with what is coming out of me, rather than on what comes out of my wife. We need to examine ourselves before we try to pick the splinter out of our spouse's eye.

c. We need to believe that God can complete His good work is us. *"Being confident of this, that he who began a good work in you will carry it on to completion until the day of Christ Jesus"* (Philippians 1:6).

Some of us need to put our lives and our marriages back in the Potter's hands and let Him form something beautiful out of our lives. We need to learn to trust God with our lives and our marriages. The first step to transformation is to see where it is needed. It's time to take an honest evaluation as to where we stand regarding Ahab or Jezebel characteristics. I invite you to mark any of the following that apply to you. Remember Ahab characteristics can be found in both men and women.

8. Ahab Characteristics (check any that are true of you):

⇨ *Ahab spirits are assigned to strip you of your dignity, authority and identity and to kill all hope that you can be a man or woman of God.* (i.e. I can never be as good a spouse or Christian as my pastor is...)

- ☐ Generational: passivity, laziness, indecisiveness, apathy and indifference.
- ☐ Excelling in evil passed on down generational lines.
- ☐ Giving up responsibility of leadership in the family, physically and/or spiritually.
- ☐ Intimidated by your wife or having a domineering wife.
- ☐ Placing your wants above all else.
- ☐ Fear of failing, so it's easier to not try especially in spiritual manners.
- ☐ Rebellion, doing what you want to do even though you know it's wrong.
- ☐ Self-justification and rationalization of patterns of behavior.
- ☐ Manipulation, use sulking, pouting, silence or anger to get your own way.
- ☐ Wants peace at all cost and does not confront issues.
- ☐ Usually not an Ahab without a Jezebel.

Ahab Prayer (Pray and reflect over each portion of this prayer — let the Holy Spirit bring change to your heart and life):

- ☐ Lord Jesus Christ, I confess you as my Lord and Savior.
- ☐ I want you, Lord, to cleanse my soul, to make me whole and to make my image as yours.
- ☐ I pray that the spirit of Ahab that has robbed me of the fulfillment of God's intended plan and purpose for my life be exposed! Please show me the areas in my life where they are.
- ☐ Where I am apathetic and not caring or involved, where I am indifferent, or where I'm not a person who makes a difference... Lord, I choose to be a person who makes a difference!
- ☐ Lord, I ask you to release your holy passion and fire in me.
- ☐ Show me, Jesus, where I am lazy and help me to be actively involved and motivated.

- ☐ Show me my rebelliousness and help me to obey you.
- ☐ Show me, Lord, where I am fearful and indecisive. Please help me be of good courage and fear not.
- ☐ Show me where I have justified or rationalized any of these behaviors and where I have given place to the spirit of confusion or fear of failing.
- ☐ Show me, Lord, where I have pulled back from my responsibility of spiritual warfare and obedience or have condoned sin around me. It is my will to regain that ground!
- ☐ Lord, show me where I have tried to manipulate you and others through my anger, silence and pouting. In Jesus' Name I turn away from this and choose to trust you and your provision.
- ☐ Lord, where I have been tolerant of sexual immorality I now choose to be sexually pure.
- ☐ Show me where I am idolatrous, and where I'm unfaithful to you, because it is my will to be one who serves you, Lord.
- ☐ Lord, please bring me to a place where I have true godly sorrow and repentance for cooperating with this vile spirit of Ahab and see it defeated in my life.
- ☐ Strengthen my will, Lord, that I may renounce these sins and strongholds and fulfill all that you have intended for my life.
- ☐ And where I have given place to the spirit of confusion or fear of failing, I cast that down in the name of Jesus.
- ☐ Now, Father, in the name of the Lord Jesus Christ, I pray that you will fill me with hope and understanding. Help me to not be paralyzed by the fear of being deceived, lied to, or taken advantage of. Please restore hope in me. Lord, I believe you right now for a change in my future. In Jesus' Name, Amen.

9. Jezebel Characteristics (check any that are true of you):

⇨ *Jezebel spirits and strongholds are assigned to strip you of your vulnerability and ability to come alongside your spouses and help them be all that God wants them to be. It also kills all hope that you can be a woman or man of God.* (i.e. I can never be as good a wife or Christian as my pastor's wife is)

- ☐ Dominates, manipulates and controls through deception.
- ☐ Control is the issue, bossy, self-willed and fiercely independent.
- ☐ Jezebel literally means "without co-habitation" — can't really get close to others or to God.
- ☐ Can't live peaceably unless I can dominate.
- ☐ Targets men of leadership and brings discouragement and fear.
- ☐ Cannot fully submit (in my heart) to authority.
- ☐ Cuts off the spiritual order that God designed for husband, wife and children.
- ☐ Uses sorcery, witchcraft, and manipulative prayers to get my way through controlling behavior and spiritual powers.
- ☐ Rebellious and has great difficulty in relationships that I can't control.
- ☐ Prideful, at times I feel like I am the only one capable of doing it.
- ☐ Prone to lying and twisting the truth.
- ☐ Prone to stirring up trouble.
- ☐ Critical, judgmental and unforgiving.
- ☐ Hates the grace of God, holiness and repentance.
- ☐ Hates prayer.
- ☐ Hates the prophetic.
- ☐ Self-promoting.
- ☐ Cunningly uses fear, jealousy or insecurity to control others.
- ☐ Blatant or subtle use of seductive sensuality (flirting or pouting).
- ☐ Can cause you to be idolatrous, "I don't have time for God or to pray. I have other priorities..."

Jezebel Prayer (Pray and reflect over each portion of this prayer — let the Holy Spirit bring change to your heart and life):

I remind you that Jezebel can affect women and men. If you pray this prayer and make these declarations with me, some things may really strike deep in your heart. Mark those things so you can pinpoint them in prayer. This is a time to seek the Lord for personal revelation. Take time to pause after each sentence and receive help and insight from the Holy Spirit.

- ☐ Lord Jesus Christ, I ask you to reveal to me any foothold that I have given to Jezebel strongholds or spirits.
- ☐ Show me, Lord, where I have rebelled against you, and against your will. I choose now to be a person who is not rebellious.
- ☐ Show me where I have given place to idolatry so I may worship only you, and look to you alone for comfort.
- ☐ Show me, Jesus, where I have been wicked, for I choose to be an instrument of righteousness and holiness.
- ☐ Show me, Lord, where I have lied and deceived, for I desire to be a person of truth, vulnerability, and reality.
- ☐ Show me, Lord, where I have given any place to sexual immorality, for I choose to live a life of purity which brings honor to you.
- ☐ Show me where I have brought division to ministry or in homes. I choose to be a minister of reconciliation. I choose to be one who draws unto you and does not resist you.
- ☐ Lord, show me where I have given place to manipulation and to control and to a cunning spirit. I choose to release those places and trust you Lord. I let go of them and consecrate my needs and the desires of my heart to you Lord Jesus.
- ☐ I choose to willingly submit to the authority you have placed over me.
- ☐ Lord, show me where there's been hatred and anger and bring peace to my heart. Let your forgiveness flow through me.
- ☐ Show me where there has been any violence or rage to the anointing or the anointed of God.
- ☐ Show me where I have been self-willed, self-centered, and self-reliant or independent of you Lord. For I declare that I choose to be a person submitted to your leading, to your plans and your purpose.
- ☐ Show me, Lord, where my selfish ambition has lead me to give place to Jezebel's witchcraft and sorcery. I choose not to be given to such ungodliness.
- ☐ I hate you Jezebel! I hate what you've done in my life and I put you on notice your work is finished in me. I shall not cooperate

- ☐ with your plan to bring destruction to my life or to others any longer.
- ☐ Holy Spirit, I now pray that you will work your work of sanctification in me.
- ☐ Father, I ask you to cast down any work of fear.
- ☐ Holy Spirit, I ask you to minister to my heart where I have been afraid of trusting God and people. Come now and minister to my need. I cast down that work of fear.
- ☐ Lord, you are a trustworthy God. Hallelujah! Thank you, Jesus.

Renouncing and Casting Down Ahab and Jezebel

Prayer helps us deal with our relationship with God and confession releases us from sin but it takes renunciation to break the bondage demons hold because of past sin. Therefore I encourage you to make the following renunciations out loud.

- ☐ Now, in the Mighty Name of Jesus Christ, I break every stronghold of Ahab and Jezebel off my life.
- ☐ I refuse to cooperate with Ahab and Jezebel any longer.
- ☐ I submit my life totally to Jesus Christ.
- ☐ I command Ahab to come off and go to the feet of Jesus, Now!
- ☐ I command Jezebel to come off and go to the feet of Jesus, Now!

Reversing Ahab and Jezebel curses in marriages:

When a husband or wife truly works through Ahab and Jezebel issues with God they often feel the need to work through them with their spouses as well. The following can be a guide for husbands to make proper confession to their wives. After this there is a similar guide for women to make confession to their husbands.

Husband to Wife:

- ☐ My Dear_____, I confess that I have often shifted responsibility and failed to love you as Christ loved the Church. I have seen some Ahab and Jezebel characteristics in my life, and I have directed them toward you. Will you please forgive me? With God's help, I will take my God given authority and lead you and our home to the glory of God.

- ☐ I thank you, Heavenly Father, for the gift_____ is to me.
- ☐ _____, I will be always be your best friend and husband; I will love you, and take care of you forever.
- ☐ I will fully listen to you and will help you realize your dreams and goals.
- ☐ I recognize my Scriptural duty to love you as Christ loved the church, and to lead you in the way everlasting. I like the way you help others when they need help, and I want to be there for you in the same way. I will walk hand in hand with you.
- ☐ With God as our guide, we will face whatever life brings, hand in hand, believing in each other and trusting in God.
- ☐ Today, I recommit to our marriage. Like rivers running together, we gain strength and vitality because we now come together as one, in Christ, forever. With His help, I will surely keep these vows. I love you.

Wife to Husband:

- ☐ My Dear_____, I confess that I have often assumed your responsibility and failed to submit to you as the Church does to Jesus. I have seen some Ahab and Jezebel characteristics in my life, and I have directed them toward you. Will you please forgive me?
- ☐ I thank you, Heavenly Father, for the gift_____ is to me.
- ☐ _____, I will be always be your best friend and wife. I will love you, and help you forever.
- ☐ I will fully listen to you and will help you realize your dreams and goals.
- ☐ I recognize my Scriptural duty to submit to you as the Church does to Christ. I will walk hand in hand with you.
- ☐ With God as our guide, we will face whatever life brings, hand in hand, believing in each other and trusting in God.
- ☐ Today, I recommit to our marriage. Like rivers running together, we gain strength and vitality because we now come together as one, in Christ, forever. With His help, I will surely keep these vows. I love you.

Scripture References about Ahab and Jezebel: 1 Kings 16-22, Romans 9, 1 Chronicles 21:13 Isaiah 47:7-10, 57.3-4, Revelation 2:19-24.

Years ago I came across a poem that is funny but beautifully poignant in its scope. I don't know who the author is but I deeply appreciate his or her insight.

Butt Prints in the Sand

One night I had a wondrous dream,
One set of footprints there was seen.
The footprints of my precious Lord,
But mine were not along the shore.
But then some stranger prints appeared,
And I asked the Lord, "What have we here?"
Those prints are large and round and neat,
But Lord, they are too big for feet."
"My child", he said, in somber tones,
"For miles I carried you alone".
"I challenged you to walk in faith",
"But you refused and made me wait".
You disobeyed, you would not grow,
The walk of faith you would not know,
So I got tired, I got fed up,
And there I dropped you on your butt.
Because in life there comes a time,
When one must fight and one must climb.
When one must rise and take a stand,
Or leave their butt prints in the sand.
— Author Unknown

PART TWO: FREEDOM SESSIONS.

In Free Indeed Seminars I lead people through corporate deliverance and deep healing sessions. In each session I cover one area of possible bondage. I begin each session with a teaching regarding the area and then lead in some self-evaluation and corporate ministry.

It is my hope and prayer that the Lord will release his healing and delivering anointing upon this portion of the book in the same way that He does in the seminars. My prayers are with you as you continue and I challenge you to deal with each one of these areas with courage and with the confidence that Jesus was anointed to heal the brokenhearted and to set the captives free.

CHAPTER TWENTY-EIGHT
DEALING WITH REJECTION ISSUES

Rejection may be the most common stronghold in many churches. Christians may struggle with feelings of rejection from things in the past, present or even what they may face in the future. People in bondage to rejection, self-rejection, perceived rejection, or fear of rejection never learn to enjoy the abundant life that Jesus offers.

But there is good news. Everyone has a choice. You can experience the abundant life. If you choose to deal with your rejection issues you can cast down rejection and begin walking as one accepted in the Lord! But it is a choice — each person has to choose the path of freedom. God has made it possible for people not to feel rejected any longer.

The Church of Jesus Christ should be the best place in the world to receive total and unconditional love, acceptance, and forgiveness. Jesus modeled that as He received those that society rejected. But the church doesn't always follow His example.

One of my first ministries was leading a youth group. In one meeting I had each teen hang a sign from their necks that said "I.A.L.A.C.". I didn't tell them that it stood for "I am lovable and capable." But whenever someone was rejected or put down in any way, I would tear a piece off their sign. Before the meeting was over many of the teens didn't have anything left to show they were "lovable and capable".

The same thing happens in many churches and homes. Right when people most need the love, acceptance, and forgiveness of Jesus Christ is when they are most likely to be shunned. Think of our first reaction to people who mess up like people going through a divorce, single people who get pregnant, people struggling with sin or addictions or behavioral problems. Many of these people fell into sin because they have been overcome with rejection issues. The church should be the one place where they can overcome rejection. Amen?

The American College Dictionary defines rejection as: 1) Act of rejecting. 2) State of being rejected. 3) That which is rejected. It gives this definition of reject: 1) to refuse to have, take, recognize, etc. 2) To refuse to grant (a demand, etc.). 3) To refuse to accept (a person); rebuff. 4) **To throw away, discard, or refuse as useless or unsatisfactory.** 5) To cast out or eject; vomit 6) To cast out or off. *Noun*: 1) Something rejected as an imperfect article. (Emphasis mine).

As I define these two words many people see themselves in them. People feel rejected by those who have refused them, by others who have ignored them and both others that have failed to recognize them and their need.

Some of them feel they have been rebuffed, thrown away, discarded. They think no one really knows them or even wants to. If they came from a broken home or marriage, they may feel rejected as useless or unsatisfactory. Even issues in the womb can bring rejection. If a woman is abused while pregnant, her fetus may pick up spirits of rejection, trauma, or panic and the like.

I worked with a beautiful fifteen year old that was caught up in lesbianism. I was brought in to minister to her after she had run away and was found several states away with some friends whom she thought accepted her as she was. Through deep healing we discovered that she felt rejected by her Dad. We dealt successfully with the issues and later found out that her Dad wasn't with her when she was being born because he was required to be in training to complete his certification for his career. Then he wasn't allowed in the room after her difficult delivery. She also had spirits of trauma that had entered while she was in the womb and we later found out that her mother had been in two automobile accidents shortly before she was born. Satan was trying to kill, steal and destroy God's destiny for her.

Perhaps some of your life experiences have been used by Satan to make you feel so rejected that you would kill yourself if you weren't so afraid of God's final rejection. I remember a lady at one of my seminars who looked really depressed. During one session I asked her if she ever tried committing suicide. She told me that she wanted to, but was afraid of going to hell. But every day she prayed that God would take her life. Her stronghold of rejection led her to the point of despair after her husband had died.

We are going to deal with rejection issues from a Kingdom perspective today. God's Kingdom is one of unconditional love, acceptance, and forgiveness. Therefore we can assume that rejection is not part of His Kingdom. Jesus came to save the world, not condemn it. He says things like *"Neither do I condemn you, go and sin no more."* Jesus came to destroy the devil's works, including the work of rejection. One way we can know that the Kingdom of God is within us is when we are freed from spirits of rejection.

Jesus said *"But if I drive out demons by the **finger** of God, then the kingdom of God has come to you"* (Luke 11:20). Matthew reveals that the finger of God is a euphemism for the Spirit of God. *"But if I drive out demons by the **Spirit** of God, then the kingdom of God has come upon you* (Matthew 12:28 — Emphasis mine).

Jesus wants to tear down every stronghold of rejection by His Blood and by His love. The devil cannot operate in at atmosphere of love and he does everything he can to destroy it. The kingdom of darkness is one of hatred and rejection with no love, no acceptance, only condemnation.

I once ministered deliverance to a lady who was overcome with rejection. Her own father had used her to teach her brothers and their friends how to have sex. She was a deeply wounded woman. We had come to a standstill in her deliverance. I was trying to cast out the spirit of hatred and it wouldn't come out. I breathed a silent prayer and asked God what to do and he told me to start singing songs like "Jesus Loves Me, This I Know". The demons literally began screaming in agony when I sang about the love of God and they soon came out.

A couple of months later this woman drove several hours to Sturgis to give testimony of how God had set her free. She brought a paper-plate with 29 psychotropic drugs on it and told us that she used to take all 29 of them before getting out of bed. But by that time her psychiatrist had her down to three pills a day.

Consider what Jesus said in John 10:10. *"The thief comes only to steal and kill and destroy; I have come that they may have life, and have it to the full."* (More Abundantly).

The enemy comes to steal acceptance from us. The Greek language describes Satan as a "klepseis" who comes to "klepsei", destroy and kill. Do you hear "klepto" — the root of "kleptomaniac" in that word? Satan is such a thief that he absent mindedly does whatever he can to steal our acceptance from God, others, and even ourselves. He does that through rejection at several levels. His scheme of rejection began in Genesis Three. I want you to see how rejection works as we study this passage.

1. Satan tempted Eve to disbelieve God's acceptance.

- *Now the snake was the most clever of all the wild animals the Lord God had made. One day the snake spoke to the woman. He said, "Did God really say that you must not eat fruit from any tree in the garden?" The woman answered the snake, "We may eat fruit from the trees in the garden. But God told us, "You must not eat fruit from the tree that is in the middle of the garden. You must not even touch it, or you will die."" But the snake said to the woman, "You will not die. God knows that if you eat the fruit from that tree, you will learn about good and evil. Then you will be like God!"* (Genesis 3:1-5).

Satan was tempting Eve to think God didn't really love her enough to give her everything she needed. He made her think that God was holding out on her. That there was more for her to have, but God was being mean and stingy about it. This made her feel like God was rejecting her.

2. Their sin made them think God couldn't love them anymore.

- *When the woman saw that the fruit of the tree was good for food and pleasing to the eye, and also desirable for gaining wisdom, she took some and ate it. She also gave some to her husband, who was with her, and he ate it. Then the eyes of both of them were opened, and they realized they were naked; so they sewed fig leaves together and made coverings for themselves. Then the man and his wife heard the sound of the LORD God as he was walking in the garden in the cool of the day, and they hid from the LORD God among the trees of the garden. But the LORD God called to the man, "Where are you?" He answered, "I heard you in the garden, and I was afraid because I was naked; so I hid."* (Genesis 3:6-10).

Why did Adam and Eve hide from God? He wasn't offended at their nakedness. They had always been naked and unashamed. There is a great scriptural truth here: God was seeking Adam and Eve AFTER they sinned. He still loved them. He still wanted to provide for them. He still wanted fellowship with them. It was people, not God, who were so strained by what they did that they tried to cover themselves and hide from God.

God was leading them to confession. Do you think He didn't know where Adam and Eve were when they were hiding in the garden? Do you think God lost track of them? When my granddaughter Alexis was four, Pam brought her into my office one day. She wandered out and we went looking for her. She was going from room to room looking for God. She would peek in a door and ask "God, are you in here?" Was God looking for Adam and Eve like that?

Do you think God was saying "Adam, I don't know where you are?" Of course not, but I emphasize this because it helps people overcome rejection. Remember, God knew what they had done and He came looking for them. The heart of the Good Shepherd is seen looking for the lost sheep. Satan makes us fear we've gone one sin too far and we will never be able to get back to God. Please catch this. It was after they had sinned that God came looking for them. Not to punish them, but to cover their nakedness. God asked "Where are you?" so Adam would own up and make confession.

3. Sin and perceived rejection strained all their relationships:

a) They became self-conscious and ashamed. They started focusing on their nakedness. I remind you, they were created perfect. They didn't have warts or wrinkles or scars to be ashamed of. But they felt shame and embarrassment. They blushed for the first time.

b) They started covering who they really were. They began pretending to be something they weren't. They didn't like what they saw in themselves so they tried to cover it. And we still do that. But now we pay psychiatrists thousands of dollars to try to uncover what we have hidden even from ourselves.

c) They began justifying themselves and passing blame.

Adam blamed God *and* his wife. *"The woman you put here — she gave me some fruit from the tree, and I ate it."* Isn't it amazing how quick people are to pass blame rather than confess responsibility? Adam says, "You see God, if I wasn't married to this woman you gave me, it wouldn't have happened." Eve blamed the serpent. And people are still blaming others rather than owning up to responsibility.

Walking in rejection is a choice. People have to choose to be overcomers or they will be overcome. Adam and Eve chose to be overcome by hiding and blaming rather than dealing with sin & rejection issues.

d) Their focus turned from being to doing. God created us to be human beings not human doings. *But sin makes us focus on what we do rather than who we are.* Many people define themselves by their work rather than by their being.

Ralph Neighbour teaches there are two types of people in the Bible. There are God rejecters who find their self image in what they do and God Followers who find their identity in God. When you read about the God followers in Genesis 4:25-5:24 you see that the number of years they lived is listed because when you follow God, every day counts. But all that is listed for the God Rejecters in Genesis 4:16-26 is what they did. Their identity was totally centered in their work.

Legalistic churches struggle with this same temptation. That is why they have to battle with works-righteousness. They define Christianity by what they do rather than who they are in Christ. They make this great little "do and not to do" list of things they think will prove whether or not they are rejected by God. The emphasis becomes self and good works rather than Christ and His perfect work. (Col 2:20-23)

Are you a saint or a sinner? Your answer depends on whether you are trusting in your good works or in His perfect work! Is salvation something you do or something that He did? Both! Being born again in spirit is the work of God. But God requires you to work out your salvation through the engrafted word which is able to save your souls. But sanctification has to start with what God did. Only God can transform sinners into saints. If we think we are saints destined to victory we have assurance of His acceptance and will conquer. If we think we are sinners destined to fall, we will. We will also be tempted to reject ourselves and think God rejects us too. But I remind you. We have a choice. We can cast off rejection. So let's choose to deal with rejection.

The devil will use anything he can to make us feel rejected. He knows that the root of rejection leads to behaviors that steal, kill, and destroy. Back in the early nineties I met a wonderful Pastor who had adopted a beautiful but troubled little girl. She had been born with fetal alcohol syndrome. They had taken the child in when she was six weeks old and adopted her when she was six months old. Shortly after the adoption her birth mother stepped out in front of a truck and was killed.

This little girl had all sorts of problems. She refused comfort. If she fell and skinned her knee she would just curl up in a chair but wouldn't let her mom or dad clean it or comfort her. She caused trouble at home, at school and at church. Never once had she told her adoptive parents or anyone else that she loved them. She got poor grades and was labeled ADD and ADHD by the schools.

For years I tried to get her pastor father to let me pray deliverance over her but he thought deliverance was too radical. I continued to pray for her and the day finally came when we were meeting for a pastor's breakfast and Dad was ready to try anything. I asked how it was going with his daughter and he said "terrible, she is bringing havoc to our home, our church and her school". He said it was so bad that they had not celebrated the anniversary of adopting her that year. Again I offered to pray deliverance over her. This time he said, "We are willing to try anything." So all the ministers prayed, and we set an appointment. A few ministers even agreed to fast on the day of the appointment.

A few days later I took my daughter, Shelby, and we went to pray deliverance. The little girl was around ten years old when we first prayed with her. She came into the living room because she was forced to. But I started speaking as the Holy Spirit gave words. I'm going to use the name "Susie" rather than her real name, but I want to share what happened.

I had asked her parents if Susie was saved and they told me that they tried to lead her to Christ but when it came to the prayer she invited Satan into her heart rather than Jesus. They asked her "why" she invited Satan into her life and she told them, "well, I needed someone in here".

So I said, "Susie, I feel like you have always wanted to be able to love people and let them love you, but you've never been able to". If you let us pray for you tonight, that will change. Up to that point she had her back to me, but when I said that she swiveled her chair around to where she could glance sideways at me. I told her that I knew she really wanted Jesus to come into her heart but something was keeping her from it and asked if I could pray and make it so she could accept Jesus.

She turned her chair right toward me and nodded her head yes. In Jesus' name we broke the veil off from her and broke Satan's hold over her and in a few minutes she received Jesus. Then we started breaking the power of rejection and abandonment off her.

Suddenly I knew I was supposed to let her practice loving on Shelby. I said, "Would you like to practice showing your love to Shelby?" She came out of her seat and almost climbed up Shelby to hug her and kiss her. We prayed for a few more minutes and I asked her if she wanted to practice loving on her mom and dad. And for the first time ever, that little girl went over and fell into her mother's arms and they hugged and kissed for the longest time. Then she went to her Dad and the same thing happened.

There was more to cover but I felt like we were on such holy ground that Shelby and I excused ourselves and left. We prayed more deliverance later but that night began a remarkable change in Susie and her family. The following Saturday they went shopping. Susie had always hung an aisle or two behind her parents, but that day she started walking arm in arm with them. She had been getting poor grades but at the end of the next marking period she had all A's with one B. Her teachers and Sunday School teachers all remarked at the wonderful change in her behavior.

The story goes on, but I will stop here. I just wanted you to hear what can happen when we really deal with the stronghold and spirits of rejection. I shared her story to illustrate that the Holy Spirit will lead us to do just the right thing as we minister deliverance. Jesus wants people free even more than we do.

CHAPTER TWENTY-NINE
FORGIVING ALL WHO HAVE REJECTED YOU

One of the greatest hindrances to deliverance, deep healing and divine healing is unforgiveness.

1. Offense ties the hand of the Lord. You need to forgive those who have hurt you or forget the miracles because offense ties the hand of the Lord. You see that when Jesus could not (note it says "could not", "not would not") do many miracles because the people were offended at him.

Jesus left there and went to his hometown, accompanied by his disciples. When the Sabbath came, he began to teach in the synagogue, and many who heard him were amazed. "Where did this man get these things?" they asked. "What's this wisdom that has been given him, that he even does miracles! Isn't this the carpenter? Isn't this Mary's son and the brother of James, Joseph, Judas and Simon? Aren't his sisters here with us?" **And they took offense at him.** *Jesus said to them, "Only in his hometown, among his relatives and in his own house is a prophet without honor."* **He could not do any miracles there,** *except lay his hands on a few sick people and heal them. And he was amazed at their lack of faith (Mark 6:1-6a — Emphasis mine).*

2. Refusing to be offended opens the way for miracles. I am speaking about personal offenses here and not about areas where Christians should be offended. There is a Gospel story that demonstrates how refusing to be offended opens the way for miracles. I will insert my comments in regular print right in the midst of the passage.

Leaving that place, Jesus withdrew to the region of Tyre and Sidon. A Canaanite woman (She faced rejection as a Canaanite and as a woman.) *from that vicinity came to him, crying out, "Lord, Son of David, have mercy on me! My daughter is suffering terribly from demon-possession." Jesus did not answer a word.* (It looked like Jesus was rejecting her.) *So his disciples came to him and urged him, "Send her away, for she keeps crying out after us."* (The disciples openly rejected her.) *He answered, "I was sent only to the lost sheep of Israel."* (I'm sure she felt Jesus was rejecting her because of her nationality.) *The woman came and knelt before him. "Lord, help me!" she said.* (She refused to give into rejection.) *He replied, "It is not right to take the children's bread and toss it to their dogs."* (Can you imagine Jesus talking this way to anyone? I think he was demonstrating how to press through rejection and win the victory.) *"Yes, Lord," she said, "but even the dogs eat the crumbs that fall from their masters' table."* (She wouldn't allow perceived rejection to keep her from doing everything she could to get help for her daughter.) *Then Jesus answered, "Woman,* **you have great faith!** (The great faith she had was refusing to give in to feelings of rejection.) *"Your request is granted." And her daughter was healed from that very hour* (Matthew 15:21-28 — Emphasis mine).

This mother never would have received a miracle for her daughter if she would have taken offense. Her refusal to be offended connected her to great faith and a miracle happened in her family.

3. We are to respond rather than react to rejection.

The way we were treated is not what makes us or breaks us. It is what we do with the way we are treated. Jesus will not let us shift the responsibility for our own hearts onto others. Vengeance is the Lord's and He will repay. But we need to deal with our own heart attitudes. *We have a choice.*

Jesus called the crowd to him and said, "Listen and understand. What goes into a man's mouth does not make him 'unclean,' but what comes out of his mouth, that is what makes him 'unclean.'" Then the disciples came to him and asked, "Do you know that the Pharisees were offended when they heard this?" He replied, "Every plant that my heavenly Father has not planted will be pulled up by the roots. Leave them; they are blind guides. If a blind man leads a blind man, both will fall into a pit." Peter said, "Explain the parable to us." "Are you still so dull?" Jesus asked them. "Don't you see that whatever enters the mouth goes into the stomach and then out of the body? **But the things that come out of the mouth come from the heart, and these make a man 'unclean.'** *For out of the heart come evil thoughts, murder, adultery, sexual immorality, theft, false testimony, slander. These are what make a man 'unclean'; but eating with unwashed hands does not make him 'unclean'"* (Matthew 15:10-20 — Emphasis mine).

I heard a powerful spiritual intercessor and mapper testify to how her father began raping her by the time she was four years old. Many with her background would have given in to what Satan wanted to do through that terrible abuse. But this woman went to Christ with her issues, worked through them with the help of godly counsel and responded in such a way that her past abuse could not break her. God can and will help people with the most abusive of pasts — but they need to respond rather than react to their situations.

Reacting could be the response of retreating rather than actually dealing with problems or it could be one of aggressively reacting according to the flesh rather than moving in the flow of the Holy Spirit and according to revelation.

4. We can't blame <u>others</u> for what's in us.

Jesus says that you can't blame others for what comes out of you. When people reject you, you need to forgive them. You need to *choose* not to hold it against them. You need to guard your heart from bitterness, anger, rejection, pay backs and the like. Forgiveness is the only way to guard your heart.

I am amazed at how people (including Christian leaders) tend to play the "blame game" rather than dealing with their own responses and reactions to things that have happened. Deep Healing and Deliverance Ministry helps people to find healing for past hurts and move beyond them.

CHAPTER THIRTY
MINISTERING TO MENTAL AND EMOTIONAL ISSUES

Not all emotional and mental issues are caused by demonic bondage. Some are social, some are physical and some are caused by hormonal or chemical imbalances. Having a mental illness should carry no more stigma than having a physical illness. But many mental and emotional issues are either caused or aggravated by wrong life styles or by demons that take advantage of people when they are vulnerable. Satan loves to use mental and emotional issues to kill, steal and destroy.

This category covers a lot of ground. We've seen remarkable changes in people when they have worked through mental and emotional bondage. Many adults and children have changed so much after receiving ministry that their doctors have reduced or discontinued their psychotropic medicines. We've seen children who were labeled ADD or ADHD who have raised their grades two whole grade points after receiving ministry.

There are a lot of otherwise victorious Christians who suffer bondage in these areas. Listen! Jesus came to destroy the devil's work and to set the captives free. Those who struggle with mental or emotional issues can receive help through deep healing and deliverance.

1. Many problems are caused by how we deal with problems.

Certain problems wipe some people out while barely affecting others. Other problems get to us at certain times but don't bother us the rest of the time. How we deal with what has happened often does more damage than what really happened. God wants to use problems to make us better. Satan uses them to make us bitter. The way Judas and Peter handled their emotional problems after they denied Jesus are good examples of this.

Early in the morning, all the chief priests and the elders of the people came to the decision to put Jesus to death. They bound him, led him away and handed him over to Pilate, the governor. When Judas, who had betrayed him, saw that Jesus was condemned, **he was seized with remorse** *and returned the thirty silver coins to the chief priests and the elders. "I have sinned," he said, "for I have betrayed innocent blood." "What is that to us?" they replied. "That's your responsibility." So Judas* **threw the money** *into the temple and left. Then he went away and* **hanged himself** *(Matthew 27:1-5 — Emphasis mine).*

a. The way Judas handled remorse. Notice the words here, "seized with remorse". Satan set Judas up to betray Jesus and then damned him because of what he had done. The consequences of his decision to betray Jesus were hidden from Judas until after the action. But as soon as he did it, Satan pounced on him with guilt.

1. Judas acted irrationally. He made confession to the wrong people. He tried to make restitution by throwing money into the temple. Then he ran away from his problems just like some try to do through drugs, addictions or other plans of escape.

2. The way Judas handled guilt. Only God can forgive sins, but Judas didn't go to God in relationship. Instead he tried formal religion, running to the priests who only made matters worse. Unfortunately, Judas did not live long enough to rejoice in the resurrection of Christ or to really conceive of what Christ is atoning sacrifice could mean for him.

3. The way Judas handled temporary problems. He committed suicide. Suicide is a permanent solution to a temporary problem but

churches are filled with people who've had thoughts of suicide. When I quiz people in churches there are always several who have been tempted to drive into the oncoming line of traffic or who have had an impulse to jump from a high place to their death. These impulses often come through demons.

b. Peter finally let Jesus help him and restore him to God and to ministry. Both Peter and Judas did the same thing. They both betrayed the Lord. Peter, in his self-confidence said that he would die rather than deny Jesus. But when the going got tough, Peter made some wrong choices. He denied Jesus before a servant girl, then another girl and finally before a group of people. The third time he called a curse down on himself.

1. The way Peter handled remorse. The Bible shows how Peter handled his failure.

Then he began to call down curses on himself and he swore to them, "I don't know the man!" Immediately a rooster crowed. Then Peter remembered the word Jesus had spoken: "Before the rooster crows, you will disown me three times." And he went outside and wept bitterly (Matthew 26:74-75).

Peter cursed himself — evidently unaware of how the enemy takes advantage of curses. Self-curses can be spoken in jest but Satan takes them seriously and uses them as an avenue to bring destruction. Saying things like "I'm never going to get it" or "shame on me" or "I'd be better off dead" may be used against you!

a. Peter wept bitterly. Crying can be a good thing. But Peter's bitter tears didn't bring healing. Even his grief was self-centered. He didn't kill himself, but he did give up on himself.

b. Peter reverted to the old way of life. Peter didn't think God could ever use him again after what he had done. He was filled with grief, inferiority, condemnation, worthlessness and despair. He didn't think he could ever be around Jesus again without being overcome by rejection, depression and guilt. That is the same reason many people run from the church when they need it the most. They think they have gone one step beyond redemption.

c. Peter isolated himself from his closest friends. Right when he needed his best friends, Peter pulled away from them. Like a hand cut off from the body loses its connection for good, so does a Christian cut off from the life of the body. But the devil loves this scheme. Think of what happens when there is a death, divorce or breakup in the church. Hurting people often feel like they can't handle being around those who love them the most and can help them the most.

2. The way Jesus handled Peter's guilt was to restore him. God always wants to restore his image in people. He wants to bring them up and not cast them down. Even though the Lord will judge the living and the dead, his desire is that people will come to him and let him transform their lives. Jesus didn't want to beat Peter down — he wanted to lift him up.

a. Jesus brought Peter to full confession. The core of Peter's problem wasn't his denial. It was his imperfect love, lack of trust and failure to understand how God can use the most horrible situations to advance His cause. Peter had been too independent and full of self to understand how Jesus could lay down his life for others. Jesus uses some specific Greek words for love to help Peter better understand his own heart.

The word phileo stands for brotherly love. It's that "I'll scratch your back if you scratch my back" type of love. Agape love, on the other hand, is like the love of God for sinful people. I will insert the words agape and phileo where they belong in this passage so you will see what really happened here.

When they had finished eating, Jesus said to Simon Peter, "Simon son of John, do you truly love (agape) *me more than these?"* (it is unclear whether "these" refers to the fish or to the other disciples — but since Peter had said "even if all the others deny you, I never will", I think Jesus was reminding Peter of his previous over confidence) *"Yes, Lord," he said, "you know that I love* (phileo) *you." Jesus said, "Feed my lambs."*

Again Jesus said, "Simon son of John, do you truly love (agape) *me?" He answered, "Yes, Lord, you know that I love* (phileo) *you." Jesus said, "Take care of my sheep." The third time he said to him, "Simon son of John, do you love* (phileo) *me?" Peter was hurt because Jesus asked him the third time, "Do you love* (phileo) *me?" He said, "Lord, you know all things; you know that I love* (phileo) *you." Jesus said, "Feed my sheep.* John 21:15-17. (Words in parenthesis and regular print are mine for explanation)

Can you sense the emotional distress Peter felt when Jesus asked him "do you phileo me?" Peter was full of perceived rejection, fear of rejection and self-rejection. He didn't like who he was, feared what others might think of him and was full of anxiety and despair.

b. Jesus brought Peter to full consecration. Jesus approached Peter right at the point of his selfish independence that made him think that he even had to fix his problems by himself.

I tell you the truth, when you were younger you dressed yourself and went where you wanted; but when you are old you will stretch out your hands, and someone else will dress you and lead you where you do not want to go." Jesus said this to indicate the kind of death by which Peter would glorify God. Then he said to him, "Follow me!" (John 21:18-19).

Peter was never really free to die to himself and live unto Christ until he was healed of his emotional and mental problems. Healing came after Jesus restored Peter and after Peter was freed from his bondage.

I think it took this type of a failure to help Peter understand how God still loved him and wanted to use him. Once Peter saw that Jesus still wanted him to "feed his sheep", he was able to surrender the reigns fully to God even in the face of martyrdom.

2. Some mental problems come from spiritual captivity. You probably know people that are held captive to anger, jealousy, hatred or other negative attitudes. All such emotions can lead to spiritual captivity if they are not properly dealt with. Simon the ex-sorcerer is an example of this.

Then Peter and John placed their hands on them, and they received the Holy Spirit. When Simon saw that the Spirit was given at the laying on of the apostles' hands, he offered them money and said, "Give me also this ability so that everyone on whom I lay my hands may receive the Holy Spirit." Peter answered: "May your money perish with you, because you thought you could buy the gift of God with money! You have no part or share in this ministry, because your heart is not right before God. Repent of this wickedness and pray to the Lord. Perhaps he will forgive you for having such a thought in your heart. **For I see that you are full of bitterness and captive to sin.**" *Then Simon answered, "Pray to the Lord for me so that nothing you have said may happen to me"* (Acts 8:17-24 — Emphasis mine).

    a. Peter discerned that Simon was <u>captive</u> to sin. Peter received a revelation from God concerning Simon's condition. That often happens in deep healing and deliverance. God revealed to Peter that Simon was full of bitterness. Bitterness comes through real and perceived hurts. Demonic captivity to sin often comes through roots of bitterness that are not dealt with.

    b. Bitterness can develop a strong root system. I minister deliverance from roots of bitterness by acting like I am pulling dandelion roots out of the heart. In the Spirit I think we can truly pull those old roots of bitterness out of a penitent Believer.

Make every effort to live in peace with all men and to be holy; without holiness no one will see the Lord. See to it that no one misses the grace of God and that **no bitter root grows up to cause trouble and defile** *many* (Hebrews 12:14-15 — Emphasis mine).

Roots of bitterness always bring defilement. Satan loves to turn hurts into roots of bitterness so he can destroy people and relationships.

    c. Roots of bitterness give the devil a foothold.

"In your anger do not sin "Do not let the sun go down while you are still angry, and **do not give the devil a foothold** (Ephesians 4:26-27 — Emphasis mine).

There are two words translated anger in these verses. The first is "orgeezesthay" which speaks of anger that flares up quickly, like straw that catches fire. The second word is "parogismoi" which can be translated "the provocation". It pictures a wrath that is more like a fire in a mud bog. This anger doesn't just flare up and burn out. Instead, it smolders until any right wind comes along to make it flare up. Long lived and somewhat stifled anger is the one that gives the devil a foothold. The word for foothold is "topon" from "topos" which is the root word for topography. A root of bitterness literally gives the devil a place to stand in our lives.

d. James compares wrath to moral filth. Few churches would ignore people who were living perverted sexual lifestyles. They wouldn't look the other way if one of their members was a pedophile, a drunkard or a drug dealer. Isn't it strange that we pay so little attention to wrath and anger? The devil pays attention every time someone gets angry. Perhaps we should pay closer attention too.

My dear brothers, take note of this: Everyone should be quick to listen, slow to speak and **slow to become angry, for man's anger does not bring about the righteous life that God desires. Therefore, get rid of all moral filth** *and the evil that is so prevalent and humbly accept the word planted in you, which can save you (*James 1:19-21 — Emphasis mine).

e. There were two prodigal sons. Most people note the drunken debauchery of the son who wasted away his inheritance until he came to his senses and returned to the Father. But the second son never seemed to come to his senses. Consider the story.

"The older brother became angry and refused to go in. So his father went out and pleaded with him. But he answered his father, **'Look! All these years I've been slaving for you and never disobeyed your orders. Yet you never gave me even a young goat so I could celebrate with my friends.** *But when this* **son of yours** *who has squandered your property with prostitutes comes home, you kill the fattened calf for him!'* "'*My son,' the father said, 'you are always with me, and* **everything I**

***have is yours**. But we had to celebrate and be glad, because this brother of yours was dead and is alive again; he was lost and is found'"* (Luke 15:28-32 — Emphasis mine).

1. There were serious character flaws in the older brother. This older brother needed deep healing and deliverance ministry. He was full of anger, resentment, rebellion, pride, jealously, envy, bitterness, and rejection. The devil loves to take hold of such things.

2. The older brother couldn't see his blessings. This man was so focused on the wrong things he couldn't see the blessings. The father had always been with him. The younger brother had squandered his inheritance, but the older brother still had a double inheritance. But he couldn't enjoy them because of his mental and emotional problems anger, bitterness, jealousy, and envy.

e. Unforgiveness grieves the Holy Spirit. The Holy Spirit simply doesn't move freely where bitterness is harbored in the heart. Paul said it well.

*And **do not grieve the Holy Spirit** of God, with whom you were sealed for the day of redemption. **Get rid of all bitterness, rage and anger**, brawling and slander, along with every form of malice. Be kind and compassionate to one another, **forgiving each other**, just as in Christ God forgave you* (Ephesians 4:30-32 — Emphasis mine).

f. Self centered bitterness is from the devil. I realize that bitterness is a work of the soulish nature, but James clearly states that the self wisdom that justifies harboring bitter envy is of the devil.

*But if you harbor **bitter envy** and selfish ambition in your hearts, do not boast about it or deny the truth. Such "wisdom" does not come down from heaven but is earthly, unspiritual, **of the devil**. For where you have envy and selfish ambition, there you find disorder and every evil practice.* (James 3:14-16 — Emphasis mine).

I've spent a lot of time looking at bitterness and anger as roots of demonic bondage. There are several other emotional and mental factors that can affect our freedom in Christ. The Questionnaire Worksheet in the Addendum reveals other ways that demons can take advantage of mental and emotional problems.

CHAPTER THIRTY-ONE
MINISTERING TO CULT AND OCCULT ISSUES

Satan is hideous and takes advantage of every toe hold he can to place people in bondage. King Saul slipped down the slippery path to destruction because of his rebellion and his visit to the witch of Endor. The Israelites were thrown off track time and again by demons that hid behind the false religions of their time and area. My daughter, who teaches Kindergarten in the Coldwater Michigan Schools told me how their school banned Pokemon cards because of the way they affected behavior. Both Billy Graham and then President Clinton spoke of the demons behind the Littleton Colorado shootings. I got my hair cut the day that I first wrote this. My barber told me about the ten or eleven old daughter of a Sturgis witch who broke up a slumber party by saying how witches are everything and how they have so much more power than God. The devil is placing his calling cards in children's games and cartoons, in music, and in every type of Cult and Occult involvement.

We live in a day where parents and grandparents need to be aware of how Satan is trying to manipulate his way in to destroy children. Jesus warned us of the devil's intentions.

The thief comes only to steal and kill and destroy; I have come that they may have life, and have it to the full (John 10:10).

When children have trouble sleeping, keep having bad dreams, or are afraid to go into certain rooms, it may well be that the devil has found a gateway into the home. We have seen such difficulties stop immediately after praying for a child or even after praying over their bedrooms and anointing them. We need to pay particular attention when children have imaginary friends or pets to make sure they are not demons.

Definition of <u>Cult</u>

American College Dictionary. 1) A particular system of religious worship, esp. with reference to its rites and ceremonies. 2) An instance of an almost religious veneration for a person or thing. 3) The object of such devotion. 4) A group having an exclusive sacred ideology and a series of rites centering on their sacred symbols.

John warned us to test the spirits so we can avoid cults. He really meant it when he told us to test the spirits to see whether they be from God. This testing may include asking spirits to confess Jesus who came in the flesh or simply looking at the fruit of doctrines that deny that Jesus came in the flesh.

Dear friends, do not believe every spirit, but test the spirits to see whether they are from God, because many false prophets have gone out into the world. This is how you can recognize the Spirit of God: Every spirit that acknowledges that Jesus Christ has come in the flesh is from God, but every spirit that does not acknowledge Jesus is not from God. This is the spirit of the antichrist, which you have heard is coming and even now is already in the world. 1 John 4:1-3.

Definition of <u>Occult</u>

American College Dictionary. 1) beyond the bounds of ordinary knowledge; mysterious. 2) Not disclosed; secret; communicated only to the initiated. (3 deals with science) 4) Of the nature of, or pertaining to, certain reputed sciences, as magic, astrology, etc. Involving the alleged knowledge or employment of secret or mysterious agencies, 5 (not applicable) 6) Rare, hidden from view. 7) Occult studies or sciences, 8) anything occult. 9. To hide or shut off from view.

There seems to be an unending line of television shows like "Crossing Over" or "War of the Psychics" that lure people into occult experiences. The Bible clearly warns us against such things.

Do not turn to mediums (Crossing Over) *or seek out spiritists, for you will be defiled by them. I am the LORD your God* (Lev 19:31).

The popular "Harry Potter" series of movies and books have lured people into forbidden sorcery. Again, the Lord warns us against to stay away from sorcery, mediums and spiritists. Manasseh was one of the most wicked Kings in the Old Testament and sorcery played a part in his downfall as seen below.

He sacrificed his own son in the fire, practiced sorcery and divination, and consulted mediums and spiritists. He did much evil in the eyes of the LORD, provoking him to anger (II Kings 21:6).

We are only aware of the Lord speaking to Josiah one time during his reign — and that was through the Pharaoh of Egypt. In 2 Chronicles 35:21-22 he refused the Lord's voice in a pagan king and it cost him his life. But there was one time in his reign that he took a strong stand against mediums and spiritists after Hilkiah the priest discovered the Book of the Law in the temple of the Lord. If even Josiah could recognize how detestable sorcery and spiritualism was, don't you think that blood bought believers should reject everything related to sorcery?

Furthermore, Josiah got rid of the mediums and spiritists, the household gods, the idols and all the other detestable things seen in Judah and Jerusalem. This he did to fulfill the requirements of the law written in the book that Hilkiah the priest had discovered in the temple of the LORD. Neither before nor after Josiah was there a king like him who turned to the LORD as he did — with all his heart and with all his soul and with all his strength, in accordance with all the Law of Moses (II Kings 23:24-25).

Paul literally accused the Galatians of coming under a witchcraft spell when they turned away from grace and started acting like their salvation was dependent upon works.

*You foolish Galatians! Who has **bewitched** you? Before your very eyes Jesus Christ was clearly portrayed as crucified... It is for freedom that Christ has set us free. Stand firm, then, and do not let yourselves be burdened again by a yoke of slavery* (Galatians 3:1, 5 — Emphasis mine).

The place where Paul preached one of his greatest sermons was also the place his ministry had the least lasting influence. Even though his doctrine was right and his preaching powerful, only a few men became disciples of Jesus Christ. Paul learned a lesson there, and from then on when he went to a town full of cult and occult idolatry, you see him engaging in power encounters against the spiritual forces of evil as he did in Ephesus against the false god Artemis.

*While Paul was waiting for them in Athens, he was greatly distressed to see that the city was **full of idols**. **So he reasoned** in the synagogue with the Jews and the God-fearing Greeks, as well as in the marketplace day by day with those who happened to be there. A group of Epicurean and Stoic philosophers began to **dispute** with him. Some of them asked, "What is this babbler trying to say?" Others remarked, "He seems to be advocating foreign gods."* (They reckoned "Anastasias" to be a Christian god) *They said this because Paul was preaching the good news about Jesus and the resurrection. Then they took him and brought him to a meeting of the Areopagus, where they said to him, "May we know what this new teaching is that you are presenting? **You are bringing some strange ideas to our ears, and we want to know what they mean.**"* (*All the Athenians and the foreigners who lived there spent their time doing nothing **but talking about and listening to the latest ideas.**)...* 29 *"Therefore since we are God's offspring, we should not think that the divine being is like gold or silver or stone — an image made by man's design and skill. In the past God overlooked such ignorance, but now he commands all people everywhere to repent... For he has set a day when he will judge the world with justice by the man he has appointed. He has given proof of this to all men by raising him from the dead."* **When they heard about the resurrection of the dead, some of them sneered, but** *others said, "We want to hear you again on this subject." A few men became followers of Paul and believed* (Acts 17:16-21, 29-34a — Emphasis mine — notes in parenthesis are mine).

There are some lessons we should learn from the seventeenth chapter of acts.

1. Idolatry distresses people with spiritual insight. The devil is trying to sell America out to witchcraft and evil in the name of political correctness and tolerance. God is not tolerant of cult or occult activity.

2. There is power behind idols. Idols, statues, Ouija boards, angel boards, tarot cards, kitchen witches, fetishes, and certain pieces of jewelry are all made by human hands but they are empowered by Satan. The demons behind the idols in Athens brought Paul's ministry almost to a stalemate.

3. People left talking and arguing about the latest ideas are easily trapped. I see this as people try the newest rage in alternative treatments, medicine, and even diets. Satan loves to take advantage of things like iridology, hypnosis, acupuncture, massages, new age imagery, and the like.

4. Reasoning with people in bondage does little good. 2 Corinthians 4:3-4 and 10:3-5 explain how we need to tear down demonic veils and strongholds even before many attempts to evangelize can be effective. Satan literally blinds people with wrong logic systems and schematics that are designed to keep them from coming into the fullness of Christ.

5. Anyone who is offended by the resurrection is blinded by spiritual forces. I remember working with one attractive young lady who seemed fairly intelligent until I would talk with her about Jesus. Then she seemed to have a bad mental block. I tried repeatedly to win her to the Lord to no avail until I finally asked her if I could pray. I then demolished the spiritual veil that was hindering her from understand the Gospel and receiving Jesus. Once that veil was broken she quickly understood the Gospel and was born again.

6. The harvest is hindered by cult and occult strongholds. Even the great apostle Paul saw only a few come to Jesus in Athens. My son mar-

ried a beautiful young woman who had been brought up and baptized as a Jehovah's Witness. I witnessed to her and shared the Gospel with her but she had a stronghold of fear that made her think God would kill her if she ever entered a Christian Church. So I called on some of my friends to really pray against those strongholds and went to visit her again. I asked her if I could pray before we started talking and I engaged in spiritual warfare and prayed against the veils that were keeping her from understanding the Gospel.

The Holy Spirit took over after that and led our discussion. That was when she told me she had been baptized at a Jehovah's Witness convention. I asked her how she felt about that baptism and she said she never really thought it was right but gave into the pressure.

I started praying silently for all I was worth and then explained to her how she could renounce that cultic baptism. She decided to do it and I helped her. Then she was able to receive Christ just a few minutes later.

Christians must not think they are exempt from witchcraft or spiritual warfare. There are times when witches or workers of iniquity do warfare against Christian Workers. I've heard the story several times of a Christian Leader who sat next to a Satanist on an airplane in the mid eighties. They started conversing and he discovered that a Satanist group was praying that key Christian Leaders would fall into immorality or greed. And there were a great number of wonderful preachers and evangelists who fell in the late eighties and early nineties.

Barbara Yoder shared a few signs of the witchcraft or warfare coming against leaders.

The signs that you are under a curse of witchcraft or that spiritual warfare is being waged against you include: 1. A diminishing sense of the presence of God. 2. Losing focus on covenantal promises. 3. Losing faith because of mental confusion. 4. Losing your sense of vision from God.

The Questionnaire worksheet in the addendum gives tools to deal further with the issues of cult and occult.

CHAPTER THIRTY-TWO
BREAKING CURSES

This is by no means an exhaustive study and people who minister deliverance will want to do further study on the subject of curses.

Deuteronomy chapter 28 gives seven major indications of a curse on a person and/or on his/her family's history:

a. **Mental and/or emotional breakdown.** The ongoing frustration of mental or emotional breakdowns in the family line may indicate a curse on the family.

b. **Repeated or chronic sicknesses** are another indication of a curse — especially if the condition is hereditary.

c. Another indication of a curse is **barrenness, multiple miscarriages, or hindering female problems,** especially if these things are generational in nature.

d. **Breakdown of marriage and/or family problems** is another indication of being under a curse. The indications of a covenant breaking curse can show up in families, church membership or a variety of other ways.

e. **Ongoing financial problems** can be a strong indicator of a curse. Some people always seem to have financial problems regardless of how much they make. That may indicate a curse of poverty.

f. **Being "accident prone"** is another indicator of being under a curse. Where the accidents are while driving, walking or working, ongoing accidents may come from a curse.

g. **Suicides, unusual or untimely deaths** may also indicate a curse.

The late Derek Prince said "there is one word that sums up a curse 'frustration'." (I highly recommend his book <u>Blessing or Curse, You Can Choose</u>). People can often discern curses by thinking about what great frustrations seem to stay in a person's life. There are several good books on diagnosing and dealing with personal and familial curses. Breaking curses is often a necessary step to walking in ongoing freedom.

When I sense that a person may have generational curses or that they have been cursed or have cursed themselves by their words, I try to teach them the power of curses and then lead them to forgive those who have brought the curses into their lives. We then break the power of those curses over them in the name and through the blood of Jesus.

The power of generational curses was brought to my attention one day when I was counseling a woman before I would release church funds to reverse a shut off order from her utility company. I went through the seven indications of a curse listed above and every one of them was true of either her, her husband or their immediate families.

I then asked her if she tithed her income and she said "no" and shared all sorts of excuses. I went on to explain from Malachi 3:8-10 that she was bring a curse upon her finances through her disobedience. I led her through confession and asked her to commit to start tithing so she could stay free from the curse. Once she did so I was able to release funds to meet her immediate need.

Since many curses originate through personal or generational disobedience to God, that disobedience must be repented of before the person can be set free from the curse.

CHAPTER THIRTY-THREE
DEALING WITH ADDICTION

Many good, sincere Christians either deal with their own addictions or with the consequences of the addictions of people they love.

There are many people of faith who wouldn't dream of smoking or drinking alcohol who are nonetheless are addicted. You can look around most churches and see people who are addicted to food or even to religion. Addictions may jump a generation, or they may come in a different form — especially to children of alcoholics that get saved.

Believers who grew up with parents who were addicted to drugs or alcohol may swear that they will never touch such things — and they don't! But they may carry their father's tendency to addiction to addictions that seem to carry the church's approval.

The converted children of drug addicts or alcoholics may be addicted to something with fewer stigmas than drugs or alcohol, while still exhibiting addictive behavior. A personal example of this is that my grandfather was an alcoholic and once I understood how alcohol might entrap me I chose to stay entirely away from it. At the same time I was addicted to reading through the Bible yearly.

Bible reading is a wonderful discipline (and my wife and I still read through the Bible each year) but for me it was the focus of addiction and I felt I had to get my "Bible fix" every morning to win God's approval. For me, making my check mark at the end of my allotted daily chapters was something that I had to do — whether or not I took time to reflect on what God was speaking through those verses.

Food addiction is seldom addressed by Christians but it destroys the health of many believers. And food addiction is one of the toughest to break because people need food to live.

The American College Dictionary defines addict as 1) one who is addicted to a practice or habit, 2) to give oneself over, as to a habit or pursuit; apply or devote habitually. The definition of addiction is the state of being given up to some habit, practice, or pursuit.

I simply define addictive behavior as any controlling behavior that a person does not have mastery and freedom over.

I've ministered in the Branch County Jail once a month since the late 80's. I usually do public ministry, but when I get to do personal ministry I always try to find out what the person is in jail for. When they tell me it is for drugs, drunk driving, or some form of addictive behavior, I ask "Did your parents or grandparents struggle with addictions". The answer is almost always "Yes".

During one hot summer service we met in the old jail in a room with high walls but no ceiling. I asked one man what he was in for. He told me it was drunk driving, third offense. I asked him what his favorite brew was. He said Pabst Blue Ribbon. So I asked if he preferred bottle or can. He liked glass best.

So I described a tall, cool, bottle of Pabst Blue Ribbon that was so cold beads of moisture were dripping down it. I pretended I placed it in front of him and asked "Would you be tempted to drink this?" He said "Yes, that and about six more." Then I pretended to stab him to death. "Now are you tempted to drink it?" He said "No... I am dead." I then preached on Romans Six about reckoning yourself dead indeed to drinking but alive in Jesus Christ. That made for some easy preaching. But it wasn't enough.

I fear Christians often lack the compassion and understanding of addictive behaviors that are needed to set people free. People who never struggled with addiction and those precious few who were automatically set free from addictions when they were saved have no idea what others have to deal with. They give trite answers: "Die to self." "You can do all things through Christ who strengthens you." "If you really loved Jesus you wouldn't drink anymore."

These statements don't deal adequately with generational addiction or with the demonic strongholds of addiction. You can die to the flesh and you can discipline the flesh. But strongholds must be broken and spirits cast out.

There are hundreds of addictions that we seldom think of, from making excuses, to rage and murder, to alcohol, lying, sexual sin, negative talk, self-protective behaviors, people pleasing behaviors, fear, love, wealth and power, religious acts, grandiose thinking, anger, possessions, demonic forces, and the like. Addictive behaviors must be dealt with for people to enjoy freedom.

I. Noah and His Sons.

Genesis 6:22 says *"And Noah did everything as God commanded him."* What do you think of when you hear Noah's name? Do you think about the ark — about animals going in two by two? Do you think of how it rained forty days and nights? Do you think how only Noah and his family escaped destruction? He did all these things. Consider some passages about Noah.

"And Noah did everything as God commanded him" (Genesis 6:22).

By faith Noah, when warned about things not yet seen, in holy fear built an ark to save his family. By his faith he condemned the world and became heir of the righteousness that comes by faith (Hebrews 11:7).

If he did not spare the ancient world when he brought the flood on its ungodly people, but protected Noah, a preacher of righteousness, and seven others (II Peter 2:5).

"Son of man, if a country sins against me by being unfaithful and I stretch out my hand against it to cut off its food supply and send famine upon it and kill its men and their animals, even if these three men — Noah, Daniel and Job — were in it, they could save only themselves by their righteousness, declares the Sovereign LORD (Ezekiel 14:13-14).

When you think of Noah you think of his righteousness and faith. What a man! But how many of you think of Noah's drunkenness when you think of him? It has almost become a hidden family secret. We tend to remember his righteous acts, but forget or ignore his addiction. Genesis 9:20-25 won't let us do that.

Noah, a man of the soil, proceeded to plant a vineyard. When he drank some of its wine, he became drunk and lay uncovered inside his tent. Ham, the father of Canaan, saw his father's nakedness and told his two brothers outside. But Shem and Japheth took a garment and laid it across their shoulders; then they walked in backward and covered their father's nakedness. Their faces were turned the other way so that they would not see their father's nakedness. When Noah awoke from his wine and found out what his youngest son had done to him, he said, "Cursed be Canaan! The lowest of slaves will he is to his brothers" (Genesis 9:20-25).

A. One cannot ignore the effect Noah's drunkenness had on his family.

1. It caused Ham embarrassment and exposure. My good friend, Pastor Mike Donahue pointed out that the word "saw" or "looked upon" used to describe Ham's glance at his father's nakedness is not the basic word "to see". Instead it is the Hebrew word "ra'ah" (see #7200 in Strong's concordance) that means "approve, enjoy, experience or look joyfully". He believes that Noah's curse upon Ham's descendants was that he would go to a place of intense homosexual filth (Sodom).

Whether or not Ham was being lustful when he saw his father's nakedness, the fact remains that Noah lay naked and drunk in his tent and that brought Ham to a place where he received a curse from his father.

2. It caused Shem and Japheth to "cover up" their father's nakedness. They took every possible precaution to protect themselves and others from seeing the one little dark spot in their family line. They were strong rescuers who needed to protect him from being exposed. That is how co-dependence works; a strong rescuer needs someone to rescue and a weak victim needs to be rescued.

3. It caused Noah to misplace blame. Noah struck out at his own son. I can understand his embarrassment at being caught naked in a drunken stew, but it wasn't right of him to take it out on his own child.

4. It caused Noah to curse his own offspring. What kind of a father would say to his own flesh and blood, "A curse be upon you and his descendants"? But that is exactly what the righteous Noah did. He actually cursed Ham and his descendants. Noah's curse against Ham brought havoc to the generations following him. It is amazing how one little curse can be felt by many generations.

B. Sin is passed down generational lines. Noah's drunkenness and curse caused a specific bent toward sin in his family line. God is very clear about the way specific sin tendencies are passed down family lines. One of the many examples of this is part of the Ten Commandments.

You shall not bow down to them or worship them; for I, the LORD your God, am a jealous God, punishing the children for the sin of the fathers to the third and fourth generation of those who hate me (Exodus 20:5).

1. Each of us is born with a general bent toward good because we are created in God's image.

2. Each of us has a general bent toward sin inherited from Adam.

3. We may also have a specific bent to sin from our ancestors. People are not punished for their forefather's sins. People do not need to be

forgiven for the sins of their forefather's. But people *do* bear the consequences of the sins of their ancestors.

The soul who sins is the one who will die. The son will not share the guilt of the father, nor will the father share the guilt of the son. The righteousness of the righteous man will be credited to him, and the wickedness of the wicked will be charged against him (Ezekiel 18:20).

The Bible speaks of the bent toward specific sins which comes from the previous four generations of fathers. Sociology has proven this. The children of alcoholics have a special tendency to alcohol addiction. The same is true of all addictions: drugs, sex, eating, abuse, and the like. The fruit doesn't fall to far from the tree apart from the Lord's intervention. This is very evident as I work in jails and as I have personal deep healing and deliverance appointments.

The type of addiction often changes. For example, the child of an alcoholic may be addicted to drugs or even to extreme forms of legalistic Christianity. Still the root of addiction often remains. Christians who have a bent toward addiction usually have it manifest in unusual or hidden ways. One who might never dream of being addicted to smoking may be addicted to food or be in captivity to pornography over the internet.

II. LOT AND HIS DAUGHTERS.

What do you think of when I mention Lot's name? Most people think about Sodom and Gomorrah and how Lot escaped with most of his family but how his wife was turned into a pillar of salt when she looked back. You may even remember how he got drunk and committed incest.

Lot and his two daughters left Zoar and settled in the mountains, for he was afraid to stay in Zoar. He and his two daughters lived in a cave. One day the older daughter said to the younger, "Our father is old, and there is no man around here to lie with us, as is the custom all over the earth. Let's get our father to drink wine and then lie with him and preserve our family line through our father." **That night they got their father to drink wine, and the older daughter went in and lay with him. He was not aware of it when she lay down or when she got up.** *The next day the older daughter said to the younger, "Last night I lay with my father. Let's get him to drink wine again tonight, and you go in and lie with him so we can preserve our family line through our father." So they got their father to drink wine that night also, and the younger daughter went and lay with him. Again he was not aware of it when she lay down or when she got up.* **So both of Lot's daughters became pregnant by their father.** *The older daughter had a son, and she named him Moab; he is the father of the* **Moabites of today***. The younger daughter also had a son, and she named him Ben-Ammi; he is the father of the* **Ammonites of today** (Genesis 19:30-36 — Emphasis mine).

a. Lot's drunkenness troubles his family line to this day! If you cross reference the story of Lot with today's newspaper about trouble in the Middle East, you'll see how long reaching his sin and addiction was. His descendants (the Moabites and Ammonites) from his incest with his own daughters have been fighting each other for centuries.

b. Lot's drunkenness caused him to do horrifying things. Few things leave greater scars on people than incest or abuse from people who are in a God given role of protector and provider. One of the greatest hurts I deal with when I lead people through deep healing and deliverance is the hurt of a father or step-father that has molested his children.

C. Lot's sin did not keep God from calling him righteous.

One of the verses that has bothered me most in the whole Bible is II Peter 2:7. Getting drunk, having sex with your own daughters and getting them pregnant are about the furthest things from godliness I can think of. But look at what God says in II Peter.

And if he rescued Lot, a righteous man, who was distressed by the filthy lives of lawless men (for that righteous man, living among them day after day, was tormented in his righteous soul by the lawless deeds he saw and heard) — if this is so, then the Lord knows how to rescue godly men from trials and to hold the unrighteous for the day of judgment, while continuing their punishment (II Peter 2:7-9).

I do not begin to fully understand this verse but I think it reveals a little bit about God's heart toward His own children who are caught in the snare of addictions. Thankfully, the blood of Jesus Christ, when appropriated through deep healing and forgiveness can set the captives free and transform sinners into saints.

There is a section on the causes and consequences of addictions found in the Deep Healing Questionnaire Worksheet appendix to this book.

CHAPTER THIRTY-FOUR
LUST AND SEXUAL BONDAGE ISSUES

It is time for the church to stand up and speak the truth about lust and sexual bondage issues. We can not afford to ignore the damage that our promiscuous society is causing our children, youth and adults.

I want to warn you concerning the graphic nature of this chapter. Most teens and many elementary school children have already learned more than you can imagine about this subject. But too much of what they know they learned in the halls at school. I wish I could share this teaching with every teenager. But the choice is up to parents whether or not they want to expose their children to this teaching.

God is love and He is all for husbands and wives enjoying the marital bed. He gave humans the wonderful gift of a sexual relationship that, unlike that of animals, is not limited to the time of estrus. Because people are both spiritual and physical, God created the possibility of two people becoming one spiritually, even as Jesus Christ and His Church are one. God calls this a one flesh union.

For this reason a man will leave his father and mother and be united to his wife, and they will become one flesh. (Genesis 2:24).

This one flesh union is so real that Greek and Hebrew words for knowledge are the very same as the words used when Adam "knew" his wife and for Joseph not "knowing" Mary until after they were married. The word implies an intimate connecting not only of body, but of soul and spirit. Paul wrote that this union illustrates the relationship between Christ and His Church.

Sex is like the world's strongest epoxy glue. You can glue two things together, and the glue is stronger than what it bonds. If you glued two pieces of wood together and later forced them apart, it wouldn't be the epoxy that breaks, but the wood. Part of one piece would be attached to the other and vice versa. That is a very clear picture of the soul tie that is created through sexual union.

A soul tie is a beautiful thing in the sanctity of marriage. But apart from marriage it kills, steals, and destroys. People who have had multiple partners often feel disconnected because they have scattered parts of themselves across the sexual horizons and have parts of other people connected to them.

I illustrate this concept in my seminars by using volunteers for a fictional but profound demonstration. I invite a young man and young woman to the front and suggest that they are getting ready to get married — but neither is aware of everything that they are bringing into the marriage because of past sexual abuse and/or promiscuity.

I have the couple join hands to symbolize the soul tie that will be created between them when they become one flesh. Then I call another man and have him hold the woman's hand. I usually say that he sexually molested her when she was young. Then I have a few other men come forward and link to her as well — suggesting that they took advantage of her vulnerability after her abuse.

After that I begin linking several women with the man who represents the groom to be. I share how he had a wild side and how he had committed fornication with each of these women. Then, with all these people linked together I share how any evil spirits that are attached to any person in the group have free access to every other person in the group as long as the soul ties remain in tact. To further demonstrate that idea I will push or pull a person at one end of the line and show how each person that is connected is impacted when even one person is attacked.

Perhaps the most telling part of this illustration is when I point out how many men will be joining the union every time the woman has relations with her husband and how many women will be joining the union every time the man joins his wife in physical relations. In a very real way the woman is being tied to several other women when she cleaves to her husband and he is being tied to several other men when he cleaves to his wife. At first there may be a certain sense of perversion or revulsion because of the same sex soul ties. But when they become calloused to these wrong soul ties they begin to feel right and may produce homosexual or lesbian desires.

When you consider the ramifications of impurity and soul ties, you understand that God is protecting us, not trying to ruin our fun with his laws. God is clear concerning sexual sin. He plainly says:

"You shall not commit adultery... Exodus 20:14

On a road trip I saw a billboard that said "What part of 'Thou shalt not, do you not understand?'... God." But many Christians ignore the laws of God to their own harm by giving into the sensual lusts of their flesh.

Moses said to the people, "Do not be afraid. God has come to test you, so that the fear of God will be with you to keep you from sinning" (Exodus 20:20).

Romans 8 says that "the law of the Spirit of life has set us free." Still, a proper fear of the Lord brings the wisdom that knows His laws are for our good. Leviticus 18 gives several specific instructions about sexual sins that create harmful soul ties and therefore destroy people rather than bringing life. They include: incest, having relations during menstruation, adultery and fornication, homosexual and lesbian relationships and bestiality. God's word declares that such sins not only pollute the people but also the land in which they live.

"Do not defile yourselves in any of these ways, because this is how the nations that I am going to drive out before you became defiled. **Even the land was defiled**; *so I punished it for its sin, and the land vomited out its inhabitants* (Leviticus 18:24-25 — Emphasis mine).

Sexual sin brings a host of physical, emotional, and spiritual sexually transmitted diseases. It is the one sin that is done against one's own body.

Trust in the LORD with all your heart and lean not on your own understanding; in all your ways acknowledge him, and he will make your paths straight. Do not be wise in your own eyes; fear the LORD and shun evil. **This will bring health to your body and nourishment** *to your bones.* (Proverbs 3:7-8 — Emphasis mine).

Proverbs 5 speaks of the "cords of sin" caused by sexual sin. These cords can be called soul ties. The entire chapter is a warning against promiscuity. Listen to how in concludes:

For a man's ways are in full view of the LORD, and he examines all his paths. The evil deeds of a wicked man ensnare him; **<u>the cords of his sin hold him fast</u>**. *He will die for lack of discipline, led astray by his own great folly* (Proverbs 5:21-23).

Peter Horrobin, who has dedicated his life to healing through deliverance, teaches that all sexual relations are spiritual worship... either to God or Satan. He teaches about the link between sexual sin and immorality, saying the body reflects what is going on inside. We have many false gods which include anything we give ourselves to worship. He says "Worship and sexuality are interrelated. Adam knew Eve... same concept as knowing God."

The Hebrew word for kiss means "come toward in worship". He concludes, therefore, that all sexual sin is idolatry... placing other people before God and making soul ties to them rather than to him. This leads to demonization by a spirit of prostitution. Is this scriptural? Yes.

*A **spirit of prostitution** leads them astray; they are unfaithful to their God.* (Hosea 4:12b — Emphasis mine).

Any sexual relationship outside of marriage shows greater loyalty to self and/or to the partner than to God. That makes it idolatry and people who seek intimate relationships outside of God's will, forsake real life, and heap destruction upon themselves.

*Has a nation ever changed its gods? (Yet they are not gods at all.) But my people have exchanged their Glory for worthless idols. Be appalled at this, O heavens, and shudder with great horror," declares the LORD. "My people have committed two sins: **They have forsaken me**, the spring of living water, and **have dug their own cisterns**, broken cisterns that cannot hold water. Is Israel a servant, a slave by birth? Why then has he become plunder?* (Jeremiah 2:11-14 — Emphasis mine).

Our world is so full of hurting and battered people that it is common for people to be addicted to sex, love hunger, or such a controlling need to belong that even Christians turn away from intimacy with God to intimacy with people outside of marriage. This creates soul ties every time.

Think of the illustration of the couple getting married with all the soul ties. Satan groups people together through soul ties so he can control them. Do you now see why we need to break soul ties, come clean, and commit to sexual purity?

Let me share a couple of amazing illustrations of what happens when a person actually deals with wrongful soul ties through Deep Healing and Deliverance. A pastor friend of mine brought a man to me who was in his forties and who was a good church member and a good husband — most of the time. But once or twice a year he would seem to disappear. He wouldn't show up at work, he wouldn't come home and when he finally would return he would honestly say he didn't know where he had been. This caused some strain in his relationships, to say the least.

The pastor had the man fill out his Deep Healing Questionnaire and brought him a few weeks later for ministry. We dealt with a lot of personal issues but the most freeing issue for this man was the section on breaking soul ties and sexual bondages.

The man was in his second marriage and had reacted to his first divorce by having promiscuous relations with a few different women, one of which was a practicing witch. He had not seen any of these illicit partners for years but he still had active soul ties with each one of them. I led him in confessing each wrong relationship to the Lord. I then prayed that the soul ties would be broken and that every part of these women that remained attached to this man would return to its owner and that any part of the man who remained attached to these women would be returned to him.

The change in this man was so drastic that within a few weeks his wife wrote me a letter to thank me for her "new husband". She said the change in him was so great that she wanted to go through deep healing and deliverance so she could grow in the Lord as quickly as he was. The man truly was a new man — set free from past bondage and released to pursue the fullness of God. Within a year he became one of the key leaders of his church.

There was another time when I ministered to a pastor who had been caught up in pornography and masturbation. He deeply grieved over his besetting sin but seemed powerless to break its control. He told me that every Saturday night he would go to his own church altar and ask God's forgiveness — promising to repent of his sinful behavior — just so he could preach the following morning. But every Saturday night found him back at the same altar confessing the same sin.

So many believers are caught in sin — confess, sin — confess patterns like this. They try to discipline their flesh; they sob and beg God's forgiveness but are powerless to find lasting victory until they actually deal with their sexual bondages and soul ties. It is always a joy to me to see these servants of God set free by the power of Christ through Deep Healing and Deliverance.

There are three major stages in breaking all soul ties, including those caused by perpetrators, sexual sin, lust and pornography.

Step one is confession. Confession deals with our connection to God. It is agreeing with God that all physical relations outside the bonds of marriage are sin. (Including pornography and lust of the heart)

Step two is renouncing and breaking soul ties. This deals with the future and says from here on out so we will not be controlled by things that happened in the past. I usually act out the breaking of soul ties by snipping them with imaginary scissors or cutting them with an imaginary sword as I pray and ask God to break them.

Once the soul ties are renounced and broken, the **final step is casting out all demons** that have attached to the person through their own sexual sin or through sexual sin against them. We have seen dozens of people set free by following these steps to set them free from Satan's grip over their pasts.

The Deep Healing and Deliverance Questionnaire worksheet in the back deals more fully with lust and sexual bondages.

CHAPTER THIRTY-FIVE
FORGIVING THOSE WHO HAVE HURT YOU SEXUALLY

People with soul ties often have those ties strengthened through unforgiveness. Unforgiveness may be the biggest block to the breaking of soul ties that there is. Physical, emotional and spiritual healing is often hindered by one's unwillingness to forgive those who have caused deep wounds.

Recently I ministered to a woman who had chronic stomach problems. In deep healing I discovered that her mother had actually led her into her father's room where years of sexual abuse began. I asked her to let the Holy Spirit take her back to that painful time in her life. She began to cry and I asked the Holy Spirit to reveal Jesus to her. Soon she saw Jesus in the room with his hand on her shoulder. I asked her what he was doing and she said he was crying because he was sharing her pain. She chose to cast her pain upon Jesus and was soon ready to forgive her mother and father for their horrendous abuse. As soon as she did that we were able to minister physical healing to her.

I do not underestimate the difficulty in forgiving someone who committed sexual crime. I've witnessed the years of deep sorrow and personal pain that victims of abuse have lived with — but I've also learned that when people choose to forgive their perpetrators and leave vengeance in the hand of the Lord that Jesus delivers them from their tormentors.

I realize that forgiveness may include confronting the offender (Matthew 18:15-18) and may include reporting perpetrators to the law so God can execute his vengeance upon them. (Romans 13:1-4). One can forgive an offender from the heart and still turn them into to the police and allow God to minister justice through those He has placed in legal authority. I would never counsel anyone to cover up the abuse of someone who might abuse others.

I also realize that forgiveness is both an immediate choice and an ongoing process. The decision to forgive is an important first step in one's healing, but the healing itself often takes months or years.

I have preached in the Branch County Jail once a month for twenty years. Recently God personally set the stage for my message by prompting a man to stand and confess that he was serving time for molesting his thirteen year old step-daughter. He testified that he found the Lord while in jail and shared how God was working on his behalf. He said he could have been sentenced for 30 years in prison but had only received a one year jail sentence.

Some women in the back started shouting that he deserved the full 30 years in prison. He admitted that he did but said that while he was caught up in that sin that he just could not stop himself. Someone suggested that he could have used a bullet and he shared how close he was to doing so but he couldn't forget the night when he was fifteen and heard a shot in the dark and ran into to his father's room to see him dying with a 12 gauge slug through his heart.

Some of the inmates, including the women (most of whom had been abused) wanted to crucify the man. The others could see God's hand working and were grateful that God's mercy was being extended to the guilty one. The chaplain wisely allowed the bickering to continue long enough for the people to fully feel what they were feeling. Then he quickly stopped the discussion before it could become a riot.

There was a powerful move of God that night as both perpetrators and victims realized their need for the forgiveness, mercy and cleansing of the Lord. Part of forgiveness is leaving things in God's hands and trusting him to execute justice upon the wrong doer.

CHAPTER THIRTY-SIX
BAPTISM IN LOVE

If we fully embrace the teaching of this chapter; most of our problems will be over. Giving, serving, reaching out to the lost, taking care of the saints and things like that will never be a problem again. When Jesus was asked to sum up the law and the prophets and when he was asked to state the most important commandment he said,

Jesus replied: "'Love the Lord your God with all your heart and with all your soul and with all your mind.' This is the first and greatest commandment. And the second is like it: 'Love your neighbor as yourself.' All the Law and the Prophets hang on these two commandments" (Matthew 22:37-40).

Paul, when writing to Timothy, outlined what the most important element of the Christian faith is,

The goal of this command is love, which comes from a pure heart and a good conscience and a sincere faith (I Timothy 1:5).

Paul said, "The greatest of these is love". As we wrap up everything that we have done together, I want to share the piece of the puzzle missing that is missing for so many Christians. Here it is: A Baptism in the Love of Jesus.

1. God's Love, Acceptance, and Forgiveness.

a. God's Love for You Is Unconditional. God loves you, not because you are lovable, but because He is Love. There isn't a single thing you can do to make God love you more. And there isn't anything you can do to make him love you less. He loves you because He is love.

b. God's Acceptance of You Is Unconditional. God accepts you, not because you are acceptable, but because His heart is open to you.

My personal strongholds of rejection from my youth used to make me think that I had to be "good enough" or that I had to work hard enough for God to accept me. I thought I had to win his approval. I went through my first fifteen years of ministry as a "workaholic for God" because I was trying so hard to make him like me and to win his approval.

It took the unconditional love, acceptance and forgiveness of God to pull me out of my most miserable time of failure. I didn't think I would ever be able to enjoy God's acceptance again because of my terrible fall from grace. But it was during my time of failure that I learned that I could never be good enough for God but He accepts us because his heart is open to us.

c. God's Forgiveness of You Is Unconditional. I realize that God forgives us IF we repent but his readiness to forgive us makes it possible for us to repent. God forgives you, not because you are perfect, but because He is. In the atmosphere of understanding God's love, acceptance, and forgiveness, we can hear and obey the words: "Neither do I condemn thee, go and sin no more."

2. As Jesus is to us, we are to be to the world. Therefore:

a. Your Love for Others Should Be Unconditional. We do not love people because they are rich or wear fancy clothes. We love them because the love of God flows through us to all people. As Jesus had a special heart for those with great need, so we are to be in the world.

b. Your Acceptance for Others Should Be Unconditional. As Jesus met us just as we were — so He wants us to meet people just as they are. And what if they do not repent? Then we either choose to store up wrath, insult and vengeance or we decide to obey God and forgive them anyway.

c. Your Forgiveness For Others Should Be Unconditional. How many of you know that is not humanly possible? But this is exactly what God calls us to. He wants us to be so baptized in His love that we can love others as He loves us.

3. Does Love Cover a Multitude of Sins or Do Sins Cover a Multitude of Love?

*The end of all things is near. Therefore be clear minded and self-controlled **so that you can pray. Above all, love each other deeply, because love covers over a multitude of sins**. Offer hospitality to one another without grumbling. Each one should use whatever gift he has received to serve others, faithfully administering God's grace in its various forms. If anyone speaks, he should do it as one speaking the very words of God. If anyone serves, he should do it with the strength God provides, so that in all things God may be praised through Jesus Christ. To him be the glory and the power for ever and ever. Amen* (I Peter 4:7-11 — Emphasis mine).

John Wesley described entire sanctification as loving the Lord our God with all our heart, soul, and strength; and loving our neighbor as ourselves. But before I can love others with God's love, I must accept His for me. So do you. I truly believe that is the work of sanctification.

4. We Need to be Sanctified. Some people think that sanctification is just a weird or contrary doctrine of holiness congregations, but sanctification is God's desire for every person.

It is God's will that you should be sanctified: *that you should avoid sexual immorality; that each of you should learn to control his own body in a way that is holy and honorable, not in passionate lust like the heathen, who do not know God; and that in this matter no one should wrong his brother or take advantage of him. The Lord will punish men for all such sins, as we have already told you and warned you.* ***For***

God did not call us to be impure, but to live a holy life. *Therefore, he who rejects this instruction does not reject man but God, who gives you his Holy Spirit. Now about brotherly love we do not need to write to you, for you yourselves have been taught by God to love each other.* (I Thessalonians 4:3-12 — Emphasis mine).

May God himself, the God of peace, **sanctify you through and through. May your whole spirit, soul and body be kept blameless** *at the coming of our Lord Jesus Christ. The one who calls you is faithful and* ***he will do it****.* (I Thessalonians 4:23-24 — Emphasis mine).

5. We Need to Be <u>Continually</u> Filled with the Holy Spirit. There has been a lot of controversy in the church concerning being filled with the Holy Spirit. The best thing for us to do is to go right back to the Scriptures to see what God has to say about being Spirit-filled.

Be very careful, then, how you live — not as unwise but as wise, making the most of every opportunity, because the days are evil. Therefore do not be foolish, but understand what the Lord's will is. **Do not get drunk on wine, which leads to debauchery. Instead, be filled with the Spirit***. Speak to one another with psalms, hymns and spiritual songs. Sing and make music in your heart to the Lord, always giving thanks to God the Father for everything, in the name of our Lord Jesus Christ. Submit to one another out of reverence for Christ* (Ephesians 5:15-21).

The Greek word translated debauchery here is a compound word. It uses the Greek word for salvation and attaches a negative to it. It literally should read "Be not drunk with wine which is salvation — NOT!"

Paul compares being filled or drunk with wine to being filled or drunk with the Holy Spirit. Some who read this can remember how long intoxication lasts. It lasts until the affect of the liquor wears off. Being filled with the Spirit lasts until a person sins or until we have power go out from us through ministry. Therefore Paul tells us to be continually filled with the Spirit.

I was a born again evangelical minister for decades before I learned the importance and the reality of being filled with the Spirit. My life was similar to that of the people of Samaria. I loved the word of God and studied it and preached it faithfully. But I lacked the power of the Holy Spirit in my life and ministry.

When the apostles in Jerusalem heard that Samaria had accepted the word of God, they sent Peter and John to them. When they arrived, they prayed for them that they might receive the Holy Spirit, because the Holy Spirit had not yet come upon any of them; they had simply been baptized into the name of the Lord Jesus. Then **Peter and John placed their hands on them, and they received the Holy Spirit** (Acts 8:14-17 — Emphasis mine).

Looking back I realize that I received very little teaching about the Holy Spirit during my early years as a child of God. I was taught about God the Father and God the Son but I wasn't taught much about God the Holy Spirit. I entered the ministry shortly after I was saved and carried on the traditions of those who introduced me to the Gospel. I was fully saved but I certainly was not empowered for ministry. Like the disciples at Ephesus I had not really heard that there was a Holy Spirit. I had the Holy Spirit living in me (Romans 8:9) but I was ignorant about His ways in me and upon me. I didn't know the release of the living waters; I didn't enjoy the fresh anointing and outpouring of the Spirit of God. I possessed a whiff of the truth but none of the power.

I am eternally grateful that God helped me to press into the things of the Spirit and that he sent teachers, preachers and friends who laid their hands on me until the Holy Spirit came upon me in power just as he did for the people in Ephesus when Paul placed his hands on them.

While Apollos was at Corinth, Paul took the road through the interior and arrived at Ephesus. There he found some disciples and asked them, <u>**"Did you receive the Holy Spirit when you believed**?"</u> *They answered, "No, we have not even heard that there is a Holy Spirit." So Paul asked, "Then what baptism did you receive?" "John's baptism," they replied. Paul said, "John's baptism was a baptism of repentance. He told the people to believe in the one coming after him, that is, in Jesus." On* hearing this, they were baptized into the name of the Lord Jesus. **When Paul placed his hands on them, the Holy Spirit came on them**, and they spoke in tongues and prophesied. (Acts 19:1-7 — Emphasis mine).

6. We Need To Be Made Complete in Love. I never really understood how much God loves me until I went through my own deep healing and deliverance. I was incapable of really loving others with the love of Christ — and God knows how desperately I tried to. But my love flowed more from personal determination to be a faithful Christian than it did from personal knowledge and baptism in the Love of God. My love paled in comparison to the New Testament standard given by John.

This is love: not that we loved God, but that he loved us and sent his Son as an atoning sacrifice for our sins. **Dear friends, since God so loved us, we also ought to love one another.** *No one has ever seen God; but if we love one another, God lives in us and his love is made complete in us.* **We know that we live in him and he in us, because he has given us of his Spirit**. *And we have seen and testify that the Father has sent his Son to be the Savior of the world. If anyone acknowledges that Jesus is the Son of God, God lives in him and he in God. And so we know and rely on the love God has for us. God is love.* **Whoever lives in love lives in God, and God in him**. *In this way,* **love is made complete** *among us so that we will have confidence on the day of judgment, because in this world we are like him.* **There is no fear in love. But perfect love drives out fear**, *because fear has to do with punishment. The one who fears is not made perfect in love. We love because he first loved us.* (I John 4:10-18 — Emphasis mine).

So what do you do with all this? I first taught this material one day when we were having a Believer's Baptism at our church. My wife came under such conviction through this teaching that she asked me to literally "baptize her in the love of Jesus". I had never heard of such a thing but was prompted to do it. After I baptized my wife "in the love of Jesus" I asked her to baptize me in the love of Jesus. We (and our congregation) can testify that the love of God was shed abroad in our hearts when we did this. Most people won't be led to receive water baptism to symbolize their baptism in love. Most will simply believe and receive and here are some steps to help you do that.

1. Accept Jesus' Love. In seminars I lead people to pray this prayer. *Heavenly Father, I now know that in Jesus. You Love me unconditionally, You fully accept me, and You have completely washed away my sin. I now receive Your unconditional Love, Acceptance, and Forgiveness.*

2. Cast Out All Fears At The Root. Perfect love casts out fear but sometimes we need to exercise our faith to make sure that fear leaves. Here again we lead people in the following prayer. *Father, Your Word says that perfect love casts out fear. Therefore, In Jesus' Name, I cast out all fear from my life. I cast out all generational fear, going all the way back to Adam and Eve.*

3. Receive Unveiling of the Spiritual Eyes and Healing for the Heart. Jesus wants to release his spirit of revelation so we can see and he came to mend those whose hearts were broken so we can all pray this prayer by faith. Prayer: *Heavenly Father, I pray that the eyes of my heart may be enlightened in order that I may know the hope to which You have called me, the riches of your glorious inheritance for me, and your incomparably great power for me. I now receive spiritual healing for my heart, In Jesus' Name. Amen.*

I close this portion of the Book by praying these Scriptures and prayers over you.

Finally, be strong in the Lord and in his mighty power. Put on the full armor of God so that you can take your stand against the devil's schemes. For our struggle is not against flesh and blood, but against the rulers, against the authorities, against the powers of this dark world and against the spiritual forces of evil in the heavenly realms. Therefore put on the full armor of God, so that when the day of evil comes, you may be able to stand your ground, and after you have done everything, to stand. Stand firm then, with the belt of truth buckled around your waist, with the breastplate of righteousness in place, and with your feet fitted with the readiness that comes from the gospel of peace In addition to all this, take up the shield of faith, with which you can extinguish all the flaming arrows of the evil one. Take the helmet of salvation and the sword of the Spirit, which is the word of God. And pray in the Spirit on all occasions with all kinds of prayers and requests. (Ephesians 6:10-17 — Emphasis mine).

Now, In the Mighty Name of Jesus, I declare to the powers of darkness: "These people know the truth and the truth has set them free." "They have been set free indeed by the Son of God." I now release them in the Name of the Lord Jesus. The old is gone. The new has come. Therefore I urge you, brothers and sisters, to walk worthy of the calling you have received.

Now unto him that is able to keep you from falling, and to present you faultless before the presence of his glory with exceeding joy, To the only wise God our Saviour, be glory and majesty, dominion and power, both now and ever. Amen (Jude 24-25).

APPENDIX:
The Free Indeed Deep Healing Questionnaire Worksheet

The following is the ministry questionnaire I prepared while working on my doctorate from Wagner Leadership Institute with proficiencies in Deliverance and Prayer. There I was exposed to some of the top practitioners in the field of deliverance, including Doris Wagner, Peter Horrobin, John Eckhardt, Chuck Pierce, Barbara Yoder, Brad Bandemer, Cindy Jacobs, Neil Anderson, Derek Prince, Ed Murphy, Frank and Ida-Mae Hammond and others. I have also studied scores of books on deliverance and spiritual warfare.

It is impossible to document all credit where it is due. Still, the main text outlined in this questionnaire originally came from Chapter 10 - 15 of <u>How to Cast out Demonic Intruders</u> by Noel and Phyl Gibson (Renew) as revised by Doris Wagner and is used by her permission. I continue to update and revise it as things are revealed through personal ministry. Permission has been extended for resourcing the following pages for use in prayer situations. This questionnaire worksheet may not be copied for sale at any time.

The way I personally use this questionnaire worksheet is that I first hand a person a copy of the questionnaire. The questionnaire is the same as the questionnaire worksheet except I eliminate the items before the place where the person fills in their personal information. I also delete the bulleted items which are given to instruct the minister how to pray for the person.

Start of the appointment:

- Turn the ringer off the phone and put a "Do not disturb sign" on the door. Eliminate distraction as much as possible, and be ready to pray against spirits of distraction as needed.
- Explain how God gives the prayer minister spiritual amnesia and that the questionnaire will be returned to the person to be filed or destroyed at their own discretion. (God chooses to forget and to let me forget)
- Pray and ask blessings over your time together.
- Ask angels to take place all around, above and below the person you are praying for.
- Pray protection over office, people taking part, families, homes, and pets.

Pray:

- That demons be cut off from communication and help from other demons and Satan.
- Pray that demons will be confused on their hold on _____.
- That _____ will recognize any demonic presence and not be afraid or confused, but willingly accept our counsel and help.
- That every strongman will be bound with the ropes of heaven.
- That God will guide us and set angels to work to break up every scheme of the enemy.
- That God will release His gifts to us: faith, wisdom, discernment, words of wisdom, knowledge, and prophecy to help us enter warfare against the enemy.

Proclaim:

Now listen to me, Satan and every present demon, you cannot stall or hide. When we command you to leave, you will obey immediately. We are seated with Christ in the heavenly realms, far above your rule and authority. Jesus in us is greater than you! When we resist you, you will flee. Jesus Christ Himself will strengthen us and protect us.

Explain how we will work:

- The appointment may last from 90 minutes to three hours or more. We will take breaks when needed.
- In the case of people who have been suicidal, a helper will accompany them whenever they leave the room.

- We will pray at times, addressing God. At other times we may address spirits that are attached to the person receiving prayer. We may need to speak to those spirits with a firm voice. Know that we are addressing them and not the one being prayed for.
- The intercessor sitting in on the appointment will have pen and paper to write down any revelation received.
- Note the wastebasket and tissue in front of the one receiving prayer.

Explain what may happen:
- Demons may manifest through coughing, sneezing, shaking, burping, urges to use the bathroom, and occasionally through vomiting. Tell the person not to resist such "exiting" of demons.
- Have the person being prayed for report things like: headaches, confusion, fear, feelings of panic, and the like. Pray against such manifestations as they happen.

Name: _____ Age: _____

Marital Status: ____single ____married ____divorced ____remarried ____widowed

Current profession: _____

Please answer the following briefly:

1. What is your church background?
- *Look for clues of any denominational or religious spirits.*
- *If change: ask what problems have surfaced in your transition?*
- *There seem to be specific demons assigned to most denominations. Pray as led.*
- *Pray against a wandering or vagabond religious spirit if the person has gone from church to church.*

2. Explain briefly your conversion experience. If you came to Christ as a teenager or older, was your life really changed? ____Yes ____No
- *Look for evidence of true salvation and repentance. I use the John 3:16 diagram here to show the difference between praying a little prayer and really turning to Christ as Lord.*

3. Were you baptized or dedicated to Christ as a child? ____Yes ____No
Were you baptized as a convert? ____Yes ____No
- *I encourage post conversion (Believer's) baptism. Before I baptize anyone I always ask, "Do you renounce the devil and all his works?" Make sure that the baptismal waters are blessed.*

4. In one word, who is Jesus Christ to you?
- *I look for any incorrect doctrine or false teaching here. Part of deliverance is discipleship.*

5. What does the blood of Calvary mean to you?
- *People who have been touched by witchcraft or false vows may show an aversion to the blood of Christ and to the Lord's Supper.*

6. Is repentance part of your Christian life? What have you repented of in the last six months?
- *Look for strongholds or disobedience here and for signs of carnality.*
- *Deliverance works best for people who are ready to repent of all known sin.*

7. What is your prayer life like? Do you sense God speaking to you?____Yes ____No
- *Look for evidence of intimacy with Christ, pray for a release of the voice of Jesus.*
- *1 Peter 3:7 for husbands. 1 Peter 3:1-6 for wives.*

8. Do you have assurance of salvation? ____Yes ____No
What did Jesus save you from?
- *Look for evidence of spirits of doubt or wrong teaching about "works" righteousness, salvation by faith but kept by works theology, legalism and the like. I like assurance verses like John 1:12, 1 Jn 5:11-12; Ro 10:0-10, 13, etc. I make sure their faith is in Jesus and not in "the sinner's prayer".*

9. Do you have a problem with doubt and unbelief in everyday Christian living?
 ____Yes ____No
- *Look for symptoms of doubt, unbelief, or faulty doctrine.*

10. Are you satisfied with your Christian walk? ____Yes ____No

If not, how would you like to see it improve?
- *Look for areas of bondage or for areas that need further discipleship.*

Dealing with Cultural Issues:

In Jesus Name we bind every cultural strongman and break every cultural stronghold over_____. We cut every cord between the strongman, any demons and _____. We use the keys of heaven to open the door of freedom and victory.

1. What is your country of birth?
- *Look for specific bondages from specific cultures and countries, i.e., the stubborn German spirit, the hot headed Irish spirit, the materialistic American spirit, etc.*

2. Have you lived in other countries? ____Yes ____No
If so, which ones?
Similar to number 1.

3. Where were your parents born?
Mother: city, state, nation
Father? city, state, nation
- *Look for specific bondages from specific cultures and countries, i.e., the stubborn German spirit, the hot headed Irish spirit, the materialistic American spirit, etc.*

4. Where were your grandparents born? (City, state, nation)
Mother's mother: city, state, nation?   Mother's father: city, state, nation?
Father's mother: city, state, nation?   Father's father: city, state, nation?
Same as # 3.

5. Do you have Native Americans in your generational lines? ____Yes ____No
If so, which tribe or nation?
- *It is helpful if they know enough about the history of their tribe to know how they worshiped and any generational patterns of iniquity. These can all be prayed over.*

- *The descendants of American Indians were often dedicated to demon gods. If that is the case the following steps should be taken.*
- *Confess the sins of the forefathers and ask the Lord to separate you completely from the iniquitous patterns of the forefathers.*
- *Renounce any dedication placed upon your life to Satan and his demons. Proclaim that you belong to Christ and will serve him only.*
- *Command all demons that took advantage of this dedicate to leave.*
- *Take authority over the curse of destruction that was activated through breaking Native American covenants with demons gods.*
- *Cast out all demons of destruction related to these curses.*

6. What life events have caused you the deepest wounds and hurts?
- *Look for forgiveness issues and possible gateways to demons.*
- *Check to see what their Ephesians 2:10 prophetic destiny might be.*

Breaking the Power of Negative Confessions:
- After looking over their responses to the following, lead them in forgiving those who have spoken harmful things against them.
- Cleanse them by washing them with what God says about them from the Word.
- Break all negative vows and curses against the person.
- Pray blessings which negate the negative things spoken against them.

1. Names: What are some of the negative names you have been called (i.e.: Stupid, dummy, loser, etc)?

2. Words that did hurt you: What are some of the negative or hurtful things that have been said about you? (i.e.: You are going to end up in jail or you will never amount to anything)

3. Hurtful self-talk: What are some of the negative things you have spoken about yourself? (i.e.: I give up, I'm never going to make it, nobody loves, I might as well be dead, there is not use trying anymore, etc.)

4. Vows: What ungodly promises or pacts have you entered into with people or organizations of spiritual forces? (Even if you weren't taking them seriously)

5. **Judgments:** What words of condemnation, rejection or judgment have been spoken to you? (i.e.: you are worthless, ugly, you don't have the brains God gave a goose), etc. What negative judgments have you spoken to others: (you're never going to get it, why can't you be like... , etc.)

6. **Curses:** What negative words have been spoken against you by people close to you such as parents, teachers, bosses, friends, classmates, co-workers, doctors, etc? (i.e.: you won't get over this, you will just get weaker until you die, you are a failure, loser, etc.)

7. **Blessings:** Have you received unconditional love and affirmation from your parents, siblings, spouse, etc.? Have you communicated blessings to others?

Breaking curses:
1. Which of the following indications of a curse is part of you or your family's history? (Dt. 28)

a. Mental and/or emotional breakdown?	____Yes	____No
b. Repeated or chronic sicknesses, especially if hereditary?	____Yes	____No
c. Barrenness, multiple miscarriages, female problems?	____Yes	____No
d. Breakdown of marriage, family problems?	____Yes	____No
e. Ongoing financial problems?	____Yes	____No
f. Being "accident prone"	____Yes	____No
g. Suicides, unusual or untimely deaths?	____Yes	____No

Check for "frustration" assignments. Break frustration off. Destroy the stronghold.
- *Derek Prince said "there is one word that sums up a curse 'frustration'." Inquire about what great frustrations seem to stay in the person's life and pray accordingly.*
- *Try to identify any possible curses and ask the person to forgive those who brought the curse(s) on their family.*
- *Renounce the curse(s) and cast out the spirits that empower the working of the curse(s).*
- *Recommended reading <u>Blessing or Curse, You Can Choose</u> by Derek Prince. Chosen Books, 1990.*

2. Do you or your children and/or grandchildren have multiple sclerosis? Yes   No
- *M.S. may be linked to spirits of death, especially if there is a history of untimely deaths in the family.*

- *Break all soul ties with the dead.*
- *Cut the "silver cord" to break ties with the dead.*

3. Do you have ringing in the ears that doesn't seem to have a medical reason?
          ____Yes ____No

- *This may come from a spirit of necromancy. If so cast it out.*

Evidence of a witchcraft curse:

1. Do you have a diminishing sense of the presence of God?	____Yes	____No
2. Have you lost your focus on God's promises to you?	____Yes	____No
3. Have you lost faith because of mental confusion?	____Yes	____No
4. Have you lost your sense of vision for ministry and service?	____Yes	____No

- *Try to discern where the curse came from and forgive those who brought it.*
- *Break the curse in the Name and through the Blood of Jesus and command all spirits that took advantage of it to leave.*

DEEP HEALING TECHNIQUES through age _____

I ask the Lord to show me what age to stop at. I usually begin by leading them in visualizing Jesus and his involvement with their conception. The more we minister through deep healing, the less "deliverance" ministry is needed.

Scriptures to consider in Deep Healing: (I usually pray these verses over people, converting these promises of God into prayer for the person — following the Spirit's lead.)

For you created my inmost being; you knit me together in my mother's womb. I praise you because I am fearfully and wonderfully made; your works are wonderful, I know that full well. My frame was not hidden from you when I was made in the secret place. When I was woven together in the depths of the earth. your eyes saw my unformed body. All the days ordained for me were written in your book before one of them came to be. How precious to {Or concerning} me are your thoughts, O God! How vast is the sum of them! (Psalm 139:13-17).

"Before I formed you in the womb I knew {Or chose} you, before you were born I set you apart; I appointed you as a prophet to the nations." (Jeremiah 1:5).

For we are God's workmanship, created in Christ Jesus to do good works, which God prepared in advance for us to do. (Ephesians 2:10).

Before I was born the LORD called me; from my birth he has made mention of my name. He made my mouth like a sharpened sword, in the shadow of his hand he hid me; he made me into a polished arrow and concealed me in his quiver. (until the kairos time) *He said to me, "You are my servant, Israel, in whom I will display my splendor." But I said, "I have labored to no purpose; I have spent my strength in vain and for nothing. Yet what is due me is in the LORD's hand, and my reward is with my God." And now the LORD says — he who formed me in the womb to be his servant to bring Jacob back to him and gather Israel to himself, for I am honored in the eyes of the LORD and my God has been my strength — he says: "It is too small a thing for you to be my servant . . ?" This is what the LORD says: "In the time of my favor I will answer you, and in the day of salvation I will help you; I will keep you and will make you to be a covenant for the people, to restore the land and to reassign its desolate inheritances, to say to the captives, 'Come out,' and to those in darkness, 'Be free!'* (Isaiah 49 1b-5a, 8 - 9a).

For I know the plans I have for you," declares the LORD, "plans to prosper you and not to harm you, plans to give you hope and a future. (Jeremiah 29:11).

During the deep healing we deal with all the strongholds and demons that come up. At the end of deep healing I usually pray as follows:
- *In Jesus' Name we tear down and demolish the stronghold of <u>Rejection of God</u>!*
- *In Jesus' Name we tear down and demolish the stronghold of feeling <u>Rejected by God</u>!*
- *In Jesus' Name we tear down and demolish the stronghold of <u>Fear of Rejection</u>!*
- *In Jesus' Name we tear down and demolish the stronghold of <u>Self Rejection</u>!*
- *In Jesus' Name we tear down and demolish the Stronghold of <u>Rejection of others</u>!*
- *In Jesus' Name we bind the strongman of rejection and command you to loose _____ and come out right now!*
- *In Jesus' Name we ask the Father to give _____ a proper self acceptance and a healthy self-image so he/she might love God and his/her neighbor and he/she loves himself/herself.*

Dealing with Issues of Rejection:
- In Jesus Name we destroy every stronghold of rejection in _____. We bind the strongman of rejection and cut every cord between the strongman, any demons and _____. We use the keys of heaven to open the door God's love, healing, acceptance and forgiveness.

1. Was your relationship with your parents: ____Good ____Bad ____Indifferent?
Explain:
a. Any special problems with your Father?
b. Any special problems with your Mother?
c. Any special problems with your brother(s) or sister(s)?
- *Look for rejection and forgiveness issues (unfulfilled revenge).*

2. Tell us about your childhood:
a. Were you a planned child? ____Yes ____No ____Don't Know
- *A child who was unwanted can suffer rejection from the womb, especially if a parent cursed the child with the words "I don't want this child."*
- *A child who was unwanted may suffer from bronchial asthma. Pray against the death curse of the mother (or grandmother) and pray healing.*

b. The "right sex?" ____Yes ____No ____Don't Know
- *A child may be confused about their sexual identity if a parent wanted the opposite sex.*

c. Were you conceived out of wedlock? ____Yes ____No ____Don't Know
- *Pray against generational spirits of lust, illegitimacy and bastard.*
- *Those conceived in rape can suffer from demons that take advantage of a situation like this: lust, violence, fears, anger and hatred for women.*

d. Were you adopted? ____Yes ____No ____Don't Know
- *Do birth parents need to be forgiven?*
- *Look for hereditary rejection and pray against the spirit of abandonment.*
- *Pray for the manifestation of the Spirit of Adoption in the person's life. (Romans 8:15-16)*

e. If adopted, do you know anything about your natural parents?
____Yes ____No ____Don't Know
- *Look for clues of generational sins or spirits.*

f. Do you know if your mother suffered any trauma during her pregnancy with you?
____Yes ____No
- *Look for spirits of trauma, violence and panic, especially if the mother was battered.*

g. Did you suffer a difficult or complicated birth? ____Yes ____No ____Don't Know
- *Look for spirits of trauma, violence and panic, especially if the cord was wrapped around the neck.*

h. Were you "bonded at birth"? ____Yes ____No
A breast-fed baby? ____Yes ____No ____Don't Know
- *Look for factors that may be a root of rejection.*

i. Do you have brothers and sisters? ____Yes ____No ____Don't Know
Names_____ Ages_____
- *Look for further roots of rejection. Were other children favored?*

Where do you fall in the sibling line?
How was your relationship with them growing up?
What is it like now? Any special problems with them?
- *Look for roots of rejection or for any special problems that need forgiveness.*

3. Are your parents living?
Father ____Yes ____No ____Don't Know
Mother ____Yes ____No ____Don't Know
- *Are there feelings of blame for the death of a parent? Rejection? Is forgiveness is needed even if the parent is deceased?*

Are they Christians?
Father ____Yes ____No ____Don't Know
Mother ____Yes ____No ____Don't Know
Living together? ____Yes ____No ____Don't Know
Divorced? ____Yes ____No ____Don't Know
How old were you when (if) they divorced?_____
How is your relationship with them now?
- *Divorce often causes feelings of rejection to parents and children. Children often feel blame.*

Have they remarried?
Father ____Yes ____No ____Don't Know
Mother ____Yes ____No ____Don't Know

How is your relationship with your stepparents?
Are they Christians?

Step-Father	___Yes	___No	___Don't Know
Step-Mother	___Yes	___No	___Don't Know

How was your relationship growing up?
How is your relationship now?
- *Does someone need to be forgiven for their hurtful behavior or rejection?*

4. Were your parents critical of you or others?   ___Yes ___No
- *Look for generational critical spirits.*

5. Are you a critical person?   ___Yes ___No ___Don't Know
- *Do you want to be critical?*
- *Look for personal and/or generational critical spirits.*

6. Do you feel emotionally immature?   ___Yes ___No ___Don't Know
- *Pray against spirits of arrested development.*
- *Pray against the spirit of emotional immaturity and break emotional bondages.*
- *Pray for the healing of emotions.*

7. Tell us about your self-image (circle where applicable):

  Low self-image   Feel insecure   Condemn myself   Hate myself
   Feel worthless   Feel inferior   Believe I am a failure
    Question my identity   Punish myself (If so, how?)

- *Show that negative self-image is agreement with Satan. Ask: "how would agreement with Jesus change the way you look at yourself?*
- *Pray against spirits of self condemnation, hopelessness, despair, and self-punishment.*
- *Pray against the spirit behind the symptoms you see here.*

8. Was (is) your father (circle):

    Passive   Strong and manipulative   Neither

Were you friends?   ___Yes ___No
Describe briefly your relationship with your father:
- *Look for personal or generational spirits of manipulation and control.*

9. Was (is) your Mother (circle):

        Passive   Strong and manipulative   Neither

Were you friends? ____Yes ____No

Describe briefly your relationship with your Mother:

- Look for personal or generational spirits of manipulation and control.

10. Do you seek to control others? ____Yes ____No ____Don't Know

- Look for personal or generational spirits of manipulation and control.
- Pray against possessiveness & clingy spirits with manipulation and control, especially in children.

11. Is someone or something else controlling you? ____Yes ____No ____Don't Know

If so, describe:

- Look for personal or generational spirits of manipulation and control.
- Look for spirit guides and/or familiar spirits — in children look for spirits from games and cartoons.

12. Was yours a happy home during childhood? ____Yes ____No ____Don't Know

Describe briefly:

- Check for forgiveness issues and possible causes of bondage.

13. How would you describe your family's financial situation when you were a child?

        Poor   Slight financial struggles   Moderate income   Affluent

- Look for spirits of poverty, shame, greed, materialism.
- Break curses of poverty and/or lack.
- You may also pray against spirits of mental poverty if their finances are always in ruin.

14. Has lying or stealing been a problem to you? ____Yes ____No

Is it now? ____Yes ____No

- Look for spirits of lying, deceit, kleptomania, and stealing.

15. Were you lonely as a teenager? ____Yes ____Sometimes ____Never

- Ask: are you lonely now?
- Look for spirits of loneliness, grief, and abandonment. Note: Jesus carried our grief and sorrow to the cross and we can leave it there with him.

16. As a child, teenager, or later in life did you ever suffer an injustice?

                                                                    ____Yes ____No

What?

By Whom?

- *Is forgiveness needed? Check for emotional or spiritual scars.*
- *Ask "has this pattern of unjust treatment repeated itself in your life?"*
- *You may want to look at Psalm 62 and counsel about yielding rights to God so Jesus has freedom to work — both on them and those around them.*
- *Look for spirits of anger, rejection, shame, grief, bitterness, resentment, unforgiveness, and victimization.*

17. Do you have trouble giving or receiving love? ____Yes ____No ____At times
- *Look for spirits of emotional coldness. Break bondages over the emotions.*

18. Do you find it easy to communicate with persons close to you?

    I have real difficulty   I am unwilling   I have trouble at times   It's easy
- *Look for spirits of emotional coldness. Break bondages over the emotions.*

19. Are you a perfectionist? ____Yes ____No ____Don't Know
Were (are) your parents perfectionist? ____Yes ____No ____Don't Know
- *Look for spirits of hereditary perfectionism, perfectionism, rejection and strife.*
- *Also check for a people pleasing spirit.*

20. Do you come from a proud family? ____Yes ____No ____Don't Know
- *Look for generational spirits of pride.*

21. Do you personally have a problem with pride? ____Yes ____No ____Don't Know
- *Look for spirits of pride, arrogance and self-aggrandizement.*
- *Consider the need to crucify the carnal nature of pride and selfishness to the cross.*

22. Do you have or have you had problems with (circle all applicable :)

        Impatience   Irritability Temper   Racial prejudice   Moodiness
                Rebellion   Violence   Anger
            Stubbornness   Temptation to murder

- *These are symptoms of rejection and aggression. It helps to ask God to reveal if self-rejection and aggressive rejection are problems. Pray about each one, and then come against spirits of self-rejection and/or aggression.*

23. Do you tend to be stubborn or rebellious?
- *Pray against rebellion, lawlessness, laziness and apathy,*

24. Have you been given to: (circle)

                Swearing   Blasphemies   Obscenities?

Do you now:

                Swear   Blaspheme   Use obscenities?

- *These are symptoms of rebellion and aggression. Look for spirits of rebellion and aggression.*

25. If you are a parent, do you have any special problems with your children?
- *Look for forgiveness issues towards the person's own parents or guardians.*
- *Look for strongholds in the family line. Ask questions like "Did your parents treat you like you are treating your children — or did you treat your parents like your children are treating you?"*
- *Minister as led.*

26. Do you have toward anyone:

Unforgiveness or anger?

Whom and why?

- *Tell them to choose to forgive. Soul ties may need to be broken and spirits of unforgiveness and/or anger cast out.*
- *Make sure to pray for the healing of wounded memories at the end of this section.*
- *If the anger has been long lived, you may also check for a spirit of wrath.*

Resentment or bitterness?

Whom and why?

- *Tell them to choose to forgive. Look for spirits of resentment and bitterness.*

Jealousy or envy?

Whom and why?

- *Tell them to choose to forgive. Look for spirits of jealousy and envy.*

Hatred?

Whom and why?

- *Spirits of hatred come out a lot better after there has been deliberate forgiving. Each person the hate is directed toward (including self and God) must be forgiven for any real or perceived hurts. Then, cast out the spirit of hate. If it refuses to come out, start speaking about the unconditional love of God and reading verses like John 3:16*

- *Other symptoms of rejection are perfectionism, materialism, immorality, control, and manipulation.*

27. What are some of the negative names or things that have been said about you?
- *Deal with forgiveness issues.*
- *Break the power of negative words and cast out spirits that took advantage of them.*
- *Ask God to bring you into your full destiny and give you confidence to war for your prophetic destiny* (Ephesians 2:10).

28. What are some of the negative things you have spoken about yourself?
- *Ask God's forgiveness and renounce these negative words and their power.*
- *Ask God to bring you into your full destiny and give you confidence to war for your prophetic destiny* (Ephesians 2:10).

Prayers for overcoming rejection issues: (You may want to have them pray these prayers)
- *Heavenly Father, You sent Jesus into the world, not to reject or condemn me, but that I might be accepted and forgiven. I confess that I have believed my sin is greater than your mercy and grace. I have given in to rejection, self-rejection, perceived rejection, and fear of rejection. I have also rejected others. I ask you to forgive me and to cleanse me of all rejection. In Jesus' Name. Amen.*
- *I repent on behalf of my generations for every place they gave place to rejection, allowing its influence to be felt in my generation. I choose that from my generation forward; love, acceptance, and forgiveness will characterize my family, and that blessing will continue to future generations.*
- *I repent for allowing myself to be controlled and manipulated by rejection and for giving place to all the wrong thoughts, attitudes, and actions that rejection has caused. In Jesus' Name. Amen.*
- *Heavenly Father, I thank you that in Jesus Christ you have forgiven me. I confess that I have not always extended that same forgiveness to others. Right now, I choose to make my heart clean by forgiving all who have offended me. I choose to forgive _____for_____... In Jesus' Name; I release these people from their offense. Amen.*
- *Heavenly Father, I thank you that in Jesus Christ you have forgiven me. I confess*

that I have not always extended that same forgiveness to others. Right now, I choose to make my heart clean by forgiving all who have offended me. I choose to forgive _____ *for* _____*, in Jesus' Name, I release these people from their offense. Amen.*

Causes and Consequences of Mental & Emotional Problems:

In Jesus' Name we demolish every stronghold of mental and emotional problems. We bind every strongman that is working mental and/or emotional problems. We cut every cord between the strongman, the demons and _____. We use the keys of heaven to open the doors of healing, soundness and courage.

1. Are you easily frustrated? ____Yes ____No ____Don't Know

Do you: ____Show it ____Bury it?
- *Look for spirits of frustration, un-yielded "rights" and expectations.*

2. Are you: ____An anxious person ____A worrier ____Easily depressed?
- *Look for spirits of anxiety, worry, tension and/or depression.*

3. Did any of your ancestors suffer from depression?
____Father ____Mother ____Grandmother ____Grandfather
- *Look for generational spirits of depression and/or nervous breakdown.*

4. Do you have a "heavy" spirit? ____Yes ____No
Do you have kidney problems? ____Yes ____No
- *Kidney failure is often linked to a spirit of heaviness.*
- *Cast out the spirit of heaviness and pray healing of the kidneys.*

5. Has any family member suffered from an acute nervousness or mental problem?
____Parent ____Sibling ____Grandparent
What problem(s)?
- *Some mental problems are tied in with evil spirits. If the problem is demon related, you may look for spirits of schizophrenia, manic depression, mental illness, paranoia, and confusion.*
- *If you discern that their mental problems may be spiritual, pray against lunacy.*

6. Have you ever personally had psychiatric counseling?

                                                                       ____Yes ____No ____Don't Know

Hospitalization   ____Yes ____No ____Don't Know

Shock treatment   ____Yes ____No ____Don't Know

Psychoanalysis   ____Yes ____No ____Don't Know

- *If they were treated badly, there may be spirits of trauma, anger, victimization and deception.*
- *Pray against spirits of clinical and/or pharmacy control.*

7. Have you ever been hypnotized?   ____Yes ____No ____Don't Know
If so, when and why?

- *Look for spirits of hypnosis and/or mind control.*
- *Say: "Now I address every evil spirit that took advantage of _____ hypnotic state and entered at that time. I bind you all, I break your power, and I command you to loose _____ and let him/her go now!*
- *You can use this same pattern for acupuncture, iridology, and the like.*

8. Have you had advanced education? Is so, what?

- *People who focus on knowledge over revelation may educate themselves into unbelief.*
- *Look for spirits of skepticism, unbelief, argumentative spirit, intellectual pride and arrogance.*
- *Pray down the stronghold of secular humanism.*

9. Have you, your parents or grandparents been in any cults?

        Christian Science   Rosicrucian
        Jehovah's Witnesses   Gurus
        Mormons   Unity
        Spiritist churches   Children of Love
        Christadelphians   Scientology
        Bahai   Religious Communes
        Theosophy   Native Religions

        Unification (Moonies)   Armstrong Worldwide COG
        New Age
        Eastern religions such as: Hinduism, Buddhism, Islam, etc.

- Cast out the spirit by the name of the cult, e.g., "Spirit of Christian Science…"

10. To your knowledge, has any close family member been a:

        Freemason   Oddfellow
        Rainbow girl   Mormon
        Eastern Star   Shriner
        Elk   Demolay
        Job's Daughter   Pythian
        Daughter of the Nile?

If so, whom?

- Cast out every spirit by the name of the lodge or group. Check for generational bondages and renounce and break every vow, curse, and covenant.
- You may want to schedule a "Masonic release prayer"

Do you suffer from (circle where applicable):

        Apathy   Hardness of emotion
        Confusion   Skepticism
        Doubt   Financial disaster
        Unbelief   Allergies
        Infirmities   Frequent illness
        Mockery   Comprehension difficulty

- All the above can be symptoms of Freemason curses. You may want to review chapter 10 on "Evicting Demonic Intruders" or use one of the prayers prepared for people with Masonic backgrounds. Cast out spirits of Freemasonry and the Luciferan doctrine.
- Cast out every spirit of antichrist(s).

Is there any Masonic regalia or memorabilia in your possession such as aprons, rings, Bibles, etc.?   ____Yes ____No ____Don't Know
If so, what?

- All regalia and memorabilia must be destroyed. Don't even keep a Masonic Bible.

11. Do you feel mentally confused?   ____Yes ____No ____Don't Know
Have mental blocks?   ____Yes ____No ____Don't Know

- Look for spirits of confusion, mental block and double mindedness.

12. Do you day-dream? ____Yes ____No
Have Mental Fantasies? ____Yes ____No
What about?
- *Look for spirits of mental fantasy, and escapism.*

13. Do you suffer from sleeplessness? ____Yes ____No
Frequent bad dreams? ____Yes ____No
What about?
- *Look for spirits relating to the theme of the dreams, such as spirits of death, violence, or fear.*

14. Have you ever been tempted to commit suicide?
____Yes ____No ____Don't Know
If so, when and why?
- *Cancel every curse of death over _____. "He/she will no longer wish to die, but will to live."*
- *Look for spirits of death, murder, and suicide. Check for generational spirits of suicide if this has occurred in the family line. Break every death wish and confess your will to live.*

15. Have you ever wished to die? ____Yes ____No
Spoken it aloud? ____Yes ____No
If so, when and why?
- *All death wishes, "I wish I were dead, etc.", must be broken. First the person confesses the death wish and asks forgiveness. Then the power of the death wish is broken by saying, "in the Name of Jesus Christ who is the Way, the Truth and the Life, I break the power of that death wish and through the blood of Jesus, I cancel every curse of death over _____"*
- *Look for spirits of death, murder and suicide. Check for generational spirits of suicide if this has occurred in the family line. Break every death wish and confess your will to live.*

16. Has there been a pattern of suicide in your family line?
- *Check for generational spirits of suicide if this has occurred in the family line. Break every death curse against the family line.*

17. Have you served in the armed forces in Muslim, Buddhist or other "non-Christian" places?
- *I have read that every plane that landed on the air strips of Vietnam was greeted with groups of Buddhist monks standing at the end of the runways performing incantations to place curses of death and destruction on every arriving soldier.*
- *Break off curses of destruction and death that were placed on them by workers of false religions. Command all demons associated with these curses to flee in the name of Jesus Christ.*

18. Are you plagued with headaches that are not medical in nature?
- *Recurring headaches are often connected with generational spirits of fear. Cast out the generational spirits of fear.*

19. Have you had a strong and prolonged fear to any of the following?

Failure	Inability to cope
Inadequacy	Death
Rape	Authority figures
The dark	Violence
Heights	Being alone
The future	Satan and evil spirits
Stores	Women
Insanity	Men
Public speaking	People's opinions
Accident	Old age
Enclosed places	Breakup
Divorce	Marriage
Terminal illness	Insects
Spiders	Snakes
Dogs	Animals
Loud noises	Water
Pain	Crowds
Flying	Open spaces
Death or injury of a loved one	

Other fears? _____

Since becoming a Christian, do any of the above fears still grip you?

____Yes ____No

If so, which ones?

- Look for specific spirits of fear by name and then cast out the strongman of fear. For example, "You spirit of fear of failure, in Jesus' Name, I break your power, and I command you to loose _____ and let him/her go now! After praying over each fear, address the strongman of fear that has manifested through the fears marked, "You spirit of fear..."
- Cast out spirit(s) of phobia.

Causes and Consequences of Cult or Occult Involvement:

In Jesus Name we demolish every stronghold of Cult or occult involvement. We break every personal and ancestral curse caused by cult or occult involvement. We bind every strongman of cult or occult involvement. We declare that every curse of cult or occult is broken through the sacrifice of Jesus Christ who became a curse for us. We cut every cord between the strongman, the demons and _____.
In Jesus' Name we use the keys of heaven to open the doors of deliverance, freedom and wholeness. We use heaven's chains to bind the enemy.

1. Have you ever made a pact with the devil? ____Yes ____No
Was it a blood pact? ____Yes ____No
What was it?
When?
Why?
Are you willing renounce it? ____Yes ____No

- People who have trouble taking Holy Communion have often been part of a satanic or witchcraft ritual involving blood. Such rituals must be confessed and renounced.
- A pact is a deal a person has made with the devil which exchanges his/her soul for a favor like money, power or love. It could sound something like this: "I will forever burn in hell if you will give me..." Sometimes a pact is sealed by extracting drops of blood from the body. Curses and vows taken at a witch's coven meeting or in satanic worship are sometimes accompanied by the blood of some sacrifice or by urine or other things. These pacts are strong, but the blood of Jesus is stronger!

2. To your knowledge, has any curse been placed on you or your family? ____Yes ____No
If so, what? By whom? Why? Explain:
- Lead the person in forgiving those who have placed curses of their family.

- *Confess the iniquitous patterns of previous generations.*
- *Break the power of every curse in the Name and through the blood of Jesus Christ.*

3. To your knowledge, have your parents or any relative as far back as you know been involved with occultism or witchcraft? ____Yes ____No ____Don't Know
To what extent?
- *Confess the sins of the ancestors.*
- *If there is witchcraft in the family background as far back as ten generations, they should forgive the one who opened the family line to witchcraft.*
- *Look for spirits of generational witchcraft and break their hold over the family line.*
- *Break any curses of witchcraft, etc.*

4. Have you ever had involvement with any of the following?

Fortune tellers	Tarot cards
Ouija boards	Séances
Mediums	Palmistry
Astrology	Color therapy
Levitation	Lucky charms
Astral travel	Horoscope
Black magic	Crystals
Demon worship	White magic
Clairvoyance	Asked for a spirit guide
New age movement	Done automatic handwriting

A witch doctor or native healer?
Boy Scout vows to Native American Guides?
Other?

- *Break any vows.*
- *Look for spirits of witchcraft, death and fear.*

5. Have you ever been involved in any other witchcraft, demonic or satanic things?
____Yes ____No
To what extent?
- *Confess and renounce your involvement.*
- *Break the strongholds this involvement brought and cast down any spirits that took advantage of the involvement.*
- *Break any curses of witchcraft, etc.*

6. Have you ever read books on occultism or witchcraft? ____Yes ____No
What and Why?
- *Same as number 4.*

7. Have you ever played demonic games such as Dungeons and Dragons?
____Yes ____No
Watched demonic files? ____Yes ____No
Do you now? ____Yes ____No
- *Look for spirits of death, suicide, fear, and other spirits that some to mind.*

8. Have you been involved in transcendental meditation? ____Yes ____No
Do you have a mantra? ____Yes ____No
If you have a mantra, what is it?
- *Confess, renounce and cast out corresponding spirits.*

9. Have you been involved in Eastern religions? ____Yes ____No
Followed a guru? ____Yes ____No
- *Confess and renounce involvement, being as specific as possible, and pledge allegiance to God the Father, Jesus Christ his Son and the Holy Spirit.*

10. Have you ever visited heathen temples? ____Yes ____No
Made offerings? ____Yes ____No
Taken part in a ceremony? ____Yes ____No
- *Follow the instructions for # 9. If symptoms such as nightmares started after visiting a temple, pray cleansing. You may want to check for spirits by the name or purpose of the heathen temple visited.*

11. Have you ever done any form of yoga? ____Yes ____No ____Don't Know
Yoga Meditation? ____Yes ____No ____Don't Know
Yoga Exercises? ____Yes ____No ____Don't Know
Renounce religious exercises, meditations & worship times. Cast out religious spirits, yoga.

12. Have you ever learned or used any form of mind communication or mind control? ____Yes ____No

Explain:
- *Confess, repent and renounce. Cast out spirits of mind control, E.S.P., mind dynamics and confusion.*

13. Were your parents or grandparents superstitious?
   ____Yes ____No ____Don't Know
Were or are you?   ____Yes ____No
- *Look for personal and generational spirits of superstition and witchcraft.*

14. Have you ever worn lucky charms, fetishes, amulets, or signs of the zodiac?
   ____Yes ____No
Do you have any in your possession?   ____Yes ____No ____Don't Know
- *It is wise to go through jewelry boxes and destroy all such items. Many have curses attached to them and bring demons with them.*
- *Confess, repent, and renounce all such items. Cast out the spirit of witchcraft.*

15. Do you have in your home any symbols of idols or spirit worship, such as:
   - Buddhas
   - Painted face masks
   - Fetish objects or feathers
   - Tikis
   - Native art — what kind
   - Totem poles
   - Idol carvings
   - Pagan symbols
   - Kachina dolls

Where did they come from and how did you get them?
- *All such items need curses broken and should be destroyed by burning or smashing.*
- *If you live somewhere with such items that belong to others, ask the Lord to seal those things off from you, and protect you.*

16. Do you have any "good luck witches" in your home?
- *Confess and renounce.*
- *Destroy them by burning or smashing.*
- *Cast down any spirits that took advantage of them.*

17. Are you "turned on" by any of the following music: (circle)
   - rock & roll
   - new age
   - rap
   - or other styles of music
   - punk rock
   - country
   - heavy metal

- Destroy any music which has lyrics encouraging sin, illicit sex, violence, suicide, bad language, and the like. Music is often an entrance for spirits of violence, sex, and suicide.

18. Have you ever practiced any of the martial arts? ___Yes ___No
If so, which? Do you practice it (them) now? ___Yes ___No

Martial Arts are linked with Buddhism. Christians should bow in respect and worship to God alone. Martial Arts are frequently an opening for spirits of anger, violence, revenge and murder. Confession, repentance and renouncing are in order.

19. Do you or your children/grandchildren suffer from hyperactivity?
- Hyperactivity is often linked to an occult background. Pray against disturbing spirits, etc.

20. Are you often told you are "just like" another relative, friend or acquaintance?
- Human spirits can be transferred, especially when someone is named after another person.
- Occult practice can lead to the transference of human spirits. Speak the name of the person whose spirit may be transferred.

21. Were you named after another relative or celebrity?
- See if the person has any of the negative or sinful traits of the person they were named for.
- Confess and renounce these sinful or negative traits.
- Cast down the spirit of the namesake by name.

22 Have you ever had premonitions? ___Yes ___No
Deja vu? ___Yes ___No
Psychic sight? ___Yes ___No
- Look for spirits of deception, deja vu, sorcery, and witchcraft.
- These are counterfeit gifts that often come on someone destined to walk in the prophetic.

23. Have you ever been involved in?
Fire walking? ___Yes ___No

Voodoo? ____Yes ____No

Any other form of religious pagan ceremony? ____Yes ____No

If so, what and when?

- These need repentance, confession, renunciation and the curses should be broken.

24. Have you been involved in witchcraft or are you close to someone who is?
____Yes ____No

- Three words expose the activity of witchcraft: manipulation, intimidation, and domination. Pray against any of these that are present.
- Break soul ties with any people that are bringing manipulation, intimidation, and domination upon the person.
- Cast out manipulation, intimidation, and domination.
- Cast out the human spirits of those working witchcraft upon the person.

25. Do you have any tattoos? ____Yes ____No

If so, of what?

- Lev 19:28 forbids tattoos. Confess and renounce any that look demonic. Pay close attention to dragons and the like. If possible, laser surgery can remove tattoos.
- Even "nice" tattoos in the hands of a demonized tattoo artist will open a person to demons.

As you close this section, be sure to cast out:
- Jezebel spirit.
- Antichrist(s) spirit.

CAUSES AND CONSEQUENCES OF ADDICTIONS:

In Jesus Name we demolish every stronghold of addiction and bind every strongman every stronghold of addiction. We cut every cord between the strongman, the demons and _____. We use the keys of heaven to open the door of healing, release and overcoming victory. We use heaven's chains to bind the enemy.

1. Did any of your family as far back as you know, have addictions of any kind?
____Yes ____No

Whom:

To what:
- *Look for generational spirits of addiction.*
- *Confess and break the sins of the fathers for four generations.*
- *Break the assignment of addictions over your family line.*

2. Have you ever been addicted to any of the following: (circle?)

Alcohol	Smoking
Food	Gambling
Spendthrift	Television
Coffee	compulsive exercise
Pornography	Drugs (prescribed or hallucinatory)
	(If so, which ones)

Are any of the above a current problem?
- *Pray over each specific spirit and command it to leave.*
- *Lead in confession.*
- *Lead them to forgive those who brought addictions into their life.*
- *Many times when casting out the demons of addiction it is necessary to break the spirit of python controlling them. At times when we have cast out spirits of addictions, we have had to break the power of python, especially when the spirits manifest and come out with choking and gagging, some people may even feel a constriction or tightness in the chest and feel like they are being choked.*
- *Cast out spirit of death.*

CAUSES & CONSEQUENCES OF LUST AND SEXUAL BONDAGE:

In Jesus Name we demolish every stronghold of lust and sexual bondage. We bind every strongman of lust and sexual bondage. We cut every cord between the strongman, the demons and _____ and any of their sexual partners or perpetrators. We use the keys of heaven to open the doors of healing, forgiveness, cleansing and purity. We use heaven's chains to bind the enemy.

Steps to breaking soul ties:
- If the person willingly participated in sexual sin he or she should ask forgiveness.
- Sever the soul tie by saying "I sever (or break) this soul tie in the Mighty Name of Jesus."

- I usually swing my hand as a sword or use my fingers like scissors while severing the soul tie.
- Command that any part of the partner and/or perpetrator that has remained with the person you are counseling to go back to the partner and/or perpetrator.
- Ask God to restore any part of the person you are praying for that has remained attached to the partner and/or perpetrator.

1. Do you have lustful thoughts? ____Yes ____No
Frequency?
Of what or whom?
- *Look for spirits of lust.*

2. To your knowledge, was there evidence of lust in your parents, grandparents, further back? ____Yes ____No
Explain:
- *Look for generational spirits of lust.*

3. Are you a frequent masturbator? ____Yes ____No
If so, how often?
Do you know why? ____Yes ____No
Do you feel it is a compulsive problem? ____Yes ____No
- *Look for spirits of masturbation, fantasy lust, addiction, guilt and shame.*
- *Break all soul-ties with those fantasized over as explained above.*
- *Share how addictive masturbation and fantasy lust is because both the person and their partner are always perfect in their relations according to their fantasy lust.*

4. Were you ever sexually molested by someone outside your family?
 ____Yes ____No
By whom?
More than once? ____Yes ____No
Explain:
Were you actually raped? ____Yes ____No
By whom?
More than once? ____Yes ____No
Explain:

- *Look for forgiveness issues, explaining that God is just and that he does and will judge.*
- *Look for spirits of lust, defilement, hatred, incest, anger, guilt, shame, unforgiveness, bitterness, a man-hating spirit, and the like.*
- *Break all soul-ties as explained above.*

5. Have you ever been a victim of incest by a family member? ____Yes ____No
By whom? Explain:
More than once? ____Yes ____No
For an extended period? ____Yes ____No
Same as # 4.

6. Were you actually raped? ____Yes ____No
By whom?
More than once? ____Yes ____No
Same as # 4.

7. Have you ever molested or raped anyone? ____Yes ____No
Committed incest? ____Yes ____No
Names:

- *Confess all sin to God. Look for spirits of violence, woman hating, incest, lust and anger.*
- *Break all soul-ties as explained above.*
- *In many states those who hear such a confession are required by law to report it.*
- *I always ask the person to make proper confession, if possible, to their victims and to the police.*

8. Have you ever committed fornication (while single)? ____Yes ____No
How many partners?
First names and when?
With prostitutes? ____Yes ____No
How many?
When?
Are you currently involved in an illicit sexual relationship? ____Yes ____No
Name(s):

Are you willing to break it off? ____Yes ____No

- *There is little use of going on if a person is unwilling to break off an illicit sexual relationship. Satan always takes advantage of such relationships and God will never bless disobedience.*
- *Confess and repent of all fornication, listing the partners by name.*
- *Look for spirits of fornication, lust, generational spirits and spirits of homosexuality, lesbianism, perverse spirits, and spirits of Sodomy. Break all soul ties.*

9. Have you ever committed adultery? (At least one partner married)
                                                                                     ____Yes ____No

How many partners?
First names and when?
With prostitutes? ____Yes ____No
How many?
When?
Are you currently involved in an illicit sexual relationship? ____Yes ____No
Name:
Are you willing to break it off? ____Yes ____No

- *Follow instructions for number 9 above.*
- *Also cast out the spirit of adultery.*

10. Women: Have you ever been pregnant out of wedlock. ____Yes ____No

- *Deal with forgiveness issues — including forgiving self.*
- *Break all soul-ties as explained above.*

11. Men: Have you ever fathered a child out of wedlock? ____Yes ____No

- *Same as number 10.*

12. Have you ever had homosexual or lesbian desire? ____Yes ____No
Do you now? ____Yes ____No
Experience? ____Yes ____No
Whom and when?

- *Look for personal and generational spirits of homosexuality, lesbianism, perversity and sodomy.*
- *Break all soul-ties as explained above.*

13. Have you ever had a heterosexual experience with someone who was homosexual, bisexual or lesbian. ____Yes ____No
Whom and When?
- Same as number 12.

14. Are you sexually frigid? ____Yes ____No
- Look for spirits of resentment, bitterness, frigidity and emotional coldness.
- There may be forgiveness issues between the person and their spouse.
- I counsel married persons according to 1 Corinthians 7 and Proverbs 5.

15. Have you ever sexually fantasized about an animal? ____Yes ____No
Committed a sex act (bestiality) with an animal? ____Yes ____No
Name all the animals involved:_____
- Cast out the spirit of (<u>name of the animal</u>) Also bestiality, guilty, shame and perverse spirits.

16. Has pornography ever attracted you? ____Yes ____No
How did you become involved? Name persons involved:
To what extent?
Is it still a problem? ____Yes ____No
Have you seen porn movies? ____Yes ____No
Videos? ____Yes ____No
Live sex shows? ____Yes ____No
Do you look at internet porn? ____Yes ____No
Do you currently rent porn or have such a channel on your TV? ____Yes ____No
- Confess, ask forgiveness, and repent. Ask the Lord to cleanse _____ from the contamination of pornography and to free him/her from the bondage.
- Cast out the spirit of erotica.
- If they were "victimized" by finding porn in someone's room, etc., have them forgive the person who introduced you to pornography.
- Look for spirits of pornography, sexual fantasy, lust, addiction, and (probably) masturbation.
- Pray for cleansing of images seared into the memory. Ask God to remove them, and press the "delete" button of the brain regarding these pictures.
- Destroy all materials and cancel TV Channels which carry porn.

- *Break all soul-ties as explained above between the person and those they have masturbated over.*
- *There is so much power in porn because it uses fantasy to help people try to escape the pain and confusion of the hurts and pain and confusion of real life. What ever you say, do, offer to the fantasy person they agree with — there is no real rejection.*
- *Deal with the underlying emotion issues and rejection.*

17. Have you ever been involved in oral sex? (Outside marriage) ____Yes ____No
With whom?
- *Confess, renounce, break the soul ties and cast out perverse sexual spirits.*

18. Have you been involved in anal sex? ____Yes ____No
With whom:
- *Break all soul-ties as explained above.*
- *Cast out spirits of homosexuality, sodomy, rejection and degradation.*
- *Pray cleansing over body parts.*

19. Women, have you ever had an abortion? ____Yes ____No
How many? Give dates and father(s)'s name(s):
- *You may want to name the child and do a committal service as you would for a still born. I always ask them to ask the Lord for the name of the child (ren). When both father and mother are present I ask them to privately write down the name God gives them. To date both mother and father have always both given the same name.*
- *Have them confess the abortion to God and tell them "you are forgiven in Jesus 'Name".*
- *Look for spirits of murder, death, grief, unforgiveness, resentment, bitterness, a man-hating spirit, self-hatred, rejection, vagabond, fugitive, or wandering spirit.*
- *Pray spirit of death out of both parents of aborted children and their siblings.*
- *You may also check for spirits of Molech, Ammonite, Chemosh, poverty, famine and sickness or pestilence.*
- *Also check for a "Rachel" spirit that grieves because the child is no more.*

20. Men: Have you ever fathered a child that was forcefully aborted?
 ____Yes ____No
How many?

When? Give dates and Mother(s)' name(s):
- *Ask forgiveness and repent.*
- *Look for spirits of lust, abandonment, murder, emotional cruelty and rape if it applies.*

21. Since the abortion, have you had any new physical problems?   ___Yes ___No
- *About 70% of people with eating disorders are said to have a wrong bonding with the dead or aborted. There may be a necromancy spirit seeking rest in the "living victim" of abortion.*
- *Signs of necromancy spirit include hearing voices, inability to "shut the mind down", ringing in ears and/or recurring death wish. Cast out necromancy if these symptoms are there.*

22. Since the abortion have you or your children had bronchial asthma?
- *Bronchial asthma often comes from a death wish spoken while in the mother's womb or a generational death wish spoken when the mother was in her mother's womb.*
- *Break the power of all such death-wishes. Command spirits that took advantage of death wishes to leave.*
- *Administer divine healing in Jesus' Name.*

23. Do you have a child or grandchild with cerebral palsy?   ___Yes ___No
- *Cerebral palsy is often linked with past abortions and/or sometimes linked with Masonry.*
- *Confess any known abortions and break the assignment of death and destruction.*

24. Have you ever been plagued with desires of having sex with a child?
   ___Yes ___No
Have you actually done so?   ___Yes ___No
- *Cast out the spirit of pedophilia. Look for generational and familiar spirits. Check to see if they were a victim of pedophilia themselves. Break soul ties.*
- *In many states those who hear a confession of pedophilia are required by law to report it.*
- *I always ask the person to make proper confession, if possible, to their victims and to the police.*

25. Have you ever had inner sexual stimulation and climax out of your control, especially at night? By this I mean, do you have dreams of a personage approaching and asking to have sex with you, or just doing it, and you "feel" a presence in bed with you, and then wake up with a sexual climax? ____Yes ____No
Describe:
- *This problem is caused by lustful spirits who approach the person in a dream and cause sexual stimulation. If it acts female it is succubus, if it acts male it is incubus. Call it by name when casting it out.*
- *Look for personal and generational spirits of lust, guilt and demonic mind control.*
- *Cast out phantom with incubus.*

26. Have you been to a massage parlor and been sexually stimulated?
 ____Yes ____No
- *Look for spirits of pornography, sexual fantasy, lust, etc.*
- *Pray cleansing over every part of the body touched by the masseuse.*

27. How would you describe your sexual relationship with your spouse?
- *You may want to counsel a couple about the Bibles view of the gift of the sexual relationship to a husband or wife and about their obligation to please their spouse sexually.* (I Corinthians 7:3-5)
- *Look for spiritual causes behind the problems and pray over them.*
- *Counseling is sometimes needed.*
- *Pray healing over the sexual relationship between husband and wife.*
- *Deal with any Ahab and Jezebel spirits.*

AS YOU FINISH THIS CATEGORY:
- *And now you strongman spirit of lust, in Jesus' Name I bind you, I break your power, and I command you to loose this brother/sister and let him/her go NOW, in the name of Jesus Christ of Nazareth, be gone!*
- *Pray cleansing and healing over body, mind, emotions and memories.*

DEALING WITH GENERAL ISSUES:
1. Do you suffer from any chronic illness or allergies? ____Yes ____No
Which? Is it Hereditary? ____Yes ____No
- *Look for hereditary spirits of infirmity as well as specific spirits of infirmity. Always pray against a spirit of infirmity if there are allergies or chronic illnesses.*

- *High fevers are often connected with a spirit of infirmity.*
- *Check with the Holy Spirit to see if there are curses to be broken.*
- *Administer healing in Jesus' Name.*

2. Do you suffer from Leukemia or cancer? ____Yes ____No
- *These diseases may be linked to guilt or generational guilt.*
- *Make sure the person knows they are forgiven.*
- *Cast out spirits of guilt, condemnation, cancer and/or leukemia. Pray healing.*

3. Have you had any severe accidents or traumas that stand out in your mind (not already mentioned above)? ____Yes ____No
Explain:
- *If you have not already dealt with trauma, now is the time.*

4. Describe yourself in as many one or two word phrases as you can.
- *This is a mirror of the person's self image. Pray against any specific problems that show up. For instance, if they put "lazy", pray against the spirit of sloth.*

5. Do you feel any resistance to Christ or Christians? ____Yes ____No
Explain:
- *Pray against spirits of resistance and/or rebellion.*

6. Is there any sin in your life you cannot gain victory over? ____Yes ____No
Explain:
- *Cast out any spirits that remain.*
- *Teach them that you can cast out spirits, but they must discipline the flesh.*

7. Do you have any other problems you feel this questionnaire hasn't uncovered? (Have them explain as fully as they can. Try to pinpoint when it began and if it was connected with a trauma of some sort, if they were victimized, or if somehow they invited the problem in.)
- *Minister as led.*

8. Have you ever undergone ministry from a deliverance team before?
____Yes ____No
If so, describe the reason for seeking the deliverance and the results of the ministry.

Wrapping up the Session:
- *Always conclude by cleansing the room and commanding all spirits to go to the feet of Jesus.*
- *Pray blessings over the person and have your partner pray or prophesy over them.*
- *Cleanse the room and tell any remaining spirits to leave the room and building and forbid them to stay attached or to go home with any of you.*
- *If you have been telling the spirits to go into the wastebasket, have the person visualize Jesus again and have them "Hand the basket" to Christ. Ask them what they see him doing.*
- *Give them Post-Deliverance instructions and try to set them up with someone to equip and mentor them in their freedom.*
- *Deliverance is about 45% pre-appointment ministry, 10% deliverance and 45% post-appointment ministry. It takes a lot to transform a convert into a true disciple.*

Please remember that deep healing and deliverance is from the Lord and this questionnaire is simply a tool for the Holy Spirit to use to guide the ministry team.

INDEX*

A

Abba Father 99
abortion 239-40
Abraham 20, 24, 54-5, 81
abuse 184-5, 188, 196
acceptance 123, 149-52, 155, 200, 205, 215, 222
accidents 178, 242
accusations 27, 63
Adam 19, 86, 134-5, 153-4, 183, 188, 190, 205
Adamic sin nature 19, 21
addictions viii, xi, 12, 15, 36, 57, 69, 70, 74, 121, 150, 164, 179-86, 233-5, 238
  personal 120
  stronghold of 233
adokimos 91
adultery 1, 131, 161, 189-90, 237
agape 166-7
aggression 220-1
agreement 218
Ahab 131-4, 139-41
Ahab and Jezebel 127, 131, 133, 144, 146
Ahab and Jezebel characteristics 144-5
Ahab and Jezebel spirits x, 130, 134, 241
Ahab and Jezebel strongholds 130-1, 133-4, 139
Ahab characteristics 132-3, 139
air 27, 86, 88, 107, 134-5
alcohol 76, 118, 179, 181
alcoholics, children of 20, 120-1, 179, 184
Alexander 66
alignment 42, 112, 114-5
  right vii, 109, 111, 113-5, 124
allergies 241
Ammonites 185, 239

ancestors 40, 183-4, 223, 229
angels 16, 25-6, 54, 133, 208
  fallen 25-6
anger 27, 33, 37, 57, 76, 83, 121, 128-9, 137, 140-1, 143, 162, 167-70, 173, 220-1, 236
antichrist 172, 225, 233
apokalupto 108
appointment 13, 29, 156, 208-9
arm 82, 157
armor 43
Athens 91, 174-5
authority v, xiii, 1, 2, 5-8, 16-8, 24, 29, 46-7, 50-1, 62, 88, 101-2, 104, 113, 115-6, 142-4
  civil 115
  demonic 51

B

Baal cults 131
babies 49, 87, 99
baptism viii, 40, 97, 176, 199, 201, 203-5, 210
battle v, vi, 14-5, 17, 19, 27, 39, 41, 43, 45, 47, 49-51, 53, 55, 100-3, 112, 117
battlefield 23
battleground 19, 21-5, 29
beasts 135
bed 36, 66-7, 131, 152, 241
behaviors 45, 51, 118, 128-9, 139-42, 155, 157, 171, 180-1
  addictive 76, 179-81
believers 6, 14, 27, 45-6, 59, 61, 67-9, 93, 97, 101, 110, 118, 173, 179-80, 192, 210
  demonized 67
  demons influence 27
bestiality 190, 238
Bible 1, 4, 8, 18, 23, 25-6, 37, 41, 45, 47, 49, 51, 120-1, 126-7, 179, 184-5
birds 86, 88, 134-5
birth 21, 42, 95, 120, 191, 211, 215
birth parents 20, 216
bitter 161, 164
bitterness 69, 168-70, 220-1, 236, 238-9
  roots of 168
blaming 132, 154
blessings 103, 170, 208, 213, 222
blood 11, 18, 49, 50, 104, 108, 114, 151, 173, 178, 183, 186, 205, 210, 214, 226, 228-9
body 39, 40, 42-3, 45-6, 88-9, 91-7, 102-3, 105, 108-10, 112, 114-5, 120, 139, 166, 190, 201-2, 241
bondage xi, 11-2, 24, 52, 55, 79, 80, 147, 149, 163, 167, 171, 175, 211, 219, 238
  demonic x, 45, 81, 163, 170
  sexual 192-3, 234
  spiritual 24, 45, 77, 120
bondage demons 144

bones   135, 190
Bosworth   111
bow   57, 121, 183, 232
boys   4, 17, 20, 94, 126, 137
break   xiii, 40, 45, 59, 71, 76, 81, 144, 160-1, 192-3, 208, 211-2, 214, 224-9, 234-7, 239-41
break bondages   220
Break curses of poverty   219
break soul ties   191, 233, 240
Breakdown of marriage   177, 213
Breaking curses   178, 213
BREAKING CURSES   viii, 177
bronchial asthma   216, 240
brothers   53, 73, 83, 93, 112, 124, 139, 151, 159, 169-70, 182, 201, 206, 216-7
burning   231
bush   15, 17

C
Canaan   54, 182
cancer   242
canoe   21-2
captive   x, 13, 20, 24-5, 76, 85, 108, 147, 163, 167-8, 186, 215
captivity, spiritual   24, 167
case study   vi, 28, 31, 33, 35, 37
cast   xi, 3, 5, 7, 34, 37, 71, 131, 144, 149-50, 205, 212-4, 221-3, 225, 227-34, 237-42
cast demons   33
casting   xi, 75, 193, 234, 241
cat   28-9
celebrate   169-70
cerebral palsy   240
chains   33
  heaven's   228, 233-4
change   45, 124, 133, 140-2, 156-7, 192, 209
child   20, 82, 120, 155, 172, 183-4, 203, 210, 216, 219-20, 237, 239-40
child abusers   20
children   xiii, 11, 20, 23, 25-6, 36, 73-4, 120-1, 128, 130-1, 163, 172, 185-7, 217, 219, 221
children of God   47, 99
choice   41, 65, 104, 132, 149, 154-5, 161, 165, 187, 196
Christ   13, 23, 39, 40, 43-7, 70, 80-1, 85-6, 96-7, 100-3, 107-10, 123-4, 128-30, 144-5, 155-6, 174-6, 208-10
  Jesus   39, 40, 53, 70, 97, 127, 144, 149-50, 172, 174, 180, 186-7, 201, 210, 222, 226-30, 241
Christ-likeness   125, 127, 129, 131, 133, 135, 137, 139, 141, 143, 145, 147
Christian   6, 11-2, 23, 27, 44, 48, 74, 82, 103, 105, 123, 130, 140-1, 166, 174, 204
Christian counseling   xi
Christian faith   199
Christian leaders   59, 70, 162
Christianity, legalistic   184

Christians   xiii, 1, 2, 6, 8, 15, 19, 20, 22-3, 25-7, 45, 49, 51, 55-9, 67-8, 100-1, 103, 217-8
church   x, xi, 1, 2, 7, 13, 23-4, 44-5, 49, 63-4, 69, 118, 124-6, 133-4, 144-5, 149-50, 165-6, 187-8
Church, Christian   99, 176
church, local   x, xiii, 32
circle   218-21, 225, 231, 234
city   7, 57, 86, 125, 133, 174, 211
cleaves   118, 189
cloud   53, 58
command   6, 28-9, 63, 103-4, 112, 174, 199, 208, 212, 214-5, 224, 227-8, 234-5, 241
Common strongholds   57, 149
compassion   ix, 128-9, 181
confess   7, 20, 40-2, 45, 48, 81-2, 119, 121, 124, 140, 144-5, 192, 222, 226, 229-34, 236-40
confess Jesus   48, 172
confessing   40-1, 81, 121, 192
confession   40-1, 59, 120, 144, 153-4, 164, 166, 178, 193, 232-4, 236, 240
conflict   42, 86, 109, 137-8
confusion   131, 141, 209, 223, 225, 231, 239
control   14, 25, 27-8, 52, 59, 76, 86, 93, 95, 105, 126-7, 131, 136-7, 142-3, 191-2, 218-9
cords   74, 190, 211, 215, 217, 223, 228, 233-4
Corinthians   12-3, 18, 25, 54, 68, 74, 80-1, 88, 93, 97, 108-9, 114, 120, 175, 238, 241
couple   7, 19, 74, 126, 152, 188, 191, 241
covenant   20, 54-5, 111, 177, 215, 225
cult   viii, xi, 63, 71, 77, 119, 171-6, 224-5, 228
curses   vii, xi, 16, 103, 125, 127, 129, 131, 133-7, 139, 165, 177-8, 183, 212-4, 227-9, 231

D
dad   126, 150, 155-7
Daniel   41, 50-1, 121, 182
darkness   14, 18, 25, 59, 66, 102-3, 105, 151, 206, 215
daughters   24, 26, 36, 120, 156, 160, 171, 184-5, 225
death   11, 19, 21, 33, 40, 42, 67-8, 76, 96-7, 127-8, 132-3, 164-7, 213, 226-7, 229-30, 239-40
   physical   67-8
death curse   216, 226
debt   21-2
deep healing   viii, 76, 122-3, 150, 159, 163, 168, 170, 185-6, 192, 195, 204, 214-5, 243
   personal   184
Deep Healing and Deliverance   191, 193
Deep Healing and Deliverance Ministry   162
Deep Healing Questionnaire   75, 77, 192
Deep Healing Questionnaire Worksheet   207, 209, 211, 213, 215, 217, 219, 221, 223, 225, 227,
   229, 231, 233, 235, 237
defeat   xiii, 56-7, 59, 69, 71, 121
deja   232
delegated authority   1, 8
deliverance   ix-xi, xiii, 1, 3, 5-9, 28-9, 31-2, 35-7, 58-9, 70-1, 75-6, 81-3, 156-7, 190-3, 207, 242-3
   corporate   31, 147
   minister   29, 31-2, 157, 168, 177

deliverance appointment   29, 122-3, 184
deliverance ministers   32, 75-6, 123
deliverance ministry   v, x, xiii, 1, 3, 4, 8, 9, 11-3, 17-8, 23, 28, 31-2, 36, 39, 83, 102, 119
  effective   75
  personal   52
demolish   14, 57, 215, 223, 228, 233-4
demon gods   212
demon-possession   160
demon worship   229
Demonic captivity   168
demonic gateways
  open   121
  personal   119
Demonic Intruders   207
demonization   62, 66-7, 191
demonized tattoo artist   233
demons   x, xi, 2-5, 7-9, 14-7, 25-9, 32-5, 37, 46-7, 56-9, 64-5, 71, 101-2, 170-2, 208-9, 211-2,
    233-4
demonstration   114, 188
denominations   23, 26, 118, 209
depression   69, 165, 223
desert   4, 54, 56, 104
destiny   25, 85, 222
destroy   11, 25, 57, 63, 71, 88-9, 104, 120, 130, 138, 151-2, 155, 163, 172, 180, 231-2
destruction   134, 144, 165, 171, 212, 227, 240
devil   4, 5, 11, 13-5, 25, 27, 32, 37, 40-1, 45-7, 55-7, 62-3, 73-4, 81-2, 101-4, 119, 168-72
devil footholds   37, 45
devil's work   11, 57, 151, 163
difference   82, 118, 134, 140, 209
disciples   x, 1, 8, 31-2, 73, 159-61, 166, 174, 203, 243
discipline   71, 130, 179, 181, 190, 192, 242
discouragement   55, 142
disobedience   103, 178, 210
disturbance   33
Divine Authority and Power   5
doctrines   118, 172, 174, 201
dogs   160
dominion   88, 134-6, 206
dreams   145, 179, 184, 226, 241
drink   6, 8, 54, 83, 180-1
drink wine   184-5
drive   2, 3, 7, 8, 54, 64, 151, 165, 190
drugs   76, 118, 164, 179-80, 184
drunk   182, 184-5, 202
drunk driving   180

E

earth   3, 5, 6, 9, 17, 24-6, 46, 55-6, 81, 86, 88, 96, 134-5, 184, 214
Egypt   55
Egyptians   55
elders   124, 132, 164
emasculating controllers   138
emotional breakdowns   177, 213
emotional coldness   220, 238
emotional issues   viii, 163, 165, 167, 169
emotions   24, 43, 88, 92-3, 96, 109, 112, 167, 218, 220, 241
enemy   x, 20, 27, 31, 47, 49, 50, 55, 58, 83, 101-2, 105, 120, 123, 152, 208, 233-4
envy   123, 170, 221
Eve   134-5, 152-4, 190, 205
Evicting Demonic Intruders   225
evil   14, 19-21, 23, 28, 39, 41, 43, 54, 64, 81, 83, 97, 122, 127-8, 139-40, 205-6
  spiritual forces of   18, 49, 50, 52, 174, 205
evil spirits   32, 34, 49, 64-6, 117, 188, 223-4, 227
evolution   86-7
Exodus   53, 55, 121, 183, 189
Ezekiel   111, 182, 184

F

faith   2, 6, 32, 40-2, 44, 47-8, 67, 80, 82, 96-7, 114, 146, 159-60, 181-2, 205, 210
families   xiii, 23, 35, 115, 118, 125-7, 134, 136, 140, 157, 160, 177-8, 181-2, 184, 213, 228
family line   177, 183, 185, 221, 226, 229, 234
father   1, 2, 4, 6, 20-1, 40-1, 99, 121, 128, 132, 161, 169-70, 182-5, 202-5, 215-8, 222-3, 239
father-in-law Ethbaal   131
fear   11, 32, 37, 47, 76-7, 102, 113, 137, 140-2, 144, 149, 153, 167, 189-90, 204-5, 226-30
Fear of Rejection   215
female   134-5, 137
fence   87
field   ix, xi, 103, 118, 135, 207
fight   13, 19, 27, 49, 70, 100-2, 108, 112, 125, 146
filthy language   128-9
First names   125, 236-7
fish   86, 88, 134, 166
flee   41, 46, 120, 124, 208, 227
flesh   6, 11, 18, 49, 50, 71, 74, 93, 95, 108, 111, 135, 161, 172, 181, 183, 187-9
flesh union   187-8
food   131, 153, 179-80, 184
food addiction   180
foothold   37, 82, 143, 168-9
forces
  demonic   18, 51, 181
  spiritual   17, 51, 175, 212
forefathers   41, 53, 184, 212

forgive   1, 59, 82-3, 125, 128-9, 144-5, 159, 161, 168, 178, 195-6, 200-1, 213-4, 221-3, 229, 234
forgiveness   6, 41, 83, 149-51, 162, 186, 196-7, 200-1, 205, 215, 217, 220, 222-3, 226, 234, 238
forgiveness issues   212, 216, 219, 221-2, 236-8
forgiving   viii, 82, 159, 161, 170, 195, 197, 212, 222-3, 228
fornication   190, 237
forsake   80-1, 191
freedom   vii, xi, 1, 29, 40, 45, 85-6, 105, 120, 123-4, 149, 170, 174, 178, 180-1, 211
fruit   81, 96, 152-4, 172, 184

G

gambling   7, 69, 76
games, played demonic   230
garden   133, 135, 152-3
gateways   37, 71, 74, 119-20, 122, 172, 212
generational curses   178
generational spirits   220, 223, 227, 231, 234, 237
generations, demonized   3
gifts   8, 67, 127, 145, 168, 187, 201, 208, 241
girl   138, 165
glory   2, 6, 40, 105, 114, 127, 144, 191, 201, 206
God   1-9, 40-8, 50-5, 61-3, 79-83, 85-6, 88-9, 91-7, 102-5, 111-7, 132-6, 139-45, 151-5, 164-9, 189-93, 199-206
  finger of   3, 151
  full armor of   18, 39, 205
  knowledge of   13, 25, 43, 92, 94, 108
God's image   88, 94, 97, 121, 183
God's Love   200
God's power   113-4
God's prophetic destiny   104, 107
God's voice   108, 110, 113
God's Word   20, 100, 104
God's workmanship   81, 214
gospel   12-4, 96, 108, 175-6, 203, 206
grace   25, 40, 46, 80, 92, 95, 124, 127, 139, 173, 200, 222
  personal   83
grandchildren   121, 213
grandparents   171, 211, 223-4, 235
Greek word   12, 14, 22, 34, 37, 44, 51, 88, 91-3, 104, 107-8, 166, 202
grief   70, 165, 219-20, 239
grievances   128-9
ground   39, 44, 86, 101, 134-5, 141, 163, 205
group   23, 51-2, 102, 165, 172, 174, 189, 225, 227
guards   44, 112, 117-8, 161-2
guide   44, 75, 85, 144-5, 208, 243
guilt   118, 164-5, 184, 235-6, 241-2
guilty   83, 121, 197, 238

H

habit 70, 180
  bad 76
hair, goat's 66-7
Ham 182-3
hate 73, 121, 143, 183, 218, 221
heal 1, 2, 5, 6, 113, 147, 159
healing 1, 5, 8, 18, 24, 32, 82, 147, 162, 165, 167, 190, 196, 205, 215, 241-2
hearts 39, 40, 43-5, 48, 54, 61-2, 82-3, 89, 111-2, 128, 130, 142-4, 156, 160-2, 168, 199-202, 205
heaviness 223
helper 135, 208
hid 153, 171, 215
hierarchy x, 18, 34, 107, 109
Hierarchy of Demonic Beings 50
Hilkiah 173
hinders 57-8, 70, 75, 126, 134
holiness 25, 100-1, 105, 119, 142-3, 168
holy 74, 80, 97, 100, 105, 112, 119-20, 128, 168, 201
Holy Spirit 1, 3, 4, 8, 9, 33-4, 41, 75, 97, 114-5, 142, 144, 156-7, 168, 170, 195, 202-4, 242-3
homes 11, 29, 35, 44, 74, 77, 87, 91, 99, 115, 118, 126-7, 132-4, 143-4, 155-6, 231
homosexual 118, 189-90, 237-8
house 21, 28, 37, 65-6, 80, 111, 159
human makeup vi, 85, 87, 89, 91
human spirits 88, 91-5, 107-10, 232-3
humans 26, 86-8, 134, 187
humility 46, 128-9
hurts viii, 8, 34, 69, 70, 76, 82, 132, 137, 159, 167-8, 185, 195, 197, 212, 239
  personal 83
husbands 27, 29, 115, 118, 125-32, 134, 136, 142, 144-5, 151, 153, 178, 187, 189, 191, 241
Hymenaeus 66

I

identity, personal 23
idolatrous 141-2
idolatry 22, 54, 64, 74, 127, 129, 143, 190-1
image of God 12, 86, 96, 108, 134
impulses 165
impurity 127-8, 189
incest 185, 189, 236
incubus 241
indifference 129-30, 140
infirmity 24, 34, 241-2
inheritance 128, 132, 169-70
intimacy 191, 210
intimidation 137, 233
inventory, personal 79

involvement   119, 137, 214, 229
Isaac   20, 54-5
Israel   11, 56, 61, 63, 69, 70, 111, 132, 160, 191, 215
Israelites   54-6, 70, 171

J

Jacob   20, 54-5, 215
jails   33, 180, 184, 196, 212
James   21, 27, 41, 45-6, 93-4, 96, 124, 159, 169-70
jealousy   142, 167, 170, 221
Jehovah   55, 64-5, 69
Jehovah's Witness   13, 176
Jesse   65, 67
Jesus   1-7, 11-3, 21-2, 24-9, 31-6, 45-8, 95-7, 99, 100, 107-10, 143-5, 151-2, 156-7, 159-61, 163-7, 199, 200, 203-6
Jesus' Name   29, 47, 83, 114, 141, 205, 215, 222-3, 228, 240-2
Jezebel   129, 131-4, 140, 142-3
Jezebel Prayer   142, 144
job   ix, 26, 80, 88, 123, 137, 182
John   1, 2, 6, 11, 21, 45, 47, 57, 80-1, 83, 95, 97, 110, 166-8, 172, 203-4, 209-10
Joseph   4, 159, 188
Josiah   173
Journey Guide Inventory   76-7
Judas   159, 164-5
Jude   102, 206
judgment   55, 62-3, 92-3, 97, 116, 186, 204, 213

K

kaloopto   12
key Christian Leaders   176
kindness   128-9
king   51, 61, 64-5, 131-3, 146, 173
King James Bible   91
kingdom   12, 14, 24, 27, 46, 63, 67, 70, 107, 134, 151
kingdom of darkness   18, 102, 151
kingdom of God   3, 151
Kingdom of God   55, 151
klepseis   152
knowledge   25, 114, 128, 135, 188, 208, 224-5, 228-9, 235
  personal   204

L

land   17, 20, 54-5, 57, 88, 190, 215
laws   17, 91, 99, 107, 111, 124, 139, 173, 189, 196, 199, 236, 240
leaders   32, 115, 176
leadership   69, 116, 140, 142

lesbian   189, 237-8
lesbianism   150, 237
lessons   50, 174-5
letters   132-3, 192
Leviticus   20, 121, 189-90
light   12, 25, 58, 81, 108, 127
likeness   86, 94, 129, 131, 134, 139
link   46, 188, 190
little girl   138, 155-7
livestock   86, 134-5
Lord   5-8, 12-3, 47-50, 88-9, 109-10, 112-3, 118-9, 124, 128, 130, 140-4, 146-7, 159-60, 165-8, 173, 201-2
LORD   54-5, 57, 62-7, 70, 74, 103-4, 111, 121, 173, 183, 190-1, 215
love   viii, 2, 4, 6, 21, 49, 50, 73, 87, 89, 115, 127-30, 144-5, 150-3, 156-7, 166-7, 199-205
   unconditional   123, 149, 151, 200, 205, 213, 221
lust   viii, xi, 9, 15, 21-2, 42, 57, 69, 70, 74, 81, 127-8, 187, 193, 216, 234-8, 240-1
Lust and Sexual Bondage Issues   187, 189, 191, 193
lusts, shameful   43, 92

M

Major Battlegrounds   v, 19, 21, 23, 25, 27, 29
MAJOR TYPES of STRONGHOLDS   vi, 73
malice   128-9, 170
manifest   24, 33, 91, 137-8, 184, 209
manipulation   117, 131, 140, 143, 219, 222, 233
   generational spirits of   218-9
mankind   88, 135
mantra   230
mark   vi, 8, 22, 24, 31, 33, 35, 37, 96, 139, 142, 159, 180
marriage   26, 58, 73-4, 125-6, 133, 139, 144-5, 150, 177, 188, 191-3, 213, 239
martial arts   232
masturbation   70, 192, 235, 238
materialistic   51, 211
materialistic world   16, 23, 25, 120
mature Christian mentor   45
mediums   67, 120, 173
mental blocks   225
mercy   ix, 35, 41, 80, 82, 160, 197, 222
Michal   66
mind control   224, 230-1
   demonic   241
minds   16, 24-5, 41-4, 55-6, 64, 88-9, 92-3, 96, 110-2, 127, 131, 199, 230, 241-2
   depraved   43, 92
mindsets   59, 131, 133
minister   ix, x, 2, 7, 20, 29, 75, 77, 112-3, 143-4, 150, 156, 195, 207, 214, 221, 242
Ministering   viii, 163, 171, 173, 175

Ministering to Cult and Occult Issues 171, 173, 175
Ministering to Mental and Emotional Issues 165, 167, 169
ministry xiii, 2-5, 8, 9, 20-3, 31-3, 36, 58, 71, 77, 81, 105, 112-4, 119, 163, 202-3, 242
  personal 180, 207
miracles 4, 32, 159-60
Moabites 185
money ix, 76, 91, 118, 164, 168, 228
moral filth 169
morning 28-9, 36, 43, 64, 66, 134, 164, 179, 192
mortal body 97, 112, 139
Moses 53-5, 70, 102, 173, 189
mother 20, 46, 73, 82, 87, 126, 135, 151, 160, 187, 195, 211, 216, 219, 223, 239-40
movies 21-2, 173
Multitude of Sins 201
murder 33, 52, 161, 181, 220, 226, 232, 239-40
music 171, 202, 231-2

N
Naboth 132-3
nakedness 153-4
  father's 182-3
name 2, 6, 8, 11, 34, 46-8, 54-5, 130-1, 135, 141, 156, 202-4, 214-5, 225-30, 232, 236-41
nation 56, 62, 70, 131, 190-1, 211, 214
natural world 16
necromancy spirit 240
negative words 213, 222
New Testament 26, 54, 66-7, 204
Noah 181-3

O
obedience 85, 103, 141
occult xi, 74, 119, 172-3, 176, 228
occult involvement 71, 171, 228
occultism 67, 74, 229-30
offenses 44, 69, 70, 132, 159-60, 222-3
Old Testament 54, 67, 173

P
pain 17, 28, 82, 136-7, 195, 239
parents 20, 73, 115, 120-2, 128, 130, 156-7, 171, 179-80, 187, 211, 213, 216-8, 221, 223-4, 229
partner 74, 96, 109, 131, 191, 235-7
passages 2, 11, 13, 17, 123, 127, 152, 160, 166, 181
pastor 2, 23, 49, 71, 113, 140, 155, 192
paths 40, 74, 103, 149, 190
pattern 55-6, 59, 70-1, 112, 121, 126, 139-40, 220, 224, 226
Paul 6, 12-3, 17, 23, 25, 40-1, 45, 48, 50, 53-4, 92-3, 104-5, 107-9, 173-5, 199, 202-4

peace 1, 41-2, 44, 46, 80, 105, 110, 119, 128, 140, 143, 168, 202, 206
pedophilia 240
pencil 47
Persia, king of 50-1
person x, 9, 34-6, 62, 73-4, 79, 95-6, 102-4, 109-13, 143, 177-8, 189, 207-9, 212-4, 220-1, 232-43
personal issues 77, 192
personification 23
perverse spirits 237-8
perversion 137, 189
pets 28-9, 172, 208
Pharaoh 54-5
phileo 166-7
Philistines 63
pictures 67, 69, 70, 131, 169, 238
plans 104, 107, 138, 143-4, 164, 215
pneumatikos 93, 109
porn 119, 238-9
pornography 22, 70-1, 77, 119, 128, 184, 192-3, 238, 241
possessions 37, 55, 76, 133, 181, 225, 231
pouting 132, 140-2
poverty 177, 219, 239
power v, xiii, 1-6, 8, 16-8, 33-4, 45-7, 50-3, 62, 178, 201-3, 205-6, 222, 226, 228-9, 239-41
  divine 13-4, 108, 114
  spiritual 113, 142
Power and Authority for Deliverance Ministry 1
Power Healing Conference 69
Power of Negative Confessions 212
pray 6, 7, 13-4, 28-9, 32, 41, 45-6, 50-1, 124, 140-2, 156, 175-6, 205-10, 213-6, 218-24, 232-4, 241-2
pray healing 216, 223, 241-2
prayer xiii, 7, 44-5, 51, 70-1, 75, 81-2, 112, 114-6, 124, 126, 142, 147, 205-7, 209, 222
presumption 101-2
pretension 13-4, 25, 108
pride 14, 21-2, 42, 46, 63, 67, 124, 129, 170, 220
priest 62, 164, 173
problems xi, 27, 37, 76, 126, 130, 132, 137, 155, 161, 164, 199, 209-10, 219-20, 223, 241-2
promiscuity 28, 118, 188, 190
Promised Land 11, 53-6, 70
promises 59, 110-1, 212
prophesy 61-2, 67, 243
prophesying 62, 65
prophetic destinies 104, 212, 222
prophets 61-2, 131, 159, 199, 214
prostitutes 169, 236-7
prostitution 191

protection 101, 103-4
psuchikos 93, 108-9
psyche 88-9, 93
psychiatrists 36, 152, 154
punishing 121, 183
punishment 120-1, 186, 204
python 234

R
rage 33, 128-9, 143, 170, 181
realms 18-9, 23-4, 29, 50, 205, 208
rebellion 62, 64, 67, 101, 119, 121, 140, 170-1, 221, 242
rebellious 142-3, 221
rebuke 46, 102
region 28, 32, 35, 52, 160
rejection xi, 9, 57, 74, 149-57, 160, 162, 165, 167, 170, 200, 213, 215-8, 220, 222, 239
  perceived 149, 154, 160, 167, 222
  root of 155, 217
rejection issues viii, 149-51, 153-5, 157, 215, 222
relationships 58, 76, 128-9, 132, 134-8, 142, 144, 154, 164, 168, 188, 191-2, 216-9, 237
release xiii, 1, 5, 12, 96, 113, 140, 143, 147, 203, 205-6, 208, 210, 222-3, 233
remorse 133, 164-5
renounce 13, 40-1, 56, 81-2, 119, 141, 176, 210, 212-3, 222, 225, 228-33, 239
renouncing 40-1, 81, 120-1, 193, 232
renunciations 144, 233
repent 45, 59, 63, 65-6, 82, 104, 119, 131, 168, 174, 192, 200-1, 210, 222, 231, 237-8
repentance 6, 25, 45, 81, 108, 120, 141-2, 203, 209, 232-3
Replacing Ahab & Jezebel 125, 127, 129, 131, 133, 135, 137, 139, 141, 143, 145, 147
reprobates 91-2, 94
reprobation vii, 91-5, 97
resentment 170, 220-1, 238-9
resist 27, 41, 46, 124, 143, 208-9
resistance 108, 242
  pockets of 57, 70
resisting 41, 46, 104
responsibility 116, 134, 140-1, 145, 154, 160, 164
Restoration vii, 99
restore 93, 97, 124, 141, 165-6, 215, 235
resurrection 40, 97, 164, 174-5
revelation xiii, 12, 23, 25, 94, 104, 108, 131, 133, 146, 161, 168, 205, 209, 224
revenge 83, 232
reverence 109, 128, 130, 202
rhema 44, 104
right spiritual alignment vii, 113, 115
righteousness 39, 44, 99, 107, 143, 181-2, 184, 206

rock   53, 56, 231
Roman Catholic Church   6
room   x, 16, 26-7, 83, 150, 153, 172, 180, 195, 208, 238, 243
roots   11-2, 14, 81, 152, 161, 169-70, 184, 205
Roots of bitterness   168
ropes   133, 208
rule   14, 50, 52, 71, 86, 134, 137, 208
rulers   17-8, 24, 27, 50, 88, 95, 107, 205
   demonic   51

S
Sabbath   24, 159
sacrifices   64, 100, 107, 120, 228
saints   24-5, 43, 80, 155, 186, 199
salvation   12, 25, 44, 46-7, 62, 96, 155, 173, 202, 209-10, 215
Samaria   131-2, 203
sanctification   42, 105, 109, 124, 155, 201
sanctify   42, 105, 202
sarkinos   93, 107
Satan   x, 11, 14, 24-5, 58, 62-4, 66-7, 71, 88, 104, 130, 151-3, 163-5, 171, 175, 208
satanic   228-9
Satan's schemes   xiii, 58, 101
Saul, King   vi, 61, 63-5, 67, 171
Saul's demonization   65-7
Savior   11, 47-8, 140, 204
scandal   117
schemes, devil's   18, 104, 205
schools   51, 117, 125, 155-6, 171, 187
scriptural world   15, 17
Scripture   ix, x, 31, 44, 46, 62, 93, 104, 114, 123-4, 127, 146, 202, 205, 214
séances   74, 77, 119
secret   44, 172
Securing Adequate Protection   vii, 103, 105
self-rejection   149, 167, 220, 222
sensual   94-5
servants   3, 62, 65, 127, 131, 191, 193, 215
set   2, 6, 12-3, 24-5, 36, 41-2, 45, 56, 76, 80-1, 108, 121-2, 146-7, 174, 192-3, 206
sever   234
sex   73-4, 137, 151, 184-5, 188, 191, 232, 238, 240-1
sexual bondage issues   viii, 187, 189, 191, 193
sexual immorality   54, 105, 120, 127-8, 131, 141, 143, 161, 201
sexual relationship   187, 191, 241
sexual sin   71, 74, 120, 181, 189-90, 193, 234
shame   123, 135, 154, 219-20, 235-6, 238
sheep   63-5, 167

Shekinah Christian Church   127
Shield of Faith   44
sinful nature   15, 19, 23, 39, 41-2, 85-6, 88, 92, 105, 109-10, 124
sinful world   15, 19, 21, 23, 31
sins   6, 19-21, 39-42, 45, 58-9, 80-1, 93, 97, 107-8, 119-24, 139, 153-4, 168, 183-5, 190-3, 200-1
sisters   73, 159, 206, 216-7
slander   128-9, 161, 170
slaves   55, 107, 128, 130, 182, 191
snakes   8, 37, 54, 70, 152
society   15, 117, 149
sodomy   237, 239
son   2, 4, 6, 20, 34, 47, 62, 64-5, 67, 74, 88, 99, 119-20, 169, 181-5, 203-4
Son of God   4, 11, 40, 47, 57, 97, 204, 206
sorcery   51, 119-20, 142-3, 173, 232
soul ties   xi, 73-4, 120, 188-93, 195, 214, 221, 234-5, 237, 239
   breaking   192-3, 234
soulish   92-5, 108-9, 133
souls   12, 42-3, 88-9, 91-7, 105, 107-10, 113-5, 137-8, 140, 155, 173, 184, 188, 199, 201-2
sovereign   65, 85, 88
Spirit of God   2, 3, 8, 9, 26, 62, 79, 93, 109, 151, 172, 203
spiritists   120, 173
spiritual authorities   46, 51
spiritual inventory, personal   vi, 75, 77
spiritual protection   109-10
spiritual warfare   12-3, 17, 23, 56, 61, 102, 141, 176, 207
spirituality   92-3
spouse   73, 140-1, 144, 213, 238, 241
Standing Strong in Battle   39, 41, 43, 45, 47
steal   87, 104, 132, 151-2, 155, 163, 172, 188
stones   33, 111, 123, 132, 174
story   vi, 28, 36, 55, 61, 63, 65, 67, 113, 131, 157, 169, 176, 185
strength   37, 61, 89, 96, 127, 137-8, 145, 173, 201, 215
Stronghold of Rejection   215
strongholds   vi, 14, 39-41, 45, 55, 57-9, 67-71, 73-6, 79, 81, 121-2, 141, 175-6, 215, 223-4, 228-9
   breaking   119
   demolish   13-4, 108
   demonic   73, 127, 181
   personal   79, 81, 200
strongman   14, 37, 46, 208, 211, 215, 223, 228, 233-4
strongman of rejection   215
struggle   15, 18, 41, 47, 49, 50, 73, 79, 85, 105, 120, 149, 163, 205
subdue   33, 134
subject   93, 175, 177, 187
submit   41, 43, 46, 104, 114-6, 124, 128, 130, 142-5, 202
substandard Christian life   45

suicide 36, 52, 58, 164-5, 178, 213, 226, 230, 232
  generational spirits of 226
sullen 132
surrender 111, 167
symptoms 210, 218, 221, 225, 230, 240
synagogues 5, 24, 159, 174

T

tattoos 233
teachers 15, 32, 117, 157, 203, 213
teenager 187, 209, 219-20
temple 97, 164, 173, 230
temptation 35, 46, 54, 110, 155
tendencies 20, 120-1, 133
test 54, 91, 103, 112, 124, 172, 189
testify 36, 88, 132, 204-5
testimony 35-6, 47, 104, 114, 152
theology vi, 2, 85, 87, 89, 91
thief 152, 172
times 35-6, 45, 47-8, 57-9, 62-4, 66-7, 75, 82-3, 91-3, 114-5, 131-3, 142, 164-5, 169-71, 173-4, 207-9
tombs 28, 32-3
tongues 8, 204
trauma 150-1, 216-7, 224, 242
treasure 22
tree 15, 17, 39, 81, 135, 152-4, 184
trusting 24-5, 137, 145, 155, 197
truth 2, 6, 25, 43, 45, 47, 50, 63, 80, 86, 142-3, 167, 170, 187, 203, 205-6
types vii, 32, 73-4, 107, 109, 154, 166-7, 171, 184

U

unbelief 82, 210, 224
unbelievers 12, 108, 110
unforgiveness 57, 71, 82-3, 129, 159, 195, 220-1, 236, 239
union 188-9
United States 51, 117

V

vengeance 160, 196, 201
verses 1, 25-6, 41, 49, 73, 86, 88, 93, 102, 120, 169, 180, 185-6, 214, 221
victims 15-6, 71, 120, 196-7, 236, 240
victorious Christian life 40
victory 14, 18, 25, 40, 45, 48, 53, 56, 59, 70, 101, 155, 160, 192, 211, 233
vineyard 132, 182
violence 14, 117-8, 143, 216-7, 226, 232, 236

voice   4, 7, 33, 64, 113, 209-10
vows   145, 212, 225, 228-9
vulnerability   134, 138, 141, 143, 188

W

Wagner, Doris   75, 207
war   x, 14, 18-22, 24-5, 37, 70, 102, 104, 222
warfare   12-3, 176, 208
waste   20, 62, 87
water, living   56, 191, 203
weapons   13-4, 39, 108
wedlock   7, 216, 237
wife   7, 20, 23, 28, 46, 73-4, 87, 125-6, 132, 134-5, 139-42, 144-5, 153-4, 187-9, 204, 241
wills   105, 112
wine   6, 65, 182, 202
wisdom   100, 128, 130, 153, 159, 170, 189, 208
witchcraft   51, 57, 77, 120, 142, 175-6, 210, 229-33
witchcraft curse   176, 214
witches   16, 171, 176, 192
wives   115, 125-8, 130, 134, 144, 187, 210
woman   1, 6, 7, 20, 24, 27-8, 34, 36, 47, 82, 99, 134-6, 138, 140-1, 152-4, 160-1, 189
womb   150-1, 214-6
women   ix, 8, 33, 119, 133, 136-9, 142, 144, 188-9, 192, 196, 216, 237, 239
woods   4, 39, 50, 188
work   2, 3, 9, 11-2, 24-5, 32, 40, 42-3, 51-2, 56-7, 75-7, 91-2, 107, 130-1, 133-7, 143-4, 154-5
  demon   57
  perfect   25, 155
work deliverance   36
workplace   117
world   3, 7, 8, 11, 13, 15, 17, 19, 21, 25-6, 52, 55, 107-8, 123, 172, 200, 204
worship   22, 33, 73, 112, 121, 143, 183, 190, 232
wrath   127, 169, 201, 221

Y

yoga   230
Young Christians   45

NOTES

Made in the USA
Monee, IL
15 September 2022